Zoë **Brân** PhD is a writer, lecturer and occasional shaman. Born in a South Wales mining town – 'a cross between Coronation Street and Wuthering Heights' – Zoë grew up and was educated in the beautiful Wye Valley. She attributes her fascination with extremes of landscape and human activity to moving between these two very different locations throughout her childhood. Her writing includes journalism, academic essays and guides to sexual health – her PhD from the Cranfield School of Management was the first on AIDS from a cultural and social perspective. Her books include travelogues on Vietnam, Burma and the Former Yugoslavia. Zoë lectures on creativity and creative guidance and works as a counsellor and healer in the core shamanic tradition (www.shaman.uk.net). She currently lives in London with her lurcher, Arlu. (For more information visit www.zoebran.com.)

★ Enduring Cuba

Zoë Brân

LONELY PLANET PUBLICATIONS
Melbourne • Oakland • London

Enduring Cuba

Published by Lonely Planet Publications
 Head Office: 90 Maribyrnong Street, Footscray, Vic 3011, Australia
      Locked Bag 1, Footscray, Vic 3011, Australia
 Branches: 150 Linden Street, Oakland CA 94607, USA
      2nd Floor, 186 City Road, London ECV1 2NT, UK

First published 2002
This edition published 2008

Printed by The Bookmaker International Ltd.
Printed in China

Map by Tony Fankhauser

National Library of Australia Cataloguing-in-Publication entry

Brân, Zoë.
 Enduring Cuba.

 ISBN 978 1 74179 519 6

 1. Brân, Zoë – Journeys – Cuba. 2. Cuba – description and
 travel. I. Title. (Series: Lonely Planet Journeys)

917.2910464

Text © Zoë Brân 2002
Map © Lonely Planet Publications Pty Ltd 2008

For my friends
Louise Williams and Jim Pett.
Even the road least travelled leads home.

Acknowledgements

With grateful thanks to the following:
I. Armas, David Bellis, Rochelle Bloch, Estela Bravo, Cadena de Turismo Islazul, Enrico Cirules, Cubana Airlines, Vivian R. Carillio, Cristina, Aristides V. Chapú, F. Ramirez García, Claire McDonald, Martin di Giovanni, Robert van der Hilst, Michael and Pebbles (especially for the title), Laurel Grant, Angel Luis F. Guerra, Jane King, Ana Rosa Lara, the late Claudia Lightfoot, the Maleta family, María Elena, E. Marquez, M. Morales, R. Monzote, Joseph Mutti, Giolvis D. Osoria, Jim Pett, R. Ramirez, F. Reyes, Raquel Rubi, David Stanley, Y. Triana, Nersa. C. Veloso, S. Wilkinson.

And to the many people who asked, for differing reasons, that their names not be included above, your help is not forgotten.

Contents

Preface

Though it is rarely possible these days to arrive at a new somewhere with no preconceptions at all, as a travel writer I avoid over-researching a destination. Before arriving in Cuba, I knew as much as most well-informed people about the country, about U.S. attitudes towards it and the problems the island had faced since the collapse of the Soviet Union over a decade earlier. The networking I'd done in the UK prior to leaving for Cuba brought me into contact with men and women who were staunchly pro-Castro. Those meetings, coupled with my own liberal, left-leaning views, gave me an optimistic outlook about what I would find there. When I travelled through Cuba in the winter of 2000–1, the Revolution had been happening for more than 40 years and was, according to the government, still underway.

Rereading now what I wrote then, I'm struck by how much the feelings of the people I met and spent time with affected my experience of the place and the way I wrote about it on my return home. Cubans are passionate people, and not only for music, dancing and rum, as international tourism promotion suggests. Cubans are passionate about many things: the rights and wrongs of a situation, the weather, freedom and food, to mention just a few. As I travelled from rainy Havana to rainy Baracoa, I began to realise that freedom and food were important to ordinary Cubans chiefly because they didn't have much of either. This didn't mean that the rum, the salsa and the wonderful musical extravagance of Cuba weren't real, but, as I travelled and met people who showed me the interiors of their homes and lives, the Cuba of my imagination quickly vanished. Alongside sun, salsa and organic farming, I found a dark, melancholy sensibility, a Caribbean Gothic that was more complex, exotic and exciting than anything I had been led to suppose by British communists' tales of youth movements and the Triumph of the Revolution. It is this unique Gothic quality, rather than *mojitos* and dirty dancing, that readers will find reflected in the pages that follow.

'Nothing will ever change here.' These were the exact words said to me by teachers, hairdressers, artists and taxi drivers from one end of Cuba to the other. Many of the people I met were too young to have known anything except Fidel Castro and his 1959 revolution. Having had only limited access to information about the vast and sweeping changes that took place in Central and Eastern Europe in the early 1990s, few Cubans could conceive that such change might also be possible in their own country. Today Cuba is at the very beginning of the end of its revolution. Fidel is no longer president, though he still leads the Communist Party and casts his tall shadow over the new president, his brother Raúl. So, although very little has changed as yet on this island, whose largely unspoilt shores lie only 145 kilometres from the extremes of Florida's hedonism, everyone knows that half a century of revolution is almost over and that, one day in the not-too-distant future, things *will* change and life will never be the same again. For most Cubans this is a thrilling and appalling prospect.

Despite the gloom most people expressed to me about their lives, I left the country with a powerful sense of the complexity of what it means to be Cuban in the 21st century. Cuban writers, musicians and athletes are world class; the country sends its doctors to treat the poorest of the poor around the world, while the West cheerfully drains those same countries of their medical professionals. While passionate about inadequate salaries, the lack of basic foodstuffs, restrictions on travel, communication, information and education, which they felt should be up to date and truly free, the Cubans I met were intensely proud of their country, of the fact that they are not a U.S. satellite, despite everything that that country has thrown at them. They were proud of their revolution which has cost them so very much.

Will the country as the world has known it for half a century change forever when the Castro brothers join José Martí and 'Che' Guevara in the great revolution in the sky? Whenever and however change finally happens, I hope, perhaps somewhat naïvely, that the Cuban people, who have endured so much for so long, will at last be allowed to decide their own future, free of pressure from within, or without, the shores of their beautiful island.

Zoë Brân, London 2008

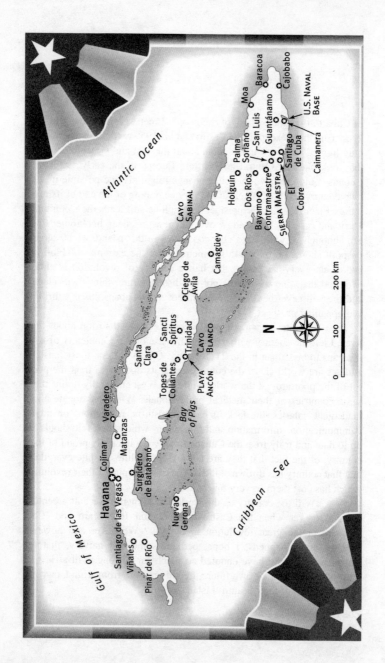

★

Arrival

> Elsewhere is a negative mirror. The traveler recognizes the little that is his, discovering the much he has not had and will never have.
>
> Italo Calvino, *Invisible Cities*

Somewhere north-east of Snug Corner we cross the Tropic of Cancer and begin our descent. Ahead is the invisible barrier of the Bahamas and Lesser Antilles, a protective chain curving casually from Florida to Hispaniola – the end of an ocean. South lies the Windward Passage: ninety shark-infested kilometres separating Haiti from Cuba's most westerly shore. Through the passage is Jamaica and beyond it, Central America and another world. Far below, the night waters of the Sargasso Sea rise and fall like breath in their moonless expanse of ocean.

Sailing towards Cuba in 1492, Christopher Columbus passed through the Sargasso Sea, through the dense *sargassum* mats that litter the ocean's surface like floating moorland. Thinking the weed an indicator of nearby land, the explorer fathomed the depths but found no bottom. He had no way of knowing it lay many kilometres below on the Nares Abyssal Plain. Columbus was fortunate to reach Cuba through the Sargasso: unknowingly he had passed through 'the Sea of Lost Ships'. But when Europeans first sailed here, drowned and tortured vessels belonged to a latent future. Post-Colombian conquistadors, finding themselves becalmed in the entropic Sargasso, jettisoned their horses in order to save water and named this area of the Atlantic the Horse Latitudes. Later it became the Doldrums and then the Bermuda Triangle, the place where whole crews disappear, entire ships melt away or are found sailing in circles, manned by skeletons or ghosts. Aeroplanes evaporate here despite radar and modern communications, for reasons science has yet to explain. Experienced divers vanish in three metres of brine. I imagine the spiralling swell far below me, its motionlessness created by the motion around it of some of the strongest currents in the world; the Gulf stream, Florida, North Equatorial, Antilles and Caribbean. The mysterious Sargasso – 'Limbo of the Lost'; a half-closed doorway to the world of the Caribbean and Central America – is Nature's masterpiece of nonconformity, a hiatus in the laws of probability.

Nothing is visible through the scratched plastic oval beside me. We are surrounded by a perfect darkness broken only by the red flashing of a wing tip. Despite the absence of light, I know exactly where I am as our route is shown with slow and painstaking precision on the brightly lit map that plays across the bulkhead wall instead of a film. A plump cartoon aeroplane twitches its way across the screen over unnaturally blue water through a broken line of green that marks the beginning of playground and revolution; the world of the Caribbean. As we turn into Cuban airspace, all is darkness. No longer over the sea, the continued absence of light implies cloud cover, a shortage of power on the ground, or maybe both – though if we were very much higher, high as a surveillance aircraft perhaps, thinly scattered lights might be visible. A satellite's view from several kilometres above the earth would reveal the small star-clusters of Caracas and Panama; the tiny distant pinpricks of Port-au-Prince, Kingston, Nassau, Guantánamo, Santiago de Cuba; and, dimming all else, the brilliant illumination that is Florida, hanging like a gaudy phallus over Cuba's northern coast.

Poised like an *orisha*'s stick between sea and ocean, between islands and a continent, between past and present, Cuba dominates the Caribbean. Now, on the point of arrival, my feelings are hopeful; my thoughts full of ideas, images and excited discussion. I'm here because Cuba is somewhere I've always wanted to be, and because there's a photograph hanging in my study at home in London – a photo of Ernesto Guevara, dead.

There's something about the space between this image of a corpse and that universally famous, iconic image of Che in his starred beret that I want to understand; between the triumph of revolution and its quietus. History is of little help, however. Cuba's turbulent past has not prepared me, and its maps are just marks on paper. Below and fast approaching is the masculine landscape of Christopher Columbus, Diego Velázquez and Henry Morgan, shaped in the image of José Martí and Fidel Castro. It is the socialist El Dorado and adopted home of that twentieth-century icon. It is also the mysterious island world of Selkirk, Stevenson and Hemingway; a place of the imagination, where anything is possible.

The plane hits an air pocket at 4,000 metres and sinks abruptly into cloud. Far below, a fisherman looks cautiously around at the dark surface of the sea before lifting a lobster basket into a small boat anchored off Baracoa's rocky shore. In a three-hundred-year-old courtyard in Santiago de Cuba, a school janitor teaches seven young women how to dance with the drum, watched by a young man who wears the Star of David and a medal of the Virgin of Charity around his neck. A *vaquero* leads a string of pack mules across a river somewhere near Bayamo and flamingos churn the salt marshes of Cayo Sabinal. In the heart of Santa Clara, a poet reads to his daughter and an artist watches his son's tiny milky mouth as he feeds. The plane banks steeply and there are lights visible now. All along the Malecón the sea hurls itself over the wall to drench the pitted road, the crumbling houses and the elderly *habanero* who lifts his arms to the flying spume and laughs for joy.

These things exist, though like Columbus suspended above the Nares Abyssal, I know nothing of them as I wait for my luggage in the shiny new airport terminal. It has taken fifteen hours to reach here from Gatwick on a 'direct' flight that gave an unexpected glimpse of Portugal through the windows of the transit lounge at Lisbon airport. The delays and winter weather have brought us south of the normal flight path because our elderly Russian plane is, we are advised, too small and fragile to face the turbulent Atlantic further north. The complaints of exhausted fellow passengers reach me through a haze of tiredness.

'My God! This has got to be one of the worst journeys of my life.'

A forty-something Englishwoman herds two blond children away from the rumbling carousel. 'I didn't want to come here, it was my husband's idea of an adventure . . . I *tried* telling him that kids don't really want adventure . . . but would he listen? I haven't left the airport yet and it's already exactly as I imagined. The sooner America takes this place over the better for everyone if you ask me.'

I don't ask, and instead wonder why she's here, what she hopes to experience, or at least, hold on to.

At four in the morning I step out of the terminal and am approached by a taxi driver who conducts me towards the only vehicle in the airport car park. The driver is large and fleshy and leans heavily on his miniskirted girlfriend as he walks towards a shiny maroon 1958 Chevrolet and opens the door. Even from the outside the car smells overpoweringly of diesel fumes. My luggage is tossed onto the back seat and I clamber in after it. The couple spread themselves comfortably across the front seat, light up dark-scented cigarettes that glow brightly in the fume-laden air, and roll down black-tinted windows.

Half an hour later, having seen no other vehicle, we enter Havana with a light rain falling.

LA HABANA

★

Centro

Strangers praised the town's colour and gaiety after
spending three days visiting its dance halls, saloons,
taverns and gambling dens . . . But those who had to
put up with the place all the year round knew about
the mud and the dust, and how the saltpetre turned
the door-knockers green, ate away the ironwork,
made silver sweat . . .

Alejo Carpentier, *Explosion in a Cathedral*

The house of Rebeca Corazón nestles between identical properties
in the heart of Central Havana. Reached from the pavement of
Neptuno Street by a long stone staircase, which opens abruptly
into a courtyard of night-scented flowers and thick-leaved plants,
the house spreads and rises in a colonial design intended to max-
imise light and minimise heat. A twisting iron staircase hangs like
a liana at the open heart of the courtyard; around it windowless
rooms filled with heavy Spanish furniture are occupied by assorted
foreigners. The staircase leads to the modern apartment of Ms
Corazón and to my small room decorated with images of wildlife,
living and dead, torn from magazines. On the roof terrace a small
green sparrow sings to a chained chow.

The minimisation of heat is not a consideration in Havana just
now. I go down onto Neptuno where rain is falling in large, sparse
drops, topping up the muddy puddles and draining into the open
cracks visible in the crumbling walls of houses and shops. The pavement is greasy and broken and I skid past men huddled in doorways,
past young women in skirts short as belts standing irritably on the
corner. The atmosphere reflects the low grey sky and the air feels
dull; everyone looks forlorn in the absence of sun and warmth.

'*Mi madre! Que frigo!*' echoes along the street as shuddering *habaneros* whisper that they are about to die of cold.

In the only brightly lit shop in the street I gaze in jet-lagged wonder at low glass cabinets half-full of biscuits, perfumes, chocolates and women's underwear. As I pay for a bottle of mineral water, a tall young black man appears from nowhere and, touching me gently on the arm, asks very politely for ten cents. Automatically I shake my head feigning ignorance, mostly from surprise. Ten cents seems so little as to hardly be worth asking for. Perhaps he said ten dollars?

In all my daydreams of Havana, this is not how I imagined the first day. There's a claustrophobic unfamiliarity, the feel of a city chill and moist with unexpected winter and heavy with a sexually charged atmosphere that increases in weight as I walk east and south into Habana Vieja and the haunts of tourists. I watch, in passing, a young light brown woman in a striped crop top and jeans wrap her arms around the hips of a much taller black man, thrusting herself hard against him. The man stares over her head along the damp street and looks bored. Near the cathedral a couple make love in the old-fashioned sense of those words. The boy wraps his arms around the girl from behind, taking her hands in his own; as he does this her eyes close and a look of ecstasy lights her face. What elsewhere might be considered a spectator sport, here elicits less than a passing glance and audiences are rare. Alone in the wet streets I am a stranger.

In the house on Neptuno the guests sit around a table draped in brown cloth, in a room filled with antiques and chandeliers. Long wooden shutters open onto two small balconies which overhang the street. The evening meal is served by a thin, nervous-looking woman in her late fifties. She brings bread, watered fruit juice and small, carefully measured portions of an unknown fish with rice. Dessert is a banana the size of my index finger and papaya carefully cut into cubes. At the end of the meal I'm still hungry and looking around the table it appears that my fellow guests, who on closer inspection are less assorted than I imagined, feel the same.

We are all British, and there's something unnerving about this discovery; as if I've walked into an early Harold Pinter play.

Beside me a tax inspector from Liverpool stares lugubriously at his empty plate. Across the table a very large white woman flanked by her two black daughters is talking about communism and the British Communist Party, of which she's a member. As she speaks I look from her face to that of her daughters – both astonishingly like her – and consider the power of genetics. The other member of our party is a student from Kent University who tells us haltingly that he's here translating drama for Rebeca Corazón's theatre company.

'That's her up there,' the student says, pointing to a wall covered in numerous black-and-white photographs of theatrical productions. I assume it is the student who speaks, as his mouth is invisible behind two shoulder-length curtains of dust brown hair.

'Nice tits,' the tax inspector comments, and we all turn towards the top of the stairs where a large image of our host as Medea or Penthesilea is displayed, palely naked and perfectly disordered. The British communist tuts and picks up her fork as if hoping to stab decadence in the heart.

'I dislike these foreign communists. Most of my people dislike them.'

The young Cuban woman I met in the transit lounge of Lisbon airport during our layover had made her feelings perfectly clear.

'They come to our country thinking it's all about "the struggle", but they see only what they are shown. Why don't they try living on two dollars a week and see how exciting life is under those conditions – how heroic.'

'Is that how it is?' I asked.

'Of course,' she replied. 'You will see after you have been in my country a short while that everything is – and is not – how it appears to be. Are you a communist?'

I shook my head.

'Do you know many communists in London?'

'I know a few people who might call themselves communists.'

'And they have told you how marvellous things are in my country, no? How wonderful our education is for example?'

I nodded.

'They are right. But what they do not see, or perhaps do not tell you, is that tools without a use are worse than no tools at all. If you are not an athlete or a musician – and if you are honest – life is very hard in my country.'

The large woman's two daughters look politely detached as their mother waves her fork and talks with animation about the volunteer brigades she's worked with over the years and her wonderful experiences during previous visits to Cuba.

'These people are magnificent,' she says. 'Magnificent. They know what sacrifice is and also what it is to be a true community, helping and supporting each other. This country puts the West to shame – you'll find that out if you travel through Cuba with an open mind.'

I think about my conversation with the young woman in Lisbon, her passion and the sense of loss she described at living in London, far from her home and family.

Rebeca Corazón sweeps into the dining room in a swirl of fabric and shouted Spanish, long dark hair streaming behind her, white arms outstretched to the world beyond the open windows. Perhaps she's rehearsing for another Greek tragedy. She dashes to the shutters and slams them shut, plunging the room into an early dusk.

'I've told you . . .' she screams at the cringing woman serving us, 'Never, *never* leave the shutters open . . . Do you want the neighbours to see what food I put on this table? Do you?'

Many weeks later I would come to understand this incident. Now, less than twenty-four hours after arriving in Cuba, it is already clear to me that forming a coherent vision of this place will be challenging.

The Malecón stretches from the Castillo de San Salvador de la Punta in the old town to another early Spanish castle at the mouth of the Río Almendares. Built by the U.S. administration in Cuba at the start of the twentieth century, the eight-kilometre road edging the city and the sea is an architectural icon, a broad ribbon of scenic dilapidation. A few newly restored buildings seem lost among the sweeping seafront's widespread decay. The road surface is crumbling, battered by a hundred years of crashing water and sinking incomes. Now the ocean forces its way up through the tarmac, spouting whale-like over pedestrians and passing cars. Between the old town and the Vedado district, car dealerships and abandoned sections of flyover are squeezed between collapsed roofs and ruined houses that were once among the most elegant in the Western hemisphere. Today, walking to the Hotel Nacional where I am to meet Cuban writer Enrique Cirules, the Malecón is busy with tourist taxis and the large, brightly-coloured Chevys and Oldsmobiles that can carry up to a dozen Cubans for a few pesos each.

The twin spires of the iconic Nacional rise above a garden of slender palms and sharp cacti near the junction of the Malecón and La Rampa. Set on an outcrop of rock overlooking the sea, the hotel's hinterland of petrol stations, pharmacies and shore is busy with history. Nearby the memorial to the crew of the U.S. battleship *Maine*, which exploded in Havana's harbour on 15 February 1898, rusts gently in the grey afternoon light. The Americans blamed the Spanish, though at the time, and since, there were rumours that the Americans blew the ship up themselves to justify going to war with Spain over Cuba. Most of the ship's officers were ashore at the time of the explosion, fuelling suspicion that ordinary sailors were sacrificed. The memorial's cannons, marble columns and statuesque women surmount a later inscription placed there by the present Cuban government: *To the victims of the* Maine *who were sacrificed by voracious imperialism in its zeal to seize the island of Cuba from February 1898 to 15 February 1961.* Beneath the Nacional is the Cave of Tanaganana, thought to be named after an Indian seeking refuge from conquistadors. Even within these few acres of land a history of desire is evident; desire for this island and its diverse riches. Desire for freedom.

Today the Nacional is full of sleek young women and dark, well-barbered men who flaunt and sway on high heels and leather soles through the lofty entrance hall and out to the garden bar overlooking the sea. They are here for the Latin American Film Festival and to flirt with the tense television journalists earnestly interviewing paunchy, self-satisfied men as pouting girls look on. It's surprisingly easy to distinguish the suave, continental Latins from the locals whose glamour is of an entirely different kind.

Behind me someone says, 'All young girls are beautiful *chica*, but they don't all grow up to be beautiful women. On the other hand, most young boys are terrible, but men get better with age.'

I turn around. A grey-bearded man in his late fifties is talking at a young woman who smiles blandly, her gaze drifting over the television reporters and the distant sea.

The history of the hotel reflects its hinterland. Built in 1930, by 1940 it was the headquarters of the U.S. Mafia in Cuba who used the island to satisfy desires of all kinds. Writer Enrique Cirules, a slender, white-haired man, is an authority on Cuban society and the Mafia in particular. As we sit in the garden bar he brings the old days to life again; the days when La Rampa was a string of Chinese theatres, casinos, restaurants and brothels and the Mafia ruled Havana. We have been introduced by the International Press Centre so I'm aware that Cirules writes 'approved' histories, but his conviction and the passion of his delivery make him a fascinating raconteur despite my problems with the language. And this place is perfect for a history lesson on the Mob.

'The Mafia began its activities here in Cuba in the early 1920s,' Cirules says, 'running rum mostly. Then, towards the end of 1933, they began to establish their criminal empire and this hotel was always at the heart of their operations.'

I gaze up from a wicker seat at the soaring, threatening brickwork, and can understand why. Built at a time when Cuba was entrenched in dictatorship, lawlessness and violence, the Nacional has been described as looking like an Arabian palace, but the elegant towers and colonnades of palms seem more like a temple of Mammon in a slightly seedy oasis. The structure's power and bleakness at first sight has a Soviet quality, but is merely reminiscent of another, criminal empire.

'When Batista began to seize power here in 1933 the Mafia saw their chance for real political infiltration. Lucky Luciano was head of the New York Mob at the time and he ordered his financier in Cuba, Meyer Lansky, to befriend Batista. So Lansky did and they began a relationship that lasted three decades. Nothing of political or business significance happened in this country during that time without his involvement either through his many agents, or through his position as adviser to Batista.' His eyes crinkle with concern that I may not be understanding everything. 'You've heard of Lansky?'

I nod, trying to remember what. 'So you're saying the Mafia ran Cuba all those years?'

'Are you surprised? It was just an extension of U.S. control here, just a different kind of annexation to what the U.S. government intended. The same year he met Lansky, Batista also met one of Roosevelt's advisers on Cuba who encouraged him in his political ambitions. Batista had never been rich, he was only a sergeant in the army until 1933. He was offered wealth by the Mafia and position by the American government; he was a clever man, but greedy and foolish, so of course he accepted both.'

Batista gave Lansky a great deal and in return Lansky made Havana the 'Paris of the Caribbean' with all that that implied. Sex, horse racing, tourism, entertainment and betting all converged. Over the years the Cuban Mob founded banks, insurance companies, television channels, usury businesses, airline companies, import and export houses and drug cartels.

'By the fifties, Cuba was the "whorehouse of the Caribbean" and almost everyone in it from Batista down became a whore.' Cirules sips thoughtfully at his lemonade. 'This is why we talk about the "Triumph of the Revolution".'

I nod uncertainly. I've been here just two days. Around us the beautiful people of Latin America laugh and drink on the terrace where Lansky fêted Lucky Luciano in 1946 at a kind of Mafia AGM. The hotel was closed to the public for several days over that

Christmas. The 1600 guests ate spiced snails and lemon-flavoured tortoise followed by breast of flamingo and garlic crayfish from Cojímar. There was venison sent by the Minister of Camagüey and, rarest of all, the succulent flesh of manatees, so human-like in their call and form that sailors once believed them to be mermaids. Frank Sinatra was the entertainment.

'The U.S. government didn't really care about Mafia activities in Cuba as long as they didn't cross each other . . . no-one opposed Mob business here. Nineteen fifty-seven was one of their best years – just before it all collapsed. Fascinating hotels were being opened, beautiful new thoroughfares built, and of course there had to be new buildings to house the administration of this criminal State. They even built the tunnel under the harbour which linked the city with the beaches to the east.'

Like any empire founded on greed and graft, it couldn't last; but it went out with a flourish of sleazy brilliance. Cirules describes those last decadent years with something bordering on nostalgia and sighs, as if thinking of all the good things done by bad people. 'They were incredibly efficient you know, amazingly so. Havana had one million inhabitants, thousands of bars and canteens attended by a legion of girls. There were exclusive mansions ruled by famous madams. Everything was organised. It was all calculated, controlled.'

'But wasn't that the start of the Revolution, fifty-seven? Castro's return?'

'Yes it was. Because while the rich criminals enjoyed themselves and grew richer, half the population was in need and Fidel saw that and knew it had to be changed. There were armies of beggars, orphans, sick people, derelicts. On every corner there was gaming: the lucky ball, the lottery ticket, bingo, dice, cards. And marijuana everywhere and cocaine . . . though cocaine was only for the rich.'

'Did no-one pay attention to Castro's landing then?'

'Not at first. It was known Fidel had landed and that his group had been surprised and almost annihilated. It was known that a few had managed to regroup and that Fidel was with twelve men in the mountains of the Sierra Maestra. Why would anyone be afraid of thirteen beaten men so far away? But then it really began and everyone was amazed.'

The rumours of revolt became certainty in the middle of 1957 along with news of death, torture and shoot-outs by the repressive government forces. In Pinar del Río a tobacco festival ended in violence; sabotage, fires and explosions were reported everywhere and the country's highways seemed to be rivers of nails and spikes. The bodies of three young people were found beneath a bridge near Matanzas; two men were found dead on a highway near Santiago; two peasants in Guantánamo were tortured, murdered and hung from a tree. In the sugar towns, refineries and villages, revolutionary flags waved. There was fire in the cane fields. Castro seemed both impossibly vulnerable and strangely unstoppable.

'It was truly an exceptional year in so many ways,' Cirules continues. I want to ask what he himself remembers of it, but there's no hint of the personal in any of his talk. 'The Mafia felt safe and the wealthy were distracted by mid-afternoon galas, dazzling all-night parties and the visits of Hollywood idols. Lots of big stars came here where they could have a good time without the press watching them as they did back home. Ava Gardner visited often and Maureen O'Hara too. You've heard of Robert Mitchum?'

'Yes.'

'He was wild when he was here, smoking marijuana and drinking. In the middle of one party he took off his clothes, doused himself with a bottle of sauce and yelled that he was the best hamburger in the world!'

I giggle.

'Hemingway lived here all through those years though he hated the Mafia. When Ava Gardner came here with Sinatra she would visit Hemingway at Finca La Vigía, but Sinatra was never invited.'

Gardner would swim naked in Hemingway's pool on these visits and as Cirules talks, I imagine the ageing writer and the beautiful actress laughing together in the pastoral comfort of La Vigía, far away from the decadent Nacional.

'Did you ever meet Hemingway?' I ask.

He shakes his head. 'No, but my neighbour met him when she was a child. Her family lived in Cojímar, before they built so many new houses. She told me that she met him on the beach when he was working on his boat. She was four years old, but she hasn't forgotten.'

Hemingway's time in Cuba is virtually unrecorded by the man himself. For someone who travelled and wrote so extensively about the world he was strangely silent on Cuba, Castro and his predecessor, Batista. When British writer Norman Lewis visited Hemingway in Havana in 1958 it was with reluctance, after hearing rumours of the writer's decline. He found a man who had lost all interest in life. Lewis asked Hemingway if he thought Castro would overthrow the government but got no response. In his report to his London newspaper Lewis wrote: 'He no longer cares to hold opinions because life has lost its taste. He told me nothing, but he has taught me more than I wanted to know.'

'Why do you think Hemingway is so memorable for Cubans?' I ask.

Cirules smiles, his blue eyes are misted with early cataracts and watering slightly, though whether from emotion at recalling Hemingway or because of the cool wind blowing across the terrace, it's impossible tell.

'Because he was kind and friendly to everyone . . . to black people, to the poor. He didn't distinguish between people – he either liked them or he didn't. They say a lot of things now about him being a depressive, an alcoholic. He wasn't, he just liked a drink . . . there are worse crimes. But mostly people still remember him with affection because he was a friend of Cuba and an enemy of Batista and the Mafia. He was from the States but he loved Cuba and he wrote about ordinary Cuban people with respect.'

We finish our drinks on the now cold terrace where a small, chill rain falls. Entering the hotel, Cirules and I walk together through the salon where Luciano and Lansky – briefly emperors of Havana – held court that Christmas more than half a century ago.

The walls are covered in photos of former guests – a few Latin, but mostly from the U.S.; women with impossibly dark lips pose, cat-like, on silk; men in tuxedos, their groomed hair reflecting light, stand nonchalantly, cigarettes dangling from pale fingers. ''Neo-colonialism'', that's what some of my colleagues call it,' Cirules says, as we pause to gaze at images of dead stars. 'We seemed politically independent but the United States owned us, it wasn't even *honest* colonialism.' That grudging nostalgia is still there in Cirules' tone. He's a patriot, he would *never* want those days again; but the glamour, the style . . . was it *really* all too decadent? We shake hands in the lobby and I watch as he walks down the steps of the hotel, past the colonnades of palms and lines of Mercedes taxis until his tall, upright figure disappears. I ask a taxi driver an approximate fare to my address. He points to the dashboard.

'Meter,' he says, tapping the ash from a thick cigar through the window and onto my shoes. 'In dollars.'

At the house of Rebeca Corazón, the chow chained on the roof has bitten a child in the face. The communist woman's two daughters have moved out. The tax inspector has not left the house in days and sits in the darkened hallway looking at the telephone. I ask if he's expecting a call.

'Not for me, no, but Rebeca wants someone to take a call for her, and Dulce is busy making the meal.'

'I thought you were on holiday,' I say.

'Oh I don't mind. I'm happy just to sit here.' His muddy brown eyes have a sad animal expression. 'I'm not feeling too good to be honest . . . stomach, must be something I ate. I've been here two weeks and I'm tired now; quite looking forward to going home.' He grins apologetically. 'I live with my mother . . . didn't think I'd miss her . . .'

The house and his mood match; an absence of windows and the brooding presence of Ms Corazón create a dark, introverted atmosphere reminiscent of Marquez at his gloomiest.

'I've enjoyed myself though,' he says, in an attempt at brightness. 'I never went out of Havana but there are lots of things to see here; some good clubs and bars. I met a woman last week, she's a teacher, a nice woman.' His voice drops confidentially. 'We went to a *casa particular*, at least she said it was . . .' he pauses, as if recalling the scene in his mind. 'It didn't look like a guesthouse, more like a bike shed.'

'She was a prostitute.'

'No! No, not a prostitute, a teacher I told you. She enjoyed it, I could tell she did – she said she did.'

'Did you pay her?'

'Well . . . it was a bit complicated. This man turned up when we went to the *casa* . . .'

'The pimp . . .'

'Pimp?' He shakes his head. 'No, no – she didn't know him, said she'd never seen him before. Then she went into the *casa* and the man told me to pay him, so I did.'

It's all I can do not to roll my eyes up to the ceiling and shake my head. 'Then after you gave her so much enjoyment, she asked to be paid, yes?'

'Yes, but I'd already paid the man, so I was confused. She said she didn't know him . . . why had I given him the money? I didn't know what to say, so I gave her money too.'

In the artificial semi-darkness his balding head just catches the light.

'That's rather an old trick,' I say. 'If he wasn't her pimp, he was probably her husband or her brother.'

He gives me a defiantly hangdog look. 'You're so cynical . . . she wasn't a prostitute, not like the others you see on the street.'

'Then why did you pay her?'

'I'm not stupid,' he says. 'I know perfectly well that no-one as beautiful as her would want someone like me, except for money.'

He gazes towards the pale rectangles of light that are the balcony and I feel almost sorry for having pressed him.

'This is a strange place, isn't it?' he says. 'Things you wouldn't do at home, no-one even notices here. Yet everyday things seem to be wrong.' He shakes his head. 'Last week I went to a pharmacy to buy eucalyptus oil for the little girl here, Dulce's niece . . . have you heard her coughing? The pharmacist asked me who the oil was for and when I told him he drew his thumb and index finger across his lips like a zip!'

'Meaning what?'

He shrugs. 'Who knows what it means. I bought it anyway; they have so little here it's shocking. You have to do something, don't you? Yesterday I went to the junior school down the road and gave away all the pens and pencils I brought with me. God! It was like a jungle, they were fighting and screaming to get at the stuff. I was mobbed by kids no higher than my waist.'

He sounds almost offended and it occurs to me to say that perhaps his action was stupid and insensitive, but he believes he's helping the poor of the world. He's also leaving Cuba in a few days, so opportunities for future damage are limited.

The following morning I decide to leave Ms Corazón's house. There's something unpleasant about the place, something Dickensian – a sort of Dotheboys Hall merged with Bleak House. Within two hours I've found alternative accommodation. The student with the curtained hair helps me carry my bag down the many flights of steps to the cab waiting on Neptuno. On the doorstep he whispers, 'You still looking for a Spanish teacher?'

'Definitely. You know someone?'

'Yeah. Meet me by the cathedral at two tomorrow and I'll take you there. She said it's okay but I want to be careful, know what I mean?'

'Yeah,' I say, though I don't. 'I'll be there.'

'Jacob,' he says as we part. 'I'm Jacob.'

I look up as the cab drives away; the tax inspector is standing on the balcony looking pale and drawn. He raises one hand in goodbye, the other shades his eyes from the light of day.

Between the university and the Malecón, Jovellar Street edges Central Havana and the district known as Vedado, a line of once fashionable tenements, modern apartment blocks and the occasional house and garden. Here, for the price of the single, windowless room, I now have an entire, post-Revolution apartment to myself in a great location. The front door has seven locks and bolts. There's a television which has to warm up before an orangey picture appears. Water in the shower is heated by a small boiler attached to the showerhead itself and controlled by naked wires and switches. The small kitchen boasts a rattling Russian refrigerator, a stone sink and four gas rings, two of which work. A balcony, filled with carefully tended pot plants and enclosed by a wrought-iron grille, hangs over the street like a cage from where I can look across the narrow street to other, older, balconies, filled with dogs, children and music. The noise of Havana is a hum that occasionally settles or rises in pitch, but it's always there, even in the ill-lit night. Dogs bark, children shriek, men shout up at darkened windows, *'Abuela, Abuela,* throw down the keys!' and, Rapunzel-like, grandmothers across the city cast down access to their homes.

That first night I lie in bed with the balcony doors open and watch unseen as people come and go in the apartments across the street. They were fine homes once, with shutters on every door and balconies swagged with laurel. Former servants now live in their masters' dwellings, but it seems a Pyrrhic victory; the things that made these homes desirable are gone, like their former owners. The dimly lit rooms are almost bare, and brown with many years of nicotine fumes. One balcony door is missing a small pane of glass and through it the wind pulls a section of dark red curtain; sucking and blowing: in, out – like the beating of a heart – as Acker Bilk's 'Stranger on the Shore' drifts by, loud and unashamed.

Walking down Jovellar that night to a local *paladar,* a private restaurant, with three tables and a locked front door that opened only after several knocks, I passed yet another balcony and glancing upwards stopped abruptly in mid-stride. Above me a large boxer dog was standing upright, front paws firmly spread on the balustrade. Its wide mouth hung open and it seemed to be laughing, or perhaps grimacing. I wasn't surprised: the pink T-shirt dress really didn't suit it – not at all the dog's colour – and I didn't know whether to laugh or pull a face myself. After another fifty metres I suddenly doubted I saw a dog in a dress, and glanced back. The boxer was still there, still upright, paws braced against some unspecified attack or foreign insult.

On the Malecón a group of small children are playing on a piece of unfinished flyover. They have made rough carts from wooden fruit boxes in which they race, unafraid and screaming with delight, down the steep concrete slope. Nearby, a group of older boys play baseball in the shadow of nineteenth-century revolutionary hero General Antonio Maceo, using their hands as bats. With a speed that leaves me standing, the sun disappears and the sky turns twilight-dark with cloud. Dust swirls around my ankles and writhes its way up my body filling my mouth and eyes. The children disappear to safety and I follow a couple of queens as they make their way towards the café in the nearby Fiat dealership. Waves crash over the low sea wall, spilling onto the cracked and crumbling road. Above the noise I can hear the continuous cursing of the queen in hot pants as he leans angrily into the wind, spiked, three-inch heels catching in the pavement; pale, shaved legs are moving beacons in the gathering gloom, arms windmills, gesticulating their fury at the weather.

I try to imagine Hemingway or Graham Greene working and drinking here – Havana as it used to be in the heady, anarchic days described by Cirules – but find only glimpses of their experience. I pass art deco houses in various states of disrepair, their metal window frames supporting expanses of curved glass in scarlet, violet, yellow. I gaze through the windows of crumbling shore-side houses: at a rocking chair with pink embroidered cushions, a chandelier hanging on bare wires from the ceiling, a deal table heavy with kitsch *objeto* – plastic flowers and plaster dogs and cats clustered around a figure of Christ, his bleeding heart held in an outstretched hand.

Outside a homeopathic pharmacy pig shoulders, dripping and red, are being unloaded and carried into the dark rear of the shop. A trail of blood is smeared into the tiled floor and marked with the soles of shoes. It looks like a crime scene and smells like an abattoir.

21

The scent is still in my nose when I reach Habana Vieja's neat web of sixteenth- and seventeenth-century houses and palaces on the peninsula of Havana thrusting across the bay. From the Avenida del Puerto the distant refineries of the Ensenada de Mirimelena are clearly visible. Flames leap, eager as napalm, from tall chimneys that bleed black smoke into the blue of the sky.

The plaque on the wall of a restored mansion, one of several which occupy three sides of a small, perfectly formed square, reads *Plaza de la Catedral*. The eighteenth-century *habaneros* called it the 'Plaza de la Ciénaga' – 'Swamp Square'. Five hundred years ago this was saline marshland; water birds and reptiles flourished among the reeds and mosquito-clouded sedge and the few human inhabitants survived mostly on fish and birds. In 1519, the same year Cuba's first governor Diego Velázquez de Cuéllar sent Hernán Cortés on a Mexican gold hunt, Havana was established here, almost precisely where I stand and wait for Jacob. It was the third Cuban settlement to include the name 'La Habana'. This was the last of Governor Diego Velázquez' 'seven towns' which started with the settlement of Baracoa in the far east of the island seven years earlier. Havana was never intended to be a place of importance, certainly not the capital of the largest island in the Caribbean. The eastern provinces and the city of Santiago de Cuba were of far greater strategic importance in the early sixteenth century because of their nearness to other Spanish island possessions. Now the old town of Havana is an uneasy combination of urban decay at its most picturesque and magnificent buildings beautifully restored.

Like many of the streets of Habana Vieja this one is narrow, and brown with history. Sunlight slants across washing hung on balconies dense with potted vegetation and reflects the face of a young woman watching the world passing by beneath her. Olive-skinned policemen with small moustaches stand at each junction of the street 'protecting' tourists from locals. Doors open into shops selling paintings and handicrafts; primary colours glaring out from the darkened interiors of haphazard galleries. Most of the artists are men, and most of the paintings feature one of three themes: Havana street scenes, American cars of the 1950s and 1960s and naked women with large breasts in imaginative poses.

Beside me, Jacob looks neither right nor left, though this may be because his hair interferes with his vision.

'Her house is just there,' he says, pointing to an eighteenth-century entrance that fills an entire archway. 'If it's okay with you, I'll go in on my own and let them know we're here. Maria knows you're coming about lessons but I want to check it's okay, just to be absolutely sure.'

'Sure about what?' I ask.

'That she won't get in trouble. That it's okay to bring you. Everyone is watched here. They have these things called CDRs, Comités de Defensa de la Revolución, and if people think you're doing stuff on the side, like making money from foreigners, maybe they'll report you. I don't want to be responsible for anything like that happening to these people.'

'Of course, no problem.'

I sit on the high kerb and listen to the salsa music echoing from a nearby hotel. A white cat slides along a wall before disappearing into the shadows. A few metres away a young man and woman are resting on a doorstep. The man moves suddenly until he's lying with his head in the young woman's lap, cheek resting against the slight overhang of her brown, naked belly. He wraps an arm round her hips to caress the small of her back while reaching up with his mouth to suck a nipple through her clothing. No-one else seems to notice.

Jacob reappears. 'It's okay,' he says, 'come on.'

An angry dog barks as we pass along a narrow, half-covered alley which leads into the former coach house of an aristocrat's mansion. Several families live here in what would be a slum if it were less spotlessly clean and aesthetically pleasing. Even the peeling paint is attractive, forming patterns of colour on the pitted walls. We pass through a half-door and into a remarkable space. One vast, high-ceilinged room has been turned into a home using partitions and a semi-mezzanine. As my eyes adjust to the cool gloom, Jacob introduces me to three generations of Old Havana women.

Maria Rosina Pereira is a handsome mulatto woman in her late thirties. Her daughter Ana, a student of mathematics, is tall and smoothly brown, with haughty Spanish features and soft African hair.

'Why didn't you bring her in with you?' Maria asks Jacob.

'I just wanted to be sure it was okay, that you wouldn't get into trouble . . . you know.'

The women laugh, as if his caution were foolish, ridiculous. Jacob blushes slightly and Ana pats him on the shoulder. We all sit and I'm offered the only chair that still has a back. Ana and Jacob chatter in Spanish about university and mutual friends. I try not to stare at the contrast of clean homeliness and overarching decay. From the bathroom-kitchen-bedroom, the ceiling of which must be ten metres high, an elderly mulatto woman appears carrying tiny cups, decorated with eighteenth-century ladies in court dress. Each holds a dose of black, bitter coffee.

'This is my mother, Antonia,' Maria says in clear, rapid Spanish. 'She is eighty-six-years old, but is very fit and healthy, as you see.'

The older woman looks at me with an expression that says there's little left in the world with the power to charm or interest her.

Haltingly, I explain that my Spanish isn't good enough to grasp most of what is being said, hence my need for lessons.

'I don't speak English,' Maria says smiling, 'so you will learn very fast.'

We agree on three hours a day, five days a week.

I make tea on a gas ring in my kitchen with a torch held between my teeth. The overhead bulb has blown. I don't know it yet, but this is good practice for more total blackouts to come. There's a choice of costume melodrama or Castro on television. I decide on Castro who's holding a press conference with President Putin.

It looks as though the Cuban leader has been speaking for some time; his voice is ponderous and very quiet, the kind of voice you have to strain to listen to, the kind that controls. The Russian President looks bored, taps his fingers on the table in front of him then seems to remember where he is and stops abruptly, only to start again almost immediately. Putin looks pale and small beside the bearded, barrel-chested Castro who, despite his age and physical stiffness, dominates the screen. Tired but content I lie on the lumpy plastic sofa with its cigarette burns, drink my tea and listen carefully to the Spanish, trying to translate. We are being told that this is an historic occasion, the first visit of a Russian head of state to Cuba since the dissolution of the Soviet Union. This is the re-forming of true friendship.

It was a strange friendship at the best of times. Half a world apart, this small island nation was taken under the extensive wing of the world's largest country. But they were never quite on the same wavelength: the Soviets chilly, yet sentimental; the Cubans extrovert, but thoroughly pragmatic. Then there was the racism: for all its pretensions to equality, the Soviet Union was a place of white, Caucasian domination. Black Cuban men who married white Soviet women found they'd made an uncomfortable bed for themselves. Cuba was a strange melting pot that both attracted and repelled the Soviets who saw the island as exotic, small and poor – to be patronised as much as helped. To Cubans, the Soviets were dull, grey alcoholics who didn't wash enough and couldn't dance.

Putin's fingers continue to drum. Perhaps he's wondering when, if ever, he'll see the twelve billion dollars Cuba owes his own impoverished country. Anti-U.S. solidarity was never cheap.

At nine sharp the following day my doorbell rings and my new teacher is standing in the hallway, refusing to enter until I invite her in in Spanish. Languages were never my strong point and Maria is relentless. I make tea and we sit on the balcony and start on the present tense. After two hours my brain shuts down and refuses to function, so we agree on simple conversation. We talk slowly about very little until Maria asks me quite suddenly if I'm a racist. It takes a few moments to find the words of denial in Spanish.

'Of course not!' I say. 'Why do you ask that?'

'Because Jacob didn't bring you straight into my house yesterday . . . I thought maybe you didn't like black people.'

Was *that* it! I laugh with relief, but I'm not left off so lightly.

'Did he think you would object to our poverty then? Was it for that reason you stayed outside?'

I think, 'My God! Is that how she sees me?' But I say, 'Jacob was concerned for you, concerned not to make trouble for you by bringing me to your house. He has much affection for your family.'

She's quiet for a moment, seeming pleased. Then she says, 'We hear there is a lot of racism in Europe, you see. Is it true? Are there many racists in Europe?'

I want to ask what Maria means by racism, feeling instinctively that her meaning and mine would not be the same, but language frustrates me. Then I remember her asking Jacob why he hadn't brought me in with him and that he'd explained and they'd all laughed at his anxieties. Has she forgotten that? Did she not believe him? Have I given her any reason to think me a racist? I'm mystified but also aggrieved, mostly with myself because I can't ask what I want. But there's the nagging suspicion of Maria's suspicion and the ground seems suddenly slippery underfoot.

She mentions France and her time there as an impoverished student in Marseilles where she experienced discrimination at first hand but was unsure if it was about her colour, her lack of money or both. I say there's racism everywhere but that most Western European countries make some effort to prevent its institutionalisation. Abruptly she changes the subject.

'Yesterday was a very wonderful day for me,' she says. 'I had tea with Ludmilla Putina, the president's wife. All of us who taught Russian at the university here met together and had tea with her.' She shakes her head. 'It was beautiful to hear Russian spoken again. Beautiful. We were all in tears,' she says, drawing her fingers down her cheeks to show me the words I don't understand. 'It has been so long, so long.'

'Are there Russians living in Havana still?' I ask.

She nods, but she doesn't know them well, they aren't friends. She no longer has Russian friends.

'Every Cuban suffered after Gorbachev . . . we lost almost everything and until three or four years ago things were terrible. We thought no country could survive such poverty. For teachers of Russian it was very hard. One day you have a good job, the next you have nothing. So I had to learn a completely different language very quickly in order to teach and I chose French. I am doing my PhD now – it's a dictionary of the relative terminologies of Spanish and French for the tourist market.'

Changing the subject abruptly once more, Maria tells me that she likes tea, especially English tea.

'The tea you made for me earlier . . . you used one bag for each of us?'

'I did.'

'That is no good. It's too strong. In my house, one tea bag makes enough for four people.'

I feel chastised. I want to say, 'But the tea bags are mine and I like it strong,' or maybe make a joke about hanging used tea bags to dry on the washing line. I do neither. Instead I think how strange and fraught with danger it is being around educated, intelligent people who are very poor. But this is not a place of desperate poverty: not the Third World, not India, Burma or Sierra Leone where the abject poor can seem almost like a different species in everything other than the most basic human requirements. In those countries there is the relief of an impenetrable language barrier, a protection and cover. Here that isn't possible, and the fact that I am being taught to speak and understand, am forcing myself to communicate, makes the potential for future complexities even greater.

'I will see you tomorrow, same time,' Maria says as I walk with her to the door. 'We will learn the past tense. It is the most difficult of all Spanish tenses, and the one we use the most.'

★

San Lázaro

> He was asleep in a short time and he dreamed of
> Africa when he was a boy and the long, golden
> beaches and the white beaches, so white they hurt
> your eyes and the high capes and the great brown
> mountains. He lived along that coast now every
> night and in his dreams he heard the surf roar and
> saw the native boats come riding through it. He
> smelled the tar and oakum of the deck as he slept
> and he smelled the smell of Africa that the land
> breezes brought at morning.
>
> Hemingway, *The Old Man and the Sea*

The first Africans arrived in Cuba in 1522, a decade after Diego
Velázquez began his colonisation of the island. That was how
long it took for Cuba's native population to be all but extermi-
nated, and in the absence of working bodies the Spanish turned to
the west coast of Africa for labour. But it was not only bodies that
filled the holds of the slaving ships leaving the palm-fringed
shores of what is now Nigeria. Spirits and gods, *orishas,* accompanied the suffering cargo on their journey west. African religion
spread across the Caribbean and the Americas with the slaving
ships and took root most deeply in the non-Anglophone colonies
of Cuba, Haiti and Brazil. In Cuba's new towns and plantations
the myths and religious practices of Africa found fertile ground
and, through careful husbandry, managed to remain as they
always had been and yet change, utterly.

Santería, 'the worship of saints', a Cuban syncretisation of
Spanish Catholicism and Yoruba religion, is a merging of tradition
and magic. Enslaved Yorubas, arriving in Cuba from the Niger

region, found that their masters also worshipped many spirits; that there was one main spirit, very like the Yoruba's creator god Olórun, and a hierarchy which included saints. It was a relatively small step for the Africans to identify their *orishas* with the icons of the Catholic Church, endowing specific Christian martyrs and virgins with all the supernatural powers of African gods and goddesses. The rather faded Christian saints got a new lease of life; their attributes of goodness, charity, self-sacrifice transmogrified into the passionate, vital and far from altruistic characteristics of Yoruba deities, who corresponded more closely to the gods of ancient Greece and Rome than with anything Christian.

Juan Perez rocks back and forth on a chair in my apartment. The legs groan and I hope the carpentry is stronger than it looks.

'You are interested in Santería?' he asks loudly. In the hallway a locksmith and a young policeman wearing a uniform as tight as his lips are attending to someone's unopenable front door. The noise is deafening, compounded by loud sax music from the adjoining apartment.

'I am. Particularly the San Lázaro's Day pilgrimage to El Rincón . . . people have told me it's worth seeing. What do you think?'

'Oh yes, definitely worth seeing.'

'You've been yourself?'

'Many years ago but I remember it.'

'Then we'll go.'

He shrugs. 'If you want. Santiago de las Vegas is quite far from here, beyond the airport. It's an all-night occasion and you may have to walk far.'

He's trying to put me off, but the annual pilgrimage in honour of San Lázaro is one of the reasons I'm in Cuba now.

'No problem, if we have to walk I'll walk.'

Juan smiles. He's short and broad, with the spreading belly of a fifty-something man who lives well. His thick hair is silver-grey over steel blue eyes set into a strong, Spanish face. Juan is a fixer, a man who makes things happen and his English, or rather, his

American, is excellent. He's worked for foreigners before, television companies and rich journalists. He knows I can't really afford him and after some discussion we agree on a fee to suit us both – only slightly more than four months salary for a full-time Havana surgeon. 'What else would you like to do?' he asks.

'Maybe a cockfight . . . whatever else you think might be interesting.'

He nods slowly. 'A cockfight is no problem. A good friend of mine is an *aficionado* of these things. I myself have never been. And maybe we could go to Cojímar?'

Without knowing why he suggests Cojímar I agree.

'So – why do you want to know about Santería?'

'Because I don't understand it,' I say. 'It's pretty complicated. Do *you* understand it all?'

He laughs. 'All, no. Enough probably. You know it came from Africa, now it's everywhere, probably the biggest religion here in Cuba. The Africans were brought here against their will so they struggled to hold onto something of their own. By merging their gods with Catholicism, the slaves made themselves a wonderful disguise. They simply call one of their *orishas* by the name of a saint and continue to worship their own gods while seeming very good Christians. The colonials never knew, or if they did they didn't care.' He smiles broadly, as if finding this mass deception appealing. 'White people follow it too, poor people, rich people, Fidel himself maybe . . . they say he's a son of Changó, *orisha* of war and fire.' He grins. 'Changó is also Santa Barbara. There's a lot of crossing of genders. Certain African gods are represented by Catholic saints: Obatalá, is Christ, though he's not really male or female so he's also associated with the Nuestra Señora de la Merced. Obatalá has a son, Elegguá, who is San Antonio and the *orisha* of destiny. It's not complicated at all when you learn their names and colours – colour is very important. You can tell what *orisha* a person follows by the colours they wear or the beads around their neck.'

'Do you believe any of it?'

He laughs. 'I was brought up a good communist, believing in Marx and Lenin.' He shakes his head, suddenly serious. 'No I don't believe it, but I respect it . . . I have seen things, things I cannot explain.'

'What kind of things?' I ask eagerly.

'Things I cannot explain,' he says.

'Santería seems to be very popular now. Was it always like that, even before the Revolution?'

'I don't know, I was a schoolkid then. It's definitely more visible now than it was even five years ago. A lot of things have changed here recently.'

'What do you remember of the Revolution?' I ask, hoping that Juan will open up more than the other people I've spoken to.

'Quite a lot as it happens. My father worked in one of the big ministries and in the holidays I would go with him to his office and sit quietly and listen to the men talking. The summer before Fidel began the fight, there was talk all the time about what would happen. Then in 1960, after the Triumph of the Revolution – I was thirteen – I went as part of a group of other schoolkids into the mountains to teach farmers to read.'

'At thirteen?'

'Why not? I could read and write so I could teach someone who had not had my opportunities. It was a very good part of my education. I taught three people to read and I am still very proud of that, because it wasn't easy. But I'm glad I did it, though I was still a child myself, taken away from my parents and my home. And it was dangerous, there were a lot of counter-revolutionaries in the mountains who didn't want the local people to get education. Some of us were killed.'

'Was it hard going back to school after all that?'

'Same as for most people I guess. We were all involved, there was no way you could not be part of what was happening around you. Then when I was fifteen we had the war at the Bay of Pigs and I was in the trenches for a long time.'

'Fifteen!' I say.

'It wasn't unusual, it was only what everyone did. We weren't heroes or anything like that.' He smiles.

'And was it worth it?' I ask, because he's in full flow and

because I've not got this far with anyone here yet, not got past the politeness and the 'Triumph of the Revolution'.

'There are at least two ways of looking at things here,' he replies. 'I can tell you the official way, you understand?'

I nod.

'The official opinion is that these people who seem to have nothing now, had an even bigger nothing forty years ago – they were diseased, illiterate *campesinos* who were little more than slaves. Now they are literate, have access to health care and university, and many work in jobs their parents couldn't even have imagined. That they get paid almost nothing for doing these jobs is, of course, irrelevant. The lack of material goods is made up for by other things.'

'What other things?' I ask, with a pretty good idea of what he's going to say.

'Neighbours, family, the chance to help other people, to make a difference, to be part of something bigger than yourself – the Triumph of the Revolution.

I nod. I can see how that might feel good. 'And is it enough?'

He shrugs. 'We make it enough, what else is there to do? Now of course there's a big gap between my generation and my son's. He has never known anything but this and because he has no knowledge of how bad it was before, he sees only how bad it is now. This is a problem for us here, this difference in the generations. It's even more difficult for the older people. Many of them are very happy now and can't understand the problems of my son's generation.'

Juan is knowledgeable on a wide range of matters, not only relating to Cuba. As he relaxes with me I learn that he's actually a senior lecturer at the university, that he teaches languages; his guide/fixer persona is a sideline.

'So when will we go to Cojímar?' he asks.

'What's in Cojímar?' I ask.

'The sea, a nice restaurant, the place Hemingway spent a lot time.'

(That name again.)

'And then there's the old man . . . the one in the story of *The Old Man and the Sea*. We could see him if you want.'

'What do you mean, "see him"?'

'Everyone goes to *see* Gregorio. He's at least 103.'

After almost a week here, my understanding of the language has come on in leaps and bounds, as long as the speaker talks very slowly and with an English accent. Maria seems pleased with my progress, though it occurs to me that she perhaps feels paid not only to teach, but to conceal frustration. The day after my meeting with Juan Perez she tells me there's going to be a performance for San Lázaro at the Casa de Africa, the African cultural centre and museum in Habana Vieja.

'You are going?' I ask.

'Me? No!' she replies, as if I've asked whether she's going to the moon. 'I have no use for these things. Santería is an interesting cultural phenomenon, but because it is from Africa people think that all black Cubans are involved.'

Maria is usually happy to tell me anything about Cuban culture, but is reluctant to talk about society and even more reluctant to discuss her own views. I have a suspicion that she looks at me and all foreigners not from the former Soviet bloc as degenerate capitalists. There's a faint air of moral superiority about her that I find fascinating and want to probe.

'So are you or your family religious at all?' I ask.

'I grew up after the Revolution, with communism, so that is what I know.'

'I've heard that Fidel is a follower of Santería, that he is a son of Changó . . .'

She turns away briefly. 'Who knows about Fidel? Myself, I have never heard this.'

The Casa de Africa is a large colonial house filled with treasures, its masks, statues and weapons reminders that Africa is part of Cuba's history. In the narrow cobbled street, which is filling with a mix of locals and foreigners loaded with cameras, three *batâ*, sacred drums of different sizes, are being set up by three grave young black men dressed in the white of Obatalá. The atmosphere among the gathering crowd is expectant; the locals gaze intently at the proceedings, their eyes fixed on the drums and the youths as if both are strange and unexpected.

A small troupe of young people, dressed in street clothes emerge from the Casa and dance to a slow drum beat. Thin girls and big girls dance with equal, flaunting grace; the smooth-skinned boys with unselfconsciousness sensuality. They're all good – really good. They stop abruptly and file back into the building. Nobody moves. Expectation tightens the atmosphere until there's not even a whisper from the locals who are looking on now with a fascination that seems part genuine respect and part excitement. The foreigners are curious but nothing more; as yet this is just another colourful tradition to be captured on film or video.

A young woman wearing the red and black of the *orisha* Elegguá leaps into the street waving a short stick bent at one end. She capers wildly with the drums – miming eating, drinking and dancing – then staggers and abruptly falls to the ground, twitching in spasm. Locals and foreigners lean forward together as the girl jackknifes on the cobbles, right at their feet. The dancers reappear around her, no longer young and carefree but old or diseased and dressed in sack-cloth, their skin blotched with sores. Together, sufferers human and divine stumble and fall in the space allowed by the pressing crowd. The writhing is horribly realistic: a *danse macabre*. The great drums thud, echoing off the eighteenth-century walls, vibrating through the cobbles. There's a tense breathlessness about this spectacle, a theatrical claustrophobia caused by the nearness of the buildings and the proximity of the silently wailing dancers.

The drumming changes as two more costumed performers appear; one female in blue and white, the other male and dressed in purple. They move towards Elegguá with help, soothing and healing, and as the *orisha* recovers so too do the humans, until all are dancing joyfully together, upright and healthy despite lingering sores.

In the final act the youngsters are themselves once more, dancing with vigour and humour as cameras flash in dark eyes and over swaying breasts. The drums reach an abrupt crescendo and it's over.

A large black woman with greying hair appears beside me and asks if I enjoyed the performance.

'Very much' I say. 'I just wish I understood it all better.'

'You are a tourist?'

I shake my head. 'A writer.'

'Ah, I too am a writer. If you have time I will explain to you what you have just seen.' She shakes my hand in a colleague-ish way. 'My name is Carmelita,' she says. 'Would you like to have coffee?'

Carmelita is a journalist, and between the Casa and a tourist bar she knows she tells me about working in Moscow, Iraq, Lebanon and Angola. She's in her late fifties or early sixties and must have been in those countries at the height of the Cold War. As a Cuban journalist she would have seen and reported the world quite differently to pretty much anyone else I know, and for some reason I'm naïvely surprised by this thought. The gulf between us yawns and the thing she thought linked us, oddly, makes her seem more remote. This feeling is all on my side of course: I've already learnt that Cubans adapt far better and faster than soft Westerners. If I were from Pluto Carmelita would accept that and suggest coffee just the same.

The pleasant courtyard bar is full of *jineteras* waiting for passing male trade. It's a pretty up-market tourist place that Carmelita would never visit alone and there's an unspoken assumption that I'm paying, which in one sense doesn't matter at all but in another matters very much because of the dynamic her expectation creates.

An excellent *son* band fronted by a young man with a piercing falsetto plays into one ear as Carmelita relays rapid Spanish into the other, describing Santería in complex terms of which I understand about half. She explains the relationship between infinite deities like the universal creator Olórun – who seems to be linked to an ancient Egyptian sun deity – and other gods like Elegguá, represented by the dancing girl in black and red whose bent stick symbolises the *orisha*. Elegguá is the god of destiny who opens and closes all doors, protecting entrances and exits. When Elegguá was in pain, the *orisha* in white and blue who helped him was Yemayá, goddess of the moon and sea. The other helper, dressed in purple, was San Lázaro, the *orisha* of illness: San Lázaro in his African form of Babalú Ayé. I ask whether it's usual for male deities to be represented by female dancers, but don't understand the answer, or perhaps my faulty Spanish makes no sense.

Carmelita says she has a son in his thirties. He currently has three girlfriends. 'I've told him I think he is sick. This is not normal, it is an insult to the women.'

'Do they know?' I ask wondering at the change in conversation and thinking that despite disapproval there's just a trace of mother's pride in the desirability of her offspring.

She shrugs. 'Who knows? Maybe they do and maybe they just say nothing.' She looks as though she despises such feminine feebleness but she chuckles, a dark, throaty gurgle. 'He thinks he is Changó, with his women and wanting his own way in all things.'

After a sandwich, two cakes and three coffees, Carmelita eventually lets me go.

'Thank you,' she says, wiping her lips, 'I enjoyed that.' Then she's gone, her large figure making its way with determination through the busy crowd of men and women window-shopping.

Anoche, yo soñé con el Che.

Che is alive. He was dead, but has been revivified by a new technological procedure; recreated from DNA extracted from his remains. Though alive, he is extremely weak and is being kept in a top secret hospital while he recovers all his former strength. In the dream it's night. I know I'm very near this hospital and that if I simply keep on walking I'll reach it and actually meet Che Guevara. The prospect of this is exhilarating and also moving, because I am about to meet someone I never thought to meet and see something I never thought to see. Though I haven't reached the building I know where he is and how he looks. He's white and emaciated; his hair and beard are long and very dark against his skin. He can't stand and is helped by two male nurses to lie down on an old-fashioned hospital bed in a small, white room. I continue walking and reach a perimeter fence. I can see a low, white building ahead despite the darkness. I crawl under the fence and . . .

I recount this dream in Spanish for Maria. She seems interested but not particularly excited and I'm faintly disappointed. Perhaps Cubans dream of heroes all the time? Because my telling is so poor, Maria suggests that we write it out together as an exercise.

'You thought up this story alone?' she asks me when we've finished.

I look at her, surprised. For half an hour we've been discussing a dream, or so I thought.

'I didn't think it up. I dreamt it, early this morning, just before I woke.'

'Dreamt it?'

'Yes, I dreamt it.'

'It's not a story then, something that you thought to write?'

I laugh. 'God no, my waking mind doesn't work like that.'

'It's really a dream?'

'Yes, really.'

She looks for a moment, weighing me with large, dark brown eyes. 'Ah, that's different,' she says and smiles. 'A real dream is different.'

> There is never a moonlight night but wicked notions
> writhe like serpents' nests in evil souls, and charita-
> ble ones sprout lilies of renunciation and dedication.
> So Medardo's two halves wandered, tormented by
> opposing furies, amid the crags of Terralba.
>
> Italo Calvino, *The Cloven Viscount*

The suburbs of Havana reach east and west along the coast and south into the interior of La Habana province. A ring of small towns and villages with sanctified names surround the largest city in the Caribbean like guardian spirits: San Antonio de los Baños; Santiago de las Vegas; San José de las Lajas; San Miguel des Casanovias.

En route to the evening climax of San Lázaro's Day at the church of El Rincón, we stop briefly at Guanabacoa, a suburb of Havana but a world away from the high rises of La Rampa and the Malecón. A bright sun burns its way across the midday sky. Streets, lined with pastel terrace houses and festooned with telegraph wires, shimmer in the extreme heat. Women queuing to use the blue Italian phone boxes that cluster like hard blossoms in the main square are wilting fast. Men dash past on bicycles heavy with the drooping, pastel stems of gladioli. This is San Lázaro's Day, when sin and success are paid for and the spiritually dead rise. Like many of Cuba's towns, Guanabacoa is quietly readying itself for the night of atonement and celebration that lies ahead.

We eat chips in a shiny, plastic café opposite the lugubrious, sixteenth-century Spanish church. Juan drinks beer from a bottle that frosts in his hand. He's good company, full of facts and information offered, but not pressed. Driving here along wide roads, past aged American cars belching oily, black smoke he shared his impressions of life, the universe and Cuba; each snippet of conversation prefaced with 'You realise the view I'm putting forward isn't necessarily my own . . .'

Now, when I ask, 'What happened to the Revolution,' he starts with the party line, 'Things have never been easy . . . there's a limit to what can be done in forty years when we are constantly violated from the outside by a country as powerful as the U.S.'

He lists some of the countless attacks the United States has made against Cuba over the years, including the current, stifling trade embargo. There was the 'illness of the hogs' (presumably swine fever) and the 'deliberate' spread of child-killing dengue fever. The many assassination attempts against Castro are enumerated in a passionless voice. When I ask what proof there is of these things he says everything is documented, that Cuba too has its secret services and is able to control what and who enters the country. (How did the diseases and would-be assassins arrive?)

Leaving Guanabacoa we drive past a large state-owned bakery with doors that open onto a dark interior. Seeing me look at the place Juan says, 'Everyone gets a bread roll a day for five centavos. That's the ration. If you want more and can afford it you go to the back of the bakery and buy as many rolls as you want at one peso each . . . that's twenty times the ration price.'

'What kind of country is this,' I ask, half-joking, 'where social deviation is displayed on the body?'

He glances down at his belly and giggles. It's a high-pitched and rather endearing sound, at odds with his sober, well-rounded appearance.

The day before his death in a skirmish with the Spanish colonial army in 1895, the great Cuban writer and patriot José Martí wrote about that other enemy in waiting, so much more dangerous than the degenerate, burnt-out Spanish – the United States of America. 'I have lived inside the monster,' he wrote. 'I have seen its entrails – and my sling is that of David.'

Like Martí, Juan knows that other America – at least, he knows San Francisco, Chicago and Washington. Like Martí, he has experienced the belly of the monster, albeit as an academic delegate . . . and loved it. He must be a pretty staunch patriot, I think as he tells me these things, a patriot who admits to being in love with the enemy.

'I believed all kinds of things before I left here for the United States: that I would experience racism or be harassed; that the entire country would be like a vicious cop movie; but it was nothing like I expected. I did what I wanted, came and went as I wanted. I partied until two and three in the morning. I did my work and no-one questioned me.' His sigh is heavy with the memory of past freedoms. 'I liked that: the autonomy, the peace, the money.' He smiles at me, his blue eyes bright. 'But Cuba is my home and I am proud to be Cuban. On one level our achievement, our continuing independence, is vast;

but on another level . . .' He grins and suddenly, like a yacht tacking in the wind, says, 'Castro – the man's a genius, but he makes me sick, you know. Every day he talks, every day, every day. Einstein was a genius but if you had to listen to him all the time, you'd go mad! By the end of a week you'd go mad, no? "Einstein?" you'd say, "Einstein? The man's crazy!" But you *have* to listen to Fidel, because that's the only way you can know what's going to happen. What he *says* is what happens, his word is law. Maybe one day he goes to a place and it's dirty and he'll talk about this . . . you know next day the garbage will be gone and the place shining clean.'

A 1959 Oldsmobile, complete with coloured lights and tailfins, clatters along the road beside us.

'I used to have one of those,' Juan says, 'a '55 Oldsmobile with a V8 engine. Now they're all converted to diesel – that's what the smoke is.' He points to the oily black cloud blooming under the vehicle. 'It may look like an Olds on the outside . . . underneath it's all Cuban tractor parts and Russian engineering. But mine was great,' he says, longing thick in his voice. 'I really loved that car.'

I ask why he doesn't give up his ill-paid university job and work with people like me all the time.

'It's in here' he says, tapping the top of his head. 'It's about status, and my job gives me status. I have thirty people working for me. Until I began this kind of work,' he indicates me with a flick of his fingers, 'I worked as a cab driver. Many of my colleagues do this because no-one could live on our salaries. Now I must keep both jobs . . . if I give up the teaching I lose status. It's simple: you move out of the system you lose contact with your friends and colleagues, with society. You have more money, but what use is money if you've lost the other things of life?'

Beyond the open car window, rough fields studded with single palms and small farm gardens, neat with rows of organic onions and cabbages, pass in rapid procession. The sun is trying to burn its way through the cloud that covers the province of Havana, and the air is heavy with invisible moisture that sticks the car seat to my back and thighs. The land we're passing through is mostly dusty savannah intersected with broad roads often empty of traffic. The roadside is dotted with posters of dead, hirsute heroes, their faces black and white above equally stark words: '*Patria o muerte!*', '*Vigilancia en la defense de la Revolución!*' When I ask Juan about the images he merely shrugs.

Thinking over Juan's comments, the dichotomies of Cuban existence appear fascinating and terrifying in almost equal measure. He sees the contradictions in what he says, even points them out. But behind Juan's humour there's resentment – though perhaps it isn't that either; perhaps what I'm seeing is a quiet desperation that has solidified into an acceptance of the division between what is and what people like Juan believe was promised. I wonder if his thoughts are typical or if he represents a privileged minority. Then I remember: there are no minorities here, and no privilege. There's not a whole lot to buy here either; the value of money is limited by the unavailability of material goods. Homes are virtually free to Cubans. Travel and petrol are restricted and you can only buy what food there is, which isn't much. Yet despite this, everyone, naturally, wants more.

'What if the United States dropped the embargo tomorrow?' I ask after we've been silent for a little while.

'Nothing will change overnight. It can't.'

I point out that things pretty much changed overnight in Russia and the Eastern bloc.

'Yes,' he replies, 'but Russia went from feudalism to communism. Russia never knew capitalism, never knew what it was like to endure that, to be a colony of the most capitalist country in the world. Until 1959 and the Triumph of the Revolution, Cuba was an unofficial part of America. We went from total capitalism to total communism – what other country in the world has chosen to do that?' he says, with unmistakeable pride.

I see the first groups of pilgrims soon after we pass José Martí Airport: men, women and children moving in single file like semi-solid ghosts against the backdrop of trees. Women carry large bunches of flowers, men have children on their shoulders and every few kilometres there's a family picnicking at the roadside. It's a long walk from here to the church at El Rincón but San Lázaro's Day is a time for penitence, for the fulfilment of vows and for celebration. Some of these people will have been walking for days, perhaps weeks, barefoot across Cuba.

It's late evening as we pass through the small town of Santiago de las Vegas where every bus and truck in Cuba seems to have gathered. The darkness is alive as people pour, ant-like, from vehicles, minor roads and houses. There are police everywhere directing traffic and trying to prevent the confusion that's already well under way. Somewhere in these humid streets that disappear into blackness in the absence of lighting, the great Italian novelist Italo Calvino was born nearly eighty years ago. As we drive helplessly round and round through swarms of eager pilgrims I think of the infant Calvino, breathing Cuban air, drawing it in like the milk of a mulatto wet nurse, until, like a character in one of his own magical realist 'fairy tales', he turned into a changeling; a Latin-European.

Magical realism, a style created and perfected by Latin American writers, is both a contradiction of and a perfect vehicle for describing revolutionary cultures. In tales like *The Cloven Viscount* and *Invisible Cities*, Calvino explored the ways in which dichotomies can merge. He described how state and individual, past and present, can coexist and how – like the heroic *barbudos* gazing down from their billboards at the pilgrims passing beneath – any past can be glorified and utilised.

Juan asks for directions to El Rincón from a blond boy who rolls his blue eyes and guttural 'r's wildly. I can't follow a single sentence, and trying instead to interpret his expansive gestures it seems fitting that Calvino's writing should be closer to Borges or García Márquez than to his European contemporaries. His magical realist stories are, like the history of Cuba itself, often brief and apparently fragmentary. Someone once described Calvino's writing as 'fire and algebra', and looking at the thickening crowd heading towards El Rincón I imagine how the fire of his Latin soul would have been drawn to San Lázaro and fascinated with his birth country's continuing dedication to the past and to martyr-dom. Yet Calvino had a clear, algebraic vision of the stultifying effects of clinging to an outworn, inflated vision of history: 'Futures not achieved are only branches of the past . . . dead branches,' Marco Polo tells Kublai Khan in *Invisible Cities*.

We drive on into the rural heart of La Habana, searching for an approach not blocked by traffic police, and then I see it – a glowing dome of silver light surrounding the church and former leper colony of El Rincón. From here I could be looking at a small stadium, a spaceship or Xanadu. It's the coldest glow I've ever seen and look-ing at it I feel its alienness.

We walk along a rough road for about half an hour guided only by the distant brightness; a light at the end of a tunnel. The road curves gently between fields and trees, between hedges of bamboo and small clumps of sugarcane that rustle in the night breeze, releasing damp, earthy scents. Surprised by foreign bodies, night birds call shrilly to each other from the depths of bushes and high grass, and giant bats swoop past on leathery wings. The shadow figures around us walk in groups or couples; most are young and seem to be enjoying themselves, chatting and laughing quietly. It's chill, but I'm sweating in air so soft and full of moisture that my lungs feel like a bath sponge.

On the outskirts of El Rincón village we join the main road from Santiago and our human trickle turns to a wide, roaring current pouring between gaudily lit houses and street lamps, past dozens of stalls selling banana chips, iced cakes, brightly coloured soft drinks and dark yellow candles that smell of the abattoir. Music shrills and thumps from every house, each playing something different. There's rock, reggae, rap, disco and, from one pink-and-yellow veranda, loudspeakers blasting Mozart's *The Magic Flute*. A small girl is dancing alone to Robbie Williams on the flat roof of a two-storey building, leaping and spinning close to the edge. Above it all, the voice of Carlos Manuel rises in the thudding strains of Cuba's number one pop song, 'Malo Cantidad', a play on the cliché of Cuban men's infidelity. '*Yo soy malo . . . yo soy malo . . .*'

Manuel yells, 'I'm bad, really bad, but if I'm *so* bad, why do you love me?' There's a real party atmosphere here and none of the hysterical, religious fervour I'd been led to expect. After more than forty secular years in which religion was pretty much suppressed and culture encouraged, tonight looks like a mix of fun, alcohol and piety – in that order.

But then there's San Lázaro. Here on the road he's in the form of the Afro-Cuban saint with his crutches and spotted dogs. He's everywhere – in life-size statues and small palm-size pictures. This San Lázaro is an impostor, not even one of the three Christian claimants for the name but a character from a New Testament parable merged with an African healing god. Looking at him I experience *déjà vu*. This is the man of my Che dream, the emaciated, bearded hero reborn. The resemblance is remarkable and for a moment I feel disorientated, wondering how I could dream something I'd never seen. Then the crowd pushes me on towards the railway station and the dream is forgotten.

Rails, glowing in the streetlights, bisect the road at El Rincón like a bracelet or manacles. This small village station is a junction through which trains must pass to Surgidero de Batabanó on the south coast and to Artemisa and Pinar del Río in the west. Names on a map that roll round the mouth heavy with the flavours of Cuba. Just beyond the lines, everything changes. At this point pilgrims start to fulfil their vows to San Lázaro, their promises. Promises made in the hope of being blessed with a child, health, wealth, everyday things that matter. Some people promise wealth, flowers, prayer. But San Lázaro is demanding and there are many who believe that their hopes and wishes will only be fulfilled through personal sacrifice. Between here and the small church a kilometre away, the promises must be fulfilled.

A few metres beyond the station a middle-aged man is lying in the road and propelling himself backwards on shoulders and feet while a companion brushes the ground in front of him with a leafy branch. A small girl with the face of a Leonardo angel is seated across his hips; her face serene, otherworldly. I try to imagine how a Western child would behave in this situation, and fail. A crowd of onlookers stare down at the man, whose thin shirt is no protection against the surface of the road, their faces a mixture of curiosity or scepticism, with the occasional dash of sympathy. The man has travelled only a few metres and he's already in pain, his face strained with effort. All around him people are pressing forwards, eager to reach the church, the food, the drink. His sacrifice seems impossibly hard and lonely in the middle of such activity and I wonder what was promised. Is this painful gesture a thank you for the child straddling him or something I can't even guess at? I approach cautiously, held back by an unfamiliar discomfort with voyeurism; but I'm entirely alone in this feeling, no-one else seems remotely awkward staring at this man in his extremity.

After 100 metres the bizarre becomes commonplace. A semi-naked man is being ridden like a pony by his teenage son whose wasted legs dangle short of the ground. There is a young black woman pushing a large box-cart lit by a dozen burning candles and filled with images of San Lázaro. At the centre of the cart sits a child, motionless as a living deity, hung with flowers. A few people, like the well-dressed, elderly white man wearing thick kneepads, have a pragmatic attitude to their vows, but most are throwing themselves into the spirit of their promise. One man has rolled up his trousers and, lacking even the padding of his clothing, crawls agonisingly slowly on bare, bony knees that are already raw and angry-looking. Music, shouted voices and the shuffle of many thousands of feet merge to drown out his low keening. His head hangs hopelessly, drooping ever closer to the ground with each bone-crunching step. Tears fall from his eyes and mucus from his nose – signs of pain or repentance, or maybe both.

The more bizarre, masochistic promises seem to have been made by young men. Clanking metal and rasping breath mark the passing of a group dragging large stones by chains attached to their ankles. The scenario is medieval, relic of an unquestioning, nightmare past. One disabled youth crawls in military fashion, all elbows and knees, despite the severe curvature of his spine and the swelling that raises one shoulder much higher than the other. Sweat glistens along his chin, dripping an invisible trail into the dirt under his face. He flinches, put off his motion, as an outstretched man rolls past him and on down the road.

The Santuario de San Lázaro at El Rincón, western Cuba's most important shrine, was built in 1917 on the site of an old leper hospital – a lazar house. In 1986, when HIV infection was considered the new leprosy, an AIDS sanatorium opened here. An HIV diagnosis once meant incarceration. These days it's rumoured Cuba's sanatoriums are so comfortable people get infected deliberately, just to be somewhere like El Rincón.

With its floodlighting and busy crowd, the place has a modern, upbeat air tonight, like a nightclub at New Year. Everything is wrapped in a chill, Nordic brightness. The grass around the church glows like spiked mercury where it's not covered with family picnics and burning candles. Juan tells me they're waiting for the midnight service. He winces as he says this, as if fearing I'll ask him to spend another two hours here. He's patient, resigned to the walking, the crowd, the noise, but he's not enjoying himself.

A woman's voice quavers through a microphone, instructing the gathered crowd not to loiter inside the church. But loitering is what everyone is here to do. The heat from flames and bodies is welcome and almost overwhelming after the night-time cold, and people are already asleep in corners. Hundreds of coloured candles have turned the floor into lakes and rivers of melted wax that flow across the tiles like blood and water. A troop of mulatto women, semi-naked in shiny purple and gold outfits, wander between pillars smoking cigars and giggling drunkenly. Serious-looking family men, candle-waving children astride their shoulders, clutch bunches of flowers. The scent of tallow and lilies offers a humid absolution to the crowd pressing forward to the altar rails where priests hand out recycled bottles filled with blessed water drawn from a fountain outside the old leprosy hospital behind the church. As candles gutter and new ones are lit, the quavery-voiced woman sings out-of-tune hymns.

By the time we leave, the crowd has swelled to many tens of thousands, as people arrive from across the country. Pilgrimage, penitence, partying: that's El Rincón tonight. The noise has increased exponentially and men are clutching bottles of rum now and weaving as they walk. The road is deep in orange peel, the misshapen ends of candles and sweet wrappers, and there's a nightmarish feel to the vision of crawling, dragging, rolling pilgrims who are almost lost now in the surging mass of upright flesh. The man with the child across his hips has travelled only a few hundred metres since I first saw him and his face is pale and contorted under the florid streetlights. A black woman crawling on all fours is sobbing openly and shaking her head against the pain. I wonder if everyone makes it to the church and what happens if they don't.

We enter Havana via the Plaza de la Revolución and the memorial to José Martí. Juan points out the image of Che made from steel railings donated by the French government. What would these Cuban heroes have thought of the things I've just witnessed – Martí who lived much of his adult life in Europe and North America, and Che who believed in nothing but communism? I gaze up at Che's face, the steel forged into a likeness of Korda's iconic 1960 photograph.

'He was so . . . picturesque,' I say to Juan who's tired and quiet now.

'Picturesque? Maybe – but he was really a great man,' he sighs. 'Che had such ideas. Ideas for change. Did you know he'd planned to go to Argentina after Bolivia? He wanted to go back to his own country and make changes there – that's what he wanted: to change all of Latin America.' He laughs, 'Then maybe he would have started on North America!'

'You remember when you learnt he was dead?'

'Of course . . . everyone remembers that, like Americans with President Kennedy. Fidel told us Che was dead and that his diary of what happened in Bolivia had been found and given to the Bolivian minister of the interior. This minister was a good man and handed over the diaries to Cuba and got into a lot of trouble in his country because the Bolivian government murdered Che, helped by the CIA.'

'What happened to the diaries?'

'We read them. I remember it clearly. I was a student and that day I walked down the steps from the university, crossed the road and stood in a long line outside the Hotel Havana Libre. They were giving away copies of the diary to anyone who asked, so every Cuban could read Che's words for free.' Juan's grin is lopsided in the light from the Lada's dashboard. 'That is socialism!'

★

Valla de Gallos

North and west of Jovellar, Vedado spreads out in a designer grid of fantasy homes set among tree-lined roads and avenues. During the building boom of the Mafia years, properties built in neoclassical styles sprang up like tasteful mushrooms in the damp of Havana. Now the place has an air of decadence without exoticism; the balconies rotting gently, the portico steps cracked and broken.

'It makes me think of New Orleans,' I say to Cecilia Vaux as we drink beer on her broad, tree-shaded balcony, 'the Garden District.'

'It reminds me of Savannah, Georgia,' she replies, 'something about the style, the pillars.'

Cecilia, an attractive fifty-something Englishwoman, has taught at the International School for more than four years. She's also a writer. Instinct tells me we're going to be friends and I'm already grateful to the London contact who put me in touch with her.

'You must really like it here,' I say.

'I do. I like it a lot. It's very relaxed most of the time. I enjoy the weather and of course Havana is a wonderful place to write about.'

'What about the food?'

'Luckily I don't have to shop. My landlady does all that sort of thing and I suppose I've got used to the limitations and sameness. You do, don't you?'

'What about friends?'

'There's a smallish expat community here, not all diplomatic. Some people have been here many years – they like the lifestyle, the lack of material pressure, the people. Have you met many expats yet?'

I shake my head.

'You should, there's a few who are really interesting and could give you some real insights. Remind me to give you their details.'

'And Cuban friends?'

'Some. Some are very good friends, with others it's hard to know. There's always a kind of edge, an uncertainty. Ultimately I have money – compared to them that is – and I can come and go as I like. That makes a difference. Even after years, it's hard to be sure of real friendship in a place like this.'

'And what about men?'

She lights a strong, dark Cuban cigarette and inhaling deeply says, 'Take it from one who knows . . . a Cuban man is for Christmas, not for life.'

We both laugh.

'Tell me about sex here,' I ask. 'It's everywhere but I can't make out if it's for real or just simmering, like in Mediterranean countries – all flashing eyes and tight knees.'

'Oh it's very real,' she says. 'There really *was* a sexual revolution here that left the rest of us way behind. Before the political revolution prostitution was rampant, mostly aimed at foreigners of course. But even then everyone was at it like rabbits, except nice, middle-class girls and after the Revolution it became acceptable even for them.'

'So what happened?'

'Lots of things probably . . . maybe the Spanish Catholic middle classes were suppressed and their morality with it and so the working class Afro-Cuban lifestyle could emerge more strongly.'

'It's quite amazing,' I say, 'to see people really getting into it in the street. It reminds me of the seventies back home.'

She grins. 'They fuck in the street here and nobody notices or cares. Imagine the fuss that would cause back home – even in the seventies!'

'And is it the same for gay men and lesbians?'

'No, it's not. Some people would have you believe this is a

great place for gay men, but it isn't. It's definitely a lot better than it was, but this is not somewhere I'd choose to come on holiday if I were a gay man.' She lights another cigarette and inhales as if her life depended on it. 'Lesbians? Not much in evidence really. This is still a *very* macho culture and anything that deviates from that is seen as problematic – culturally and politically. But there *has* been a big gathering of lesbians at the cathedral the last few Christmas Eves, so they are out there!'

'Why Christmas Eve?'

'Oh, that's when gay Havana is really on show! It's great. All the queens are there outside the cathedral and the lesbians line the square. We should go!'

Cecilia's apartment is large and comfortable with *faux* Louis XIV in the sitting room. But most impressive is the dark, Chevrolet-green bath.

'Do you like it? I think it's rather good: hard-wearing, water-proof. Car paint is great when the enamel on your bath is past it. It's really difficult to get lots of things here, including paint, but I'm always amazed at how adaptable Cubans are. The embargo makes things so bad of course, but it must have been very much worse six, seven years ago when the Special Period was really biting.'

When she disappears to get her address book I stand in the kitchen and examine the wall covered in art postcards and photos of home. There is something very familiar and English about this wall, something 'corner of a foreign field'-ish. I wonder what Cecilia's Cuban friends think when they stand here.

'These two you really should get in touch with,' she says, handing me a piece of paper. 'Simon works for a Havana radio station and Martin for the foreign press. Martin's been here years, his wife is Cuban. Simon is a British socialist . . . gay. Give them a call, say I gave you their names.'

I look down: Simon Wollers and Martin di Giovanni. They sound like a couple of cardinals

★

At the International Press Centre on La Rampa I enquire, for the fourth time, about my visa extension. Each previous occasion has met with polite assurances that all will be well, that these things take time. It's becoming clear, however, that if you don't have time then you must have money to expedite officialdom.

Sitting in the large, empty lobby of the Centre I look around and wonder what it is about male photojournalists. Do they all have a bald patch with compensatory thin, grey ponytails? Bald or hirsute, today we're all the same, all waiting for someone. My someone – the British press liaison person, a handsome woman whose emerald, almond eyes record Chinese ancestry – thinks I'm beneath notice. Polite remarks on how long I've been waiting to leave Havana fall on ears veiled against me by a perfect, grey bob.

'President Putin is here,' she says by way of explanation. 'I must attend every day as a translator, so you see it's not possible for me to make anything for you.'

'But I already have my ticket for Santiago de Cuba,' I say, 'the flight leaves on Saturday and you have my passport.'

'No, the ministry has your passport . . . *I* can do nothing.'

'Nothing?'

'You can pay thirty dollars more and you will get it in three days certain.'

'But I handed it in ten days ago and paid thirty dollars for it to be returned in seven days.'

She shrugs. 'President Putin . . . '

Cornered, I hand over the second thirty dollars. I've already paid for an obligatory press pass that no-one recognises or understands. I would shrug myself, but my shoulders lack the necessary flexibility.

From the Press Centre I walk around the Malecón to the Paseo de Martí, a dramatic pedestrian boulevard of marble and sculpted lions. A group of young schoolkids are skating on the Paseo's glossy surface with their teachers. A slender black boy and a tall blonde girl with caramel skin manoeuvre together with consummate speed and skill around an obstacle course of orange traffic cones. One very small boy is heartbreakingly touching in his smiling attempts to stay upright on old-fashioned skates far too large for his feet. Watching them all I'm reminded of Cuba's remarkable successes in world-class athletics and of how much I always wanted Cuba to win their events at the Olympics or the World Championships, especially against rich Western competition. Looking at these kids it's easy to see why Cuba is a force on the sports field.

Four youngsters sit beside me on the wall and watch their classmates. Their grinning faces are a collage of history: Chinese, African, Spanish and all of these together. Seeing my recorder they ask what it's for, so I hold it in front of them and encourage them to speak. '*Hola! Hola!*' they shout. The look of surprise and shock on their faces at the tinny echo of their own voices is something I will always remember.

It's not easy to find food in Havana and what there is, is there to be endured rather than enjoyed. Even with money, you can't have what doesn't exist, and few tourist hotels offer decent food outside meal hours.

I eat a dry, three-dollar sandwich in a tourist place off the Paseo. It has a bad atmosphere and is full of miserable-looking *jineteras* and their pimps. *Jineteras. Jineteros.* Prostitutes, pimps; pimps and prostitutes. Men and women for sale. The word comes from the Spanish *jinete*, a rider or horseman, but Cubans have turned it into something new, extended the meaning. The horseman, in the words of exiled Cuban writer Gabriel Cabrera Infante, has become the 'whoresman'.

A young, tired-looking woman joins me and lays a large chameleon between us across the table. She tells me that I can stroke Tita if I want. The reptile coughs nervously as I run my fingers along its smooth, grey-green back, and the woman complains of being hungry, of having lost her job. In the background a man, probably her *chulo*, is gesticulating at her and she is ignoring him. Leaving, I give her a dollar to help feed Tita who has fallen off the table and lies stunned beside bare, dusty feet and green-painted toenails.

Before midnight on 24 December 1956, Fidel Castro, Ernesto Guevara and eighty other men left Tuxpan, Mexico in a small white boat called *Granma*. They landed on the south-east coast of Cuba to start the Revolution against corruption, capitalism and President Batista. It didn't begin well. Within a week most of the men were dead or captured. Castro hid in a sugarcane field, sucking stalks to stay alive, while elsewhere Guevara was trying to extract water from a rock with a device for controlling his asthma attacks. A week later, between twelve and fifteen men – no-one who was there can agree on the exact number or names of their *compadres* - were reunited and the Revolution began in earnest. Today, the little boat that carried them to Cuba sits in a large glass box – the 'Pavillión *Granma*' – in a square in Old Havana. An elderly tank, a rocket launcher, an aeroplane and bits of destroyed U.S. hardware from the Bay of Pigs fiasco surround the boat like tributes laid at the feet of an icon.

This is the holy of revolutionary holies, the Lenin Tomb, the Ho Chi Minh Mausoleum, of Cuba. Crossing the square I think of another tale of political upheaval and small boats, and the famous paeon to romanticised failure that begins: 'Sail bonny boat like a bird on the wing/Over the sea to Skye/Carry the lad who's born to be King/Over the sea to Skye'. Only in that case of course, the politico in question – The Young Pretender, James Stuart – was running rather than arriving, leaving behind him horrors that still lay ahead for Cuba in 1956.

But a monument to the famous craft wasn't enough for the grateful Fidelistas. *Granma* has an entire province named after her, and a newspaper – which Graham Greene described as 'the daily paper with what seems to be an odd nursery title' – which replaced the dozen or so published in Cuba prior to the Triumph in January 1959.

A block or so beyond the monument, I'm climbing flights of stairs so dark their corners are invisible, to knock on the door of Angel Luis Guerra. 'You should visit Angel,' an acquaintance in London said to me shortly before I left, 'he's unique.'

And so he is.

'Welcome!' he says as I step into the high-ceilinged room. 'Welcome to Cuba! This is my mother . . . Mother, here is the British writer I told you about.'

Angel Luis is a tall and slender man in his fifties. His hair is sandy red, his pale skin lightly freckled with gold. He's the only Celtic-looking Cuban I've ever met. We sit near each other in large wooden armchairs and I can see the delight in his face that someone from 'outside' is here in his home, another writer, wanting to talk . . . in English.

'My mother is over eighty,' he says, 'but as you see she is very fit and healthy. It's from climbing up and down those steps several times a day! Mother, let us have tea. You like tea, yes?' he turns to me. 'Earl Grey?'

'Earl Grey?' I say. 'Oh yes please!'

It arrives in an antique Chinese tea set, with neat slices of lemon laid carefully on a small dish; an oasis of liquid charm at the top of unlit stairs.

For the next two hours I am entertained and educated by a man who turns out to be a wonderful caricature. His rendition of 'I Love Paris in the Springtime' is wonderful, but his Lady Bracknell is superb.

'A handbag!' he shrills ecstatically. 'A *handbag*!' Then smiling broadly he points to the volumes of Oscar Wilde on his bookshelves. 'He was such a wonderful writer' he says. 'He captured so many of the human emotions and made it seem so easily written because it was easy to read. Do you like Wilde?'

I nod and sip the best tea I've had in Cuba.

In a street far below the shuttered windows of Angel's large apartment, an Afro-Cuban band is tuning up.

'What kind of music is that?' I ask.

He laughs. 'Who can say! They *think* they're playing folkloric music, but only in their imagination. Tell me about your travels. Where are you going next?'

'There were always foreign visitors in Cuba,' he says after we've chatted about my plans. 'Our literary history has been much tied up with movement and with people coming and going from Spain and the Caribbean. One of our most famous writers of travel and memories was a woman – Mercedes Santa Cruz y Montalvo, the Condesa de Merlín. She was born in Havana in, I think, 1789. Her family were Creole aristos, so she was sent to Spain for her education and then married a French nobleman. She was a great lady in Paris, you know, the sort that had a literary circle – wouldn't that be *wonderful*, to have a literary circle! Then she started to write about Cuba.'

'From what angle?'

'Oh almost everything interested her: national identity, independence, education, the role of women. She visited Havana in 1840 and wrote the very first travel book on Cuba, *Viajes a la Habana*. She wrote about the *criollos*, Cuban-born Spanish, and was very interested in slavery, an important subject at that time with debate about emancipation happening across the Western world.'

'Was she against slavery?'

'Oh no . . . she wrote about it objectively. Her own view was that slavery was acceptable if it was humanitarian.'

'So she didn't exactly forward the argument for emancipation then . . .'

He grins. 'Not really, but travellers of all kinds, especially British and North Americans, during the eighteenth and nineteenth centuries were very important for Cuban thinking. It was from the British that Cuba received the pragmatic notion that free labour would be more effective than slavery; something the *peninsulare* Spanish government would never have thought of! But for a woman of the Condesa de Merlín's class to even be raising the subject was very unusual. She would have been a good person to have tea with I think!'

'What does Creole mean precisely?' I ask. 'I've only heard it used about Cuban cuisine.'

He laughs. 'In the past it meant Cuban-born Spanish. For us today it means to be *very* Cuban, to be patriotic; you could be black or white or any colour and be a *criollo*. That was the mistake the Spanish made in the eighteenth century. They were too stupid and arrogant to realise that their policies, mostly about power and who owned what, would make the *criollo* aristos so very angry and that being angry the aristos would begin to be blind to colour and class and think that anyone who was on their side was a good *criollo* too. The Spanish had military and political power, the Cubans had land and money and couldn't understand why that didn't entitle – is that the right word? Entitle?' I nod. '– entitle them to political power as well. And of course, the *peninsulare* Spanish were stubborn, lazy, brutal . . .'

'Understandably unpopular then.'

'Exactly. But it's ironic that it was Spanish attitudes to their Cuban brothers that brought Cubans together and gave us our non-racist society. Even before the Revolution, racism was officially forbidden here; President Batista was a mulatto after all. Did you know that he was not allowed to enter white-only clubs owned by Americans here in Cuba? He was a very bad president, but he was still president and he was not allowed in, in his own country!' He shakes his head in disbelief. 'Then we had the Soviets and we thought socialism was forever. The Russians, the Ukrainians, the Georgians – all of them, they were so warm and loving that we made a marriage.' He smiles; for a moment his face is sad and distant. 'But like many modern marriages, ours couldn't survive poverty and then we became like children, weaned suddenly and violently –' he mimes a child being torn from the breast.

'But you've survived,' I say. 'Cuba has survived.'

'Of course, what else is there to do but survive, endure . . . and now things are getting better,' he says cheerfully. 'Slowly, very slowly, but they are definitely better.'

As I prepare to leave we talk briefly about San Lázaro, the saint in many forms, and about Che and iconography.

'Did you know,' he says, smiling at the thought, 'that in Bolivia there are people who believe Che is a saint and pray to him, with candles and offerings?'

Remembering my own unconscious conflation of the Argentinean asthmatic with San Lázaro, the idea seems perfectly reasonable.

★

Juan picks me up around eight the next morning. Cockfights start early and we want to be sure of meeting Juan's neighbour Fernando who's taking us. Juan has made it very clear that this isn't something *he* would normally have anything to do with.

The weather is cooler than when I arrived, pleasanter, at least for me. The *habaneros* are all wearing thick jumpers and jackets; I see a young woman looking like a black Inuit in a fur-lined parka. The wind is strong again along the Malecón. Dust mixed with spume smears the windscreen and the imminent sea alternately pours over the wall and forces high, white blowholes through weaknesses in the road. Through the foam I glimpse a deeper turquoise. The sea is halfway up the wheels of the car now and Juan is thinking about corrosion. Out among the high waves, brown pelicans flow and dive, cutting the churning water with tight-creased wings, to rise, salt-drenched and victorious. Sunlight strokes the Malecón's crumbled, multi-coloured houses making them beautiful; it touches the old, pale stones of the Castillo de San Salvador de la Punta until they glow, unnatural, against the slate grey of the sky. Across the harbour, the statue of Christ oversees the changing colours of his domain – the sea, the land, the distant chimneys pumping red and yellow flames like rents in the blackening sky.

Havana's suburbs continue the theme of industrial pollution. Smoke pours from refineries that take in oil from Venezuela, Iran and whatever other countries are prepared to defy the U.S. embargo. Many of the buildings look as though they started decaying centuries ago, but men and women work in the vast, rambling chaos of refineries that appear almost as dilapidated as London's Battersea power station.

The big, brightly coloured Chevys and Olds chug past us, black smoke pouring from beneath their bodies. I remember Juan telling me about the Russian and Cuban parts hidden under the voluminous hoods and looking at them now it seems to me that these cars are a kind of metaphor – shiny and bright on the outside, inappropriate and potentially poisonous within.

Vultures circle overhead, eyeing the movement on rubbish tips far below. Approaching the suburb of Playa I see small groups of shirtless men hauling household rubbish.

'There's no organised waste collection out here,' Juan says, 'so these guys take it away for about ten cents a time and dump it in a central location from where the authorities are forced to remove it.'

'Havana seems very clean to me,' I say, 'much cleaner than London.'

'You have more things to throw away,' Juan says as the car slows and he waves to a man standing on a corner of the street.

Fernando has the air of a man who understands life's seams. He sits in the back of the car as we head further west out of the city on a wide, almost empty road and, in a hoarse burr that I don't even try to understand, gives Juan a brief history of cockfighting in Cuba.

'The place where we're going, where the fight happens,' Juan says, 'it's called the *valla de gallos – gallos* are cocks.' Fernando is saying that the sport was introduced here by the Spanish who brought aggressive birds with them to establish the sport, then later different strains were introduced from India and Japan to add strength and endurance to the Spanish breeds.

Fernando talks fast, excitedly, waving his hands in mock battle.

'It's what they are born for,' Juan translates. 'Cocks love to fight, it's all they want to do. They are the most aggressive creatures in the world.'

I wonder how true this is, how much Fernando and his fellow fight-lovers believe this, to make the sport acceptable. 'Is cock-fighting legal?' I ask, aware there's an element of hole-and-corner about this trip.

'It's not legal or illegal,' Juan says with perfect Cuban ambiguity. 'It's tolerated.' Fernando, who understands more English than he lets on, mutters from the back seat.

Juan continues, 'He says it's the other forms of gambling that are not acceptable to the authorities – cards, dice and such things. When there was a cockfight, all these other kinds of gambling would spring up too and then there would be problems. After the Triumph of the Revolution, cockfighting was banned because of that.' Fernando talks on and Juan continues to translate. 'But then Celia Sanchez . . . you have heard of her?'

I nod. Castro's amanuensis, *compadre*, faithful follower through jungle and street battle, a woman described with typical sourness by the writer Gabriel Cabrera Infante as 'a feminine factotum'.

'In the early seventies Celia took a personal interest in cock-fighting because she saw that Cuban breeds were dying out and should be preserved. She wanted to breed birds for export to other Latin countries where fighting is big sport and big business. So she had breeding and fighting decriminalised.' He Juan grins. 'Cubans love to gamble; we're very good at it! Always have been.'

Graham Greene was fascinated by the Cubans love of gambling and appalled, with stereotypical English anxiety about pleasure, by what he saw of pre-revolutionary excesses. These excesses – as Cabrera Infante, whilst dismissing Greene's pro-Castro stance, admits – were fairly spectacular:

> Greene probably meant to say . . . that there were gaming houses in Havana under Batista – and of course long before him for surely Batista didn't invent roulette or create the croupier. There were casinos then and cabarets and brothels and even a peep show featuring a black man with an oversized penis who called himself Superman without the benefit of having read Nietzsche.

The fight location is a long way off the main road, down a bumpy dirt track, deep into the countryside. The city feels far away and we are becoming slowly invisible, dissolved in green and swallowed by palms and scrub. A few parked cars are the only indication that we've arrived at our destination. Juan hands over a couple of pesos to a rough-looking man and we enter a fenced-off enclosure at the centre of which is the *valla* itself, a round, palm-thatched arena. Thirty or forty mostly white men stand around in clusters talking rapidly and eyeing each other and the empty ring. A few women hang onto the arms of men who ignore them. There are children too, though Juan told me it's illegal for children under fourteen to watch a fight.

Now we're here it occurs to me that this may not be a pleasant experience. Before arriving, it was distant, cultural, a sport. Watching the groups of men and excited boys it's brought home to me that this is about blood, an event whose sole purpose is that something dies violently. As time passes and the sun gets stronger overhead, it all starts to feel like some kind of test. I asked to come. I'm here. I suppose I should make the best of it.

Under the trees beside the ring the owners are preparing the birds. I move in close, camera in hand. The crowd parts to let me through and no-one notices as I click only centimetres away from the beady eyes and combless heads. The combs are removed because they're vulnerable and bleed too much. Most of the feathers are also gone, plucked out from the lower body; only the back and wings are still covered. This apparently makes wounds easier to see and clean. (This also surely makes wounds easier to make?) Cocks weigh less without feathers and weight is crucial as each bird is publicly suspended in a sling and weighed, its details recorded on a blackboard for all to see and interpret in the betting.

Even to an outsider it is clear that much of the preparation is ritualistic and turns to theatre as the owners select spurs: judging, weighing, measuring. Owners straddle long benches, surrounded by minions and the paraphernalia of the business: thread, wax, matchboxes and artificial spurs that might be cut from dead cocks. The smell of hot wax and melting keratin fills the air as the owners prepare their fighters. A wiry, white-haired man holds his bird with practised ease, fining down the stumps of its natural spurs with a file before attaching long artificial spikes and securing them with thread and wax. The weapons are pale and deadly, designed to stab and slash. The owner's manner is cool, detached: he chews a feather and exudes a confidence and experience quite different to that of his rival on the next bench; a young, heavy-set man who sweats as he ties off the spurs on his own bird and swears at his helpers. The ritual climaxes as the opponents open their match-boxes and swap spurs in a gesture that could mean a great many things. The cocks sit placidly between their owners' legs, eyes flashing only as some stranger moves too close.

When it starts the ring is cleared of everyone but the owners, the referee and the caged birds. Every seat is filled, the front row packed with angry-looking men with large bellies and hot eyes. Young boys hang, simian, from the *valla*'s struts and supports. Fernando explains that betting starts before the fight and continues up to the moment when one animal dies. Soon everyone but myself and Juan seems to be shouting. The noise escalates. The rules are broken when someone vaults the barrier quickly followed by others. Then there's a large, hirsute man in the ring, sidestepping his way around the sanded floor. Gesturing towards the invaders I notice he's holding a long, broad-bladed knife at arm's length.

'It's the owner of the *valla*,' Juan whispers in the brief silence that follows. 'If people get into the ring then everything has to stop, all the betting is finished and everyone is very, very angry. There's a lot of money bet here; maybe five, six hundred dollars on each bird.'

No-one but me seems surprised by the weapon. Anxiety is focussed on the possibility of the fight being stopped. The white-haired, feather-chewing bird owner crouches in one corner of the ring and says nothing. As unruffled as the cock, his cool is glacial. Had I been a betting woman I would have laid odds on this man's *gallo* without ever having seen it. The younger man is sweating more profusely now. It must be his bird's first (and only?) fight and it's clear the creature doesn't want to be here and doesn't stand a chance. The pair flutter together, kicking and gouging in a rather desultory way. So much for the most aggressive creatures in the world.

In the end tiredness and fear wear the loser down. It stopped defending itself within a few minutes of the start, probably having recognised an alpha male when it saw one. Now it stands, backside in the air, beak resting in the dirt. It has already tried the old playing dead trick, but that just goaded the other bird into pecking at its head experimentally. The losing bird's periods of immobility grow longer, each one measured by an egg timer held in the referee's hand; as the sand runs fully through the timer the birds are separated and placed in the holding cage for a cooling-off period. This has been going on for about forty minutes and I'm finding it at once boring and excruciatingly unpleasant to watch. Already bloody and exhausted, the losing bird revives a little on finding itself alone, only to be dropped back into the fray thirty seconds later.

Before the bout resumes, the owners are allowed to 'encourage' their birds. As Fernando whispers this information the white-haired man blows cool breath on his animal's head and on the bald skin under its wings. His thin lips pucker as he blows, the feather still firmly clamped between his teeth. The sweaty man blows hot air and sucks his bird's bleeding head to warm it and dispel shock. The whole thing is a performance, a performance by the owners as much as by the birds: there are fights happening on many different levels here, the birds in the ring are merely the centrepiece.

After an hour, the losing bird can no longer lift its head and stands bow-legged to prevent collapse. I blink to squeeze away the tears that stop me seeing clearly, but water is now running freely down my face and I hide behind the camera.

'How long is it going to go on for?' I ask Juan without turning round.

'Until one of them is dead. Look,' he points to the sweaty man and his minions, 'they are still betting on their bird. It could suddenly get up and kill the other one, that is why the fight has to go on to the end.

I look at the pathetic creature in the middle of the ring and wipe my face. 'Okay,' I say, 'let's go, I've had enough. Have you had enough?'

'Quite enough.'

Juan whispers to Fernando and discreetly presses the money I gave him earlier into the other man's hand. As we rise to leave everything stops, the fight has been terminated though both birds are still alive.

'Why?' I ask Juan as we walk away.

'Oh, some technicality I expect.'

The white-haired man is cradling his bloody, triumphant bird in his arms. There's no sign of the loser.

It's early afternoon when we reach Cojímar, twenty kilometres east of the *valla*. Despite misgivings, Juan has persuaded me to visit Gregorio Fuentes, the village's main claim to fame.

'He's the Old Man, the fisherman Santiago in the story . . . *everyone* goes to see him,' he giggles. 'It's incredible you know, the older he gets the more money he makes. In the story he was very poor, almost starving, now he charges tourists ten dollars just to talk to him.'

Hemingway has been dead forty years; realising that someone he considered 'old' in 1951 is still alive, momentarily turns my notion of the passage of time on its head. Fuentes and Hemingway were almost exactly the same age. Maybe the fictional Santiago's fight with the great fish was about Hemingway's own ageing and fight against nature. How strange that Hemingway's alter ego is still alive and living where he always has.

Hot and dusty after the drive, we head for the relatively glossy La Terraza, a government-owned restaurant overlooking the mouth of the Rio Cojímar. Hemingway kept his boat, *El Pilar*, nearby. There are no boats in the harbour creek now, just a handful of small, near-naked boys diving and splashing and screaming in water the same chestnut brown as their skin.

La Terraza's lobster tank is full, the wine cooler golden with the tops of *cava* bottles imported from Spain. Whitewashed walls are lined with black-and-white photographs of Hemingway, Fuentes, and Hemingway with Fuentes. The barman asks if I want a mojito or a daiquiri and looks surprised and slightly offended when I say no. Perhaps all foreigners – and who else is likely to patronise La Terraza? – are supposed to order a version of Hemingway's favourite drinks. After only a short while I find the glossy wooden bar, slow-turning overhead fan and polished brass foot-rail unnatural; the contrast between this place and the *valla* is too extreme, too sublime and ridiculous.

Out near the seashore, the Hemingway Memorial is equally bizarre; a neo-Baroque folly of white pillars and curving lines. As I mount the few shallow steps to the plinth on which the bust is set, I wonder what the big, bearded guy would have had to say about all this. His bronze self is small and dark, its expression constipated and bemused.

During the half-kilometre drive between the seafront and the Old Man's house I wonder what I'm supposed to ask Gregorio Fuentes. Rumour says he's almost completely gaga and the thought of paying a drooling centenarian to dredge up fifty-year-old memories fills me with gloom. I recall Norman Lewis' tragic experience with Hemingway more than half a century ago, and quail.

Juan can't remember where the house is and asks directions of an almost-naked man sitting half in and half out of a large hole in the road; I assume he's repairing it, but who knows? Dense stubble and the soggy cigar butt dangling from beneath an enormous *bigote* make him look like a character from a spaghetti Western – one of those guys who sit around while Franco Nero listens to the musical watch and rolls his eyes. Black hair curls over a broad chest and black eyes shine with eagerness out of a craggy, dirt-streaked face. Even Juan seems to be having difficulty understanding the man's directions, and looking at him up to his waist in a pothole, grinning, I wonder if he's the whole *panetela*. But he must know what he's talking about because moments later we draw up outside a clean and newly painted house complete with fence and flowers.

The door marked *Fuentes* is closed and hung with a polite sign saying: *I'm sleeping, please do not disturb.* Relief washes over me; I'm not going to have to think up original, interesting questions after all.

'I suppose we should go then,' I say to Juan.

'Oh, for sure he's not asleep – old people don't sleep much.

There are probably ten Italians in there now. We can wait, no problem.'

I shake my head and ask him to drive on.

The photos in La Terraza show Gregorio Fuentes as already grizzled when he and Hemingway met, though he was only in his forties. An onlooker then would have said he'd aged badly, that life had not been kind, but more than half a century later he's still around and it strikes me that the Old Man is an aspect of the writer that has survived everything: revolution, changing literary tastes, the feminist movement, suicide. Fuentes, like the old fisherman Santiago, is a survivor against all the odds. What could I have asked him that would not diminish that? As Havana springs up around us, I'm happy we didn't meet. For me, at least, he will always be asleep and dreaming of lions.

★

The Cardinals

> He [Arenas] was a homosexual – and a very obvious
> one: now a Havana *loca*, a mad girl. He didn't do
> anything to suppress or even hide it. He belonged to
> the younger generation of homosexuals which pro-
> duced the gay movement elsewhere.
>
> Gabriel Cabrera Infante, *Mea Cuba*

Water pours down the slope of Jovellar towards the Malecón. For
two days it has rained so hard I've been unable to leave the apartment. There's something ironic about so much water as nothing
has come out of a tap for almost forty-eight hours. The telephone
works intermittently and this part of the city has had only occasional electricity in the last thirty-six hours. Water seeps through
the unglazed shutters and trickles down the plastic sofa as I watch
'La Fuerza del Deseo' with almost the same eagerness in which it
is viewed in every other home around me; after days alone with
Cuban television, anything is preferable to a Castro monologue. In
Maria's absence I study alone, but it's not the same without her
confrontational conversation and enlivening presence.

Despite the rain my apartment seems constantly filled with the
aggravating scent of roasting pork. Aggravating because my own
larder consists of a bucket of water in the bathroom, a packet of
cornflakes, a packet of rice and two small onions. Wiping rain-
water from the sofa with a piece of precious toilet paper, I wonder if my chief sensory memories of Havana will be the scent of
roast meat and damp, closely followed by the sounds of coughing
and barking.

During an interlude when the phone is working I call the
International Press Centre to chase my visa extension. The

woman with green eyes is unavailable, though Putin is long gone. Instead I speak to someone who tells me all is well; my passport, complete with visa, is in her hand. She would have called me, but she had a hospital appointment.

'Parasites,' she says, having seen the title 'Dr' on my passport. 'I got them in Africa many years ago and now I have them again. I thought they had gone. Do you think this means they were still there, hiding inside me, all that time?'

'I don't know. What did the doctors say at the hospital?'

'Oh, the specialist wasn't there for my appointment, they told me she had to go to a professional meeting. I must go again next week . . . maybe someone will see me then.'

Oddly, this conversation with a stranger makes me feel more cheerful. Boiling rice with a torch held between my teeth seems much less problematic knowing that other people make appointments that don't happen; that other people have parasites, while I do not.

During an easing of the downpour, I meet Simon Wollers. His thirteenth-floor apartment seems full of life and sound after two stir-crazy days. There's the local man and his Amazonian partner who tells me she's a political exile from the United States because of her involvement in black rights. Cuba is the alternative to prison or death back home now. She's occupied with the emerging Cuban rap movement and helps bring rap artists here from the United States.

'Cubans like rap music,' she says, 'and it helps raise consciousness about political prisoners in the States and draws attention to the blockade of Cuba.'

But she has no money. The tank in her Havana flat is pouring water into the neighbouring apartment below and she can't do anything about it. I wonder what 'political exile' means in her case; she doesn't look quite old enough for the Black Panthers. I want to like her, but there's something unsettling there, and when she appears behind me and starts kneading my shoulders I feel as much disquiet as comfort in her smooth, powerful hands.

Then there's the young woman from Los Angeles who's been here for a month with a film crew working on a documentary about Cuba. She's on her way out when I arrive but she stays just long enough to say isn't this place just wonderful, isn't it . . . but the food, *ohmigod*, the food . . . and she can't wait to get home and go to a supermarket and buy those cartons of ready-prepared egg whites and make a proper omelette . . . you know, the kind without yolks because after all each egg is thirty grams of fat, isn't it, and that just can't be good for your cholesterol and *of course* an omelette made only with whites tastes just the same so it's no problem throwing the yolks away . . . There's the stilt-walker Joel who occasionally stays here in a room he's hung with costumes and tight little T-shirts. He has the face of a Caravaggio angel, all geometric cheekbones and pouting lips, set among swags of curls.

Giolvis, Simon's partner, is a nurse at the nearby hospital. A country boy from Guantánamo, Giolvis moves like a sleek, dark brown cat. When the noise escalates he curls neatly on a sofa, puts on headphones and flicks through the brochure of the Latin American Film Festival, which has just ended. That's an art, I think looking at him, that ability to withdraw quietly and gracefully from a situation and do exactly what you want.

In the middle of it all is Simon, an attractive, slender man of forty-five. He's neither as prim nor as dour as I expected; my image of a gay British socialist being somewhat distorted by a London lens. He looks comfortable among his family photos and houseplants as he puts wine into my hand and shows me the balcony from where I can see the northern sweep of the Malecón and the lights of Linea leading down towards the sea.

After the black woman and her partner have left, the atmosphere shifts perceptibly. Giolvis removes his headphones and Simon opens his laptop as he talks to me about his work as a radio broadcaster.

'Some people see me as a kind of Lord Haw-Haw,' he says and grins, 'but I never broadcast anything if I don't believe it or am unsure of the source. It's not always easy, there's a fine line to walk and being non-Cuban there's always that feeling of being the outsider. But I like it here . . . I like the lack of violence, the non-materialism, the concern for others. I came here when they started bombing Yugoslavia – I found it hard to live with that level of jingoism.'

He presses a key on the laptop and smiles at the screen. 'Come and look at this,' he says to Giolvis. 'It's a photo you haven't seen, of me in Thailand.'

I peer over Giolvis' shoulder at a badly manipulated photo of Simon's head in a wig stuck on the body of a Thai bar girl. I laugh. Giolvis stares at this new aspect of his lover, nonplussed by the fakery, then realising it's a joke, laughs too.

We talk about books, then about the new film based on Reinaldo Arenas' novel *Before Night Falls*, and those days of homosexual repression in the sixties and seventies that Arenas records. Simon explains how things have changed.

'I really believe that Havana is probably the safest place for gay men to visit in all Latin America.'

'And is that true for gay men who live here too?'

'From a safety point of view, yes, though to be honest, it's probably slightly easier to live here as a gay person if you're a foreigner. But compared with El Salvador or Venezuela, which has some of the best pro-gay legislation in Latin America, this is paradise.'

'And do gay men remember what it was like before? Do young guys like Giolvis and Joel know how it was for people like Arenas? Is there much political awareness?'

'You have to realise Arenas really overstated things in *Before Night Falls*. A bit like Genet maybe, hard to sort fact from creativity.' He turns to Giolvis and asks what he thinks about sexual politics, to which Giolvis replies that he's never thought about it.

'There's very little analysis you know, this isn't an overly analytical culture; people aren't stuck in their heads all the time like us.'

Joel sweeps into the room flinging his wet curls around to dry.

'What do you know about how things were for gay men here in the past?' I ask him.

'Not much,' he says.

'It makes me cross sometimes,' Simon says, shaking his head pedagogically, 'this lack of interest in history, both as Cubans and as gay men.'

'Maybe all those bearded heroes at too young an age put them off?'

But Joel isn't done talking and now his hair is drying right he starts an unexpectedly impassioned conversation. Giolvis puts the headphones back on again. I wrap my arms around my knees and try to stop myself grinning. I've missed this.

'It's *not* easy here,' Joel says. 'I've *always* felt discriminated against because I'm gay.'

And he launches into a personal history that includes exile from the family home after coming out to his father as a young teenager, and his subsequent life in a *beca,* boarding school, which includes battery, near rape and molestation by adults.

Clearly distressed by this story, Simon says, 'But this isn't something unique to Cuba, Joel. What you're talking about happens everywhere – in England, in America, and much more in El Salvador or Jamaica. This is about being gay, not about being gay in Cuba.'

'But I've never been to America or even Jamaica . . . I can only talk about what it feels like *here* and here I have no rights, because I don't hide. Because I dress like I want and perform in the streets I am called *maricón*. Little children call me *maricón*, before they even know what it means . . .'

I can see his anger bubbling close to the surface and Simon's appearance of detachment fuelling that.

'But that's just it,' Simon says reasonably, 'it *doesn't* mean anything here, just like *negro* or *chino;* they aren't insults . . . there's no violence intended.'

'It feels violent to *me*,' Joel says passionately, 'it affects me psychologically! When I told my father I was gay he attacked me; isn't that violence?'

I hear the words 'three ribs'. His father beat him up and broke three of his ribs. He was thirteen, small and delicate. Nice one Dad. Simon turns to me to translate.

'I got it,' I say, 'his father broke his ribs . . .'

'No, no, no,' Simon says, '*he* broke three of his *father's* ribs.' (First rule of language learning, never assume.)

Joel grins and, perching on the arm of my seat, strokes my hair. 'My father never spoke to me after that, which is okay with me, and none of the neighbours ever gave me trouble . . . because although they knew I was a *maricón,* they knew I was a *vicioso maricón*!'

'I thought you said they aren't analytical,' I say to Simon.

Simon gestures to Giolvis who's been watching the interaction with the headphones still in place. 'Do you feel discriminated against as a gay black man?'

'I'm glad I'm not black,' Joel interjects, waving his arms. 'If I was gay *and* black I wouldn't stand a chance, I'd probably be dead by now! My black friends get stopped by the police all the time . . .'

'No, I've never had a problem,' Giolvis says calmly.

'Of course you never have a problem,' Joel bellows. 'You're completely conservative – look how you dress! You're a nurse, the government loves you, you help the sick, you have a clean record *and* you're not out to your family who live a thousand kilometres from here! But we can't all live like you and why should we . . . why should *I*?'

'Getting stopped by the police is also about fighting crime, not necessarily about discrimin–' Simon starts to say, but Joel is deaf to everything but his own voice.

'*You* never have a problem either,' he says, eyes wide and hot now. 'You're white and foreign and you wear a shirt and trousers. Why would the police stop you? I choose to be who I am in an open way . . .'

'I'd rather be stopped by Cuban police officers than by British or American ones,' Simon says.

'Of course you would,' I reply, 'you're a respectable foreigner. But do you think you'd feel the same if you wanted to wear a dress and a moustache?'

'I've made decisions too', he says, 'on the side of reality. You learn to look at the world realistically. I have many friends here, black and white, who get into trouble over things because they've not yet learnt to choose their battles, to decide which ones are worthwhile and which ones are unwinnable. I choose which ones I fight now and so I win most of them.'

Looking at the deceptively fragile Joel with his skintight turquoise vest and pierced nose, nothing about him would raise an eyebrow in London or Los Angeles, though he would certainly turn a few heads. I wonder what kind of choices he'd had as a kid in Havana.

'I can see you're angry,' I say to Joel. 'Are you angry with how things are in general, or just about how gays are treated?'

'Only about gays,' he says and I believe him. 'I love how it is here. I love the education and the beautiful free health system. In general our system is *very* beautiful, it really is about the people. But that's the problem, there are things undermining that beautiful system and people's confidence in it; things like homophobia and sexism and racism and violence against women and children.'

Simon says quickly, 'There's almost no abuse of children here, it just isn't tolerated; neighbours report things like that, it's simply not part of the culture.'

Joel looks at me and raises his eyebrows.

Giolvis is listening now with interest, and I ask him, 'If you came out to your family, how do you think they'd react?'

He pauses and I notice that the whole room is reflected on the curved surface of his almost black eyes. 'My mother and sister would support me for sure . . . my uncles and brothers would be a problem, but if they didn't like it they could fuck off; I'm not dependent on them in any way, what I do is only my business.'

Joel tuts and shakes his head as if to say 'dream on'.

It's late when I leave, the city is silent and deserted save for the occasional taxi. On Linea the potholes have become pools of water and the few streetlights reflect silver-black on the ragged tarmac. Like most people here I have no adequate clothing for this weather. Rains are an annual event in Cuba – though not normally at this time of year – yet everything grinds almost to a stop. The suspended animation reminds me of Britain when it snows. During the day when people are forced onto the streets by work or shopping they look horrified – as if the rain and cold were a personal affront – and talk about dying. If it rains tomorrow, perhaps I'll go out wearing head-to-toe bin-liners as Cubans do.

The next day is overcast but it's no longer raining. At Maria's house the lesson moves slowly, as if the low air pressure has invested everything with a layer of dullness. Large patches of damp have appeared along the external wall of the sitting area. Maria shakes her head at it.

'What can we do?'

Her daughter appears briefly and asks if I've heard from Jacob. I say no.

'No-one knows where he is,' she says. 'You know he moved from that house where he was staying, with that actress? I hope he's alright.'

'He seems able to look after himself,' I say.

The girl shakes her head, 'He drinks too much . . . maybe he fell down . . .'

After two weeks of lessons I can actually talk in Spanish. Not very well, but well enough that I am no longer so appalled at the prospect of my own ignorance. I feel enormously grateful to Maria, who, I can tell, feels enormously grateful to me for the money I'm giving her on an almost daily basis. There are sweets on the table now, and fish with rice, and fried bananas. The rest of the money is for Maria's new house, in the remote Stepford-like suburb of Alamar. She seems delighted at the prospect of a modern home, and gazing at the Rorschach damp blots above my head I suppose there would be advantages.

Her eyes glisten as she whispers, 'It's mine. Not my husband's, or my mother's. Mine. And it will be my daughter's if she wants it.'

With small cups of black tea before us we talk about my imminent departure from Havana, about the books I've written and the book on Italy I plan to write in the future. Maria disappears for a moment, returning with a photo album.

'I was in Italy once,' she says, flicking through the stiff pages. 'look, there's me in Rome by the Trevi Fountain and here in the Colosseum.' She pauses, her lips parting momentarily. 'The very best thing was when I went up in the dome of Saint Peter's to where you can walk around the outside of the building, and oh, it was wonderful.' Her smooth, unlined face takes on a secret, distant expression. 'I walked around the dome and looked across the whole of Rome . . . places where Julius Caesar walked, and . . . and Garibaldi. And I looked and looked . . . and I thought, "This is *me*, Maria . . . I'm *here* looking at *Rome*!" And I felt like Cleopatra, Queen of Egypt.'

An entirely unexpected lump forms somewhere in my throat and threatens to choke me. The tears stinging my eyes run down my face as I blink. Maria looks at me surprised, but squeezes my hand.

'What is it?'

I smile, shake my head and wipe the tears away. 'Nothing,' I say, 'just the thought of you like Cleopatra.' I can't begin to explain the rush of complex feelings that precipitated my reaction: this woman's capacity for joy; her imagination, alive and well despite curtailing; her longing for the outside and her inability to go there now; my discomfort at an excess of freedom. I can't explain any of these things: my Spanish isn't *that* good.

Martin di Giovanni sits behind a desk in the office of an international news agency just off the Malecón. There are two sandwiches on the desk, and handing me one, he tells me he works for an international newspaper, that this isn't actually *his* desk, he's just filling in for an absent colleague. He seems disarmingly frank for a journalist.

He tells me his wife is Cuban, that he has a twenty-year-old son; that his ten-year-old daughter is a pupil at the school where Cecilia teaches. He tells me he loses sleep over the regime and thinks about it almost obsessively; that he feels ambivalent about the prospect of his children growing up here yet believes at the same time that here is where they belong. I'm surprised that after so many years he still feels strongly about things; his emotions seem all on the surface: anger, anxiety, frustration. I ask what positive changes he has seen since he arrived here.

'It has improved a lot since the mid-1990s when things were terrible. There was a real loosening of the reins then, there had to be. Now things are a bit better the government is subtly pushing the Revolution forward again in an attempt to counter the effects of outside influences like tourism and the dollar.'

He moves as he talks – his hands, his face and most of his body. 'I don't know if you noticed yet, but there's this huge conflict between reality and rhetoric here, between what Castro says to the wider world and what he actually permits inside the country. It's ironic; he accuses the U.S. of being Goliath to his David, but here *he* is the Goliath and the people are David. He's an overgrown cuckoo in the people's consciousness, an ageing megalomaniac who doesn't know his time is past.' He continues to talk quickly, almost impatiently, as if unburdening himself.

'Cuba is split three ways, between generations – there's the sixty-plus population who remember the years before Castro, who probably fought in the war and who retain some of those youthful ideals. To them Castro is still a hero. Then there's the lost generation, people of our age, who, being on the periphery, suffered the most and perhaps understood the least, having neither the ideals nor the advantages. Then there are the under-thirties who have never known anything else, who are bewildered and blankly angry because none of the stuff drilled into them as education had any personal relevance. Castro is seventy-four, what can he have to say to the youth of this country?' He grins and looks positively cheerful. 'One of the things the government hates most about my reporting is that I always mention Fidel's age. They see it as a suggestion that he's failing in some way; but then, I think he is. He talks longer and less coherently than in the past, he shuffles papers, takes long pauses and goes off on tangents. I think that's about his age and so I say it.'

It occurs to me that he is being *remarkably* frank for someone in his position, that he doesn't know me, or what I intend to do with this interview. Perhaps I have a particularly honest face, or am automatically trustworthy simply by not being a journalist. Or maybe he really doesn't care any more.

'So what happened to the Revolution?' I ask.

His answer is as direct and simple as others' have been complex. 'It was kidnapped by one person and turned into a tool for personal power. Back in the fifties it really was a genuine movement for social justice, no question about that. But then Castro, for a number of reasons, began forcing it to fit a communist model. Now he's a kind of Frankenstein – his vision has turned into a nightmare, but it's the nightmare of eleven million people.' He leans forward, arms spread on the desk. His youthful face, made more youthful and open-seeming by the fair hair and blue eyes, is tense. 'It should have worked – the social contract between State and people was simply a good life in return for allegiance to the party/State/Revolution. It worked at first because of the support of the Eastern bloc, and then after 1990 when the government here couldn't deliver, things changed. There have been far-reaching economic developments in the last decade – the increase in tourism and small businesses, the liberalisation of the dollar. But all these things weakened the social contract – if the people provide for themselves, what happens to their allegiance to the State? Now of course it's too late to roll back the system, but the government is trying, in small ways, to do just that by constantly pointing to the failures and failings of capitalism in the outside world.'

'And the things we hear praised – like free education, health care?'

'You can give people education of course, but what is it worth if you don't allow freedom of thought or action. No-one here really knows what the outside world is like. Even if they have relatives abroad they still see only bits and pieces of the whole picture.' He picks up a copy of *Granma* and waves it at me. 'All they have is *this*,

this utter, utter rag. Everything that appears in this *thing* is simply a repetition of the party line, no divergence is tolerated. The press is so very tightly controlled, even the foreign press. I've never been able to write freely here and since 1998, foreign journalists have been denied visas if they aren't sufficiently "objective"!' He shakes his head. 'There should be a solution, but I can't see one . . . that's why I don't sleep.'

'And what happens to those who step out of line?'

'The huge police presence is meant as a deterrent to crime and as a reminder of State power, and if you push against all that? Well, the first response would be to ignore you, to isolate you. The State has an almost total monopoly on jobs, of course, which is a very powerful weapon, and then there are the CDRs, which makes about 90 per cent of the population collaborators in the repression and control of dissidents. The second response would be to crush you. I know they could get rid of me at any moment and actually I'm beginning to expect it.' The chair swivels. 'They do these reports on foreign journalists, you see, and the last one on myself and another correspondent strongly criticised us both. The *very* worst thing they can say about you is that you work for the U.S. and the report said I'm too busy working for the American news at the expense of my British commitments and my own embassy. Those are the kind of below-the-belt digs you get used to here, but they're a lot more pointed and frequent just now.'

'And how does Castro justify all this,' I ask, 'to himself I mean?'

'He sees himself as a political colossus bestriding the world . . . *the* opposer of U.S. domination, not just regionally but globally. He truly believes that he's a leader of vast international significance and thinks Greenspan should call him every morning to discuss the world's finances. The rest of the Caribbean islands, they're just specks on his ocean. Of course, the U.S. has behaved appallingly towards Cuba from the outset. It could have been so different if the Revolution hadn't come at the end of McCarthyism and if men other than Eisenhower and Nixon had been in control. Now we have this pointless embargo which plays directly into Castro's hands, and hurts ordinary Cubans.'

I ask if Castro's sense of greatness is ideological or actual . . . if Castro always had a sense of destiny as an international colossus, or whether it developed with time and age.

'I'm sure he always had it and there were always those, even people close to him, who questioned it or felt it had too strong a flavour of megalomania.'

He gets up very suddenly and strides across the small office to a filing cabinet from which he draws a sheaf of papers – handwritten notes about an anti-Castro microconspiracy in 1968. Looking at them I feel a slight *frisson,* not dissimilar to the experience of opening rare, seventeenth-century books while working in the British Library years ago. Written on cheap, yellowing paper, and stapled together by a nameless journalist, the documents detail how several hardline socialists, led by a Francisco Brito, hatched a plot to overthrow *Comandante* Castro. As with all anti-Castro plots, this one was foiled and the men were 'purged'. I ask what 'purged' meant in this instance and Martin shakes his head.

'No idea, but I've certainly not heard of Brito again . . . though that doesn't mean much.'

I wonder if he's still alive somewhere, an old man now, like Castro himself, looking back at what might have been. At his trial, Brito apparently gave his reasons for wanting to rid Cuba of its leader. It was Castro's state of mind, he said. 'Fidel wants to change the world, to be bigger than Marx. He is completely mad.'

We are both silent for a moment. Then I ask, 'And the embargo? If it were lifted tomorrow, what would happen?'

'There are enough safeguards in place in the short term at least to ensure that very little would change on the ground. More importantly Castro is easily clever enough to use something like that to the max. It would be the justification of everything he'd ever done. Can you imagine it? If and when American tourists come here officially, they'll only be allowed in in small, tightly-controlled batches. Then they'll be milked dry while being told that their evil regime has caused economic backwardness and poverty, so now they have to do without decent facilities and if they want better they'll have to pay for them in compensation.'

'Sounds like a bloody excellent idea to me,' I say, grinning, 'and it even has some justification.'

'Perhaps,' he says, 'and this government would almost certainly get away with it.'

Unexpectedly he asks me what I think about it all, about Cuba.

'I haven't been here long enough or seen enough to answer that, but I do know I couldn't live here. A first impression is that it's oddly prosaic and surreal. For example, I saw a dog in a dress the other day, a boxer. I mean, how weird is that?'

He looks at me for a moment and says, 'We have a boxer and we put it in a T-shirt.'

'Yeah, right!' I say, grinning, then realise he isn't, that actually he's looking deadly serious.

'No, we have a boxer and we put it in a T-shirt because it gets cold.'

'You're joking, right? This is Cuba, dogs don't get cold. Anyway they've got fur . . .'

'My dog has bronchitis,' he says tartly.

My God, I think, what kind of place is this when even the dogs get respiratory infections if the temperature drops more than a degree.

As we walk to the lift, Martin wishes me luck on my journey around the island. 'You'll love it,' he says, 'it really is a beautiful place. Let me know when you're back, we can meet up and you can tell me about it.'

That evening I watch a documentary history of the Revolution on television, the grainy black-and-white images a fascinating reminder of that time. There are people everywhere, happy people, black and white mixing together, laughing and embracing. The camera focuses on Fidel, his mouth moving rapidly and violently, one arm raised with pointed finger above his head. The only difference between youth and age seems to be that he also smiled and laughed back then. You can see the energy and the hope and the need in the film, especially Castro's. You can see the amazing thing the Revolution achieved . . . a moment of freedom that felt like it might go on forever.

A little after nine o'clock on Christmas Eve, Simon and I walk the short distance between his apartment and the hospital where Giolvis is on intensive care night-duty. The Avenida de los Presidentes is divided by a swathe of machete-cut grass, trimmed trees and the busts of revolutionary heroes. We walk in the middle of the empty traffic lane to avoid the crumbling pavement, and for the first time I notice a few homeless people lying in doorways. Simon says this their choice.

'Isn't that what the right wing say back home?' I ask, surprised.

'Nothing is perfect, there's no point expecting it to be. Mistakes are made here just like everywhere else but people get more care here than they'd receive in Britain or the U.S.'

'So, what happened to the Revolution?'

'It stagnated to a degree. All the leaders are old and there's no young blood. Despite that the government has accepted that change is inevitable, that sexuality, the Internet, the dollar, tourists etcetera – all the things they were wary about – are here and *must* be here if Cuba isn't to be left behind. They don't want isolation of the kind that North Korea has suffered, but at the same time it's still an ideological problem for them.'

'People have told me they feel infantilised.'

'Cubans are incredibly spoilt. So much has been given to them – they are constantly pampered by the State in everything but their monthly wage packet.'

Taken aback, I say, 'Perhaps they'd like to make their own decisions and not be "given".'

'Perhaps,' he says, ever reasonable, 'but they have the feeling that the grass is greener everywhere else, and though in some ways that's true, in other ways their lives here are incredibly easy. Many people who have left here for the States are trapped by the money they feel obliged to send home every month: that 100 dollars seems like nothing at first, but for many it becomes a huge burden that keeps them in low-paid jobs. In the beginning they think how wonderful everything is in their new country, then realise that nothing is free and that they need at least two jobs just to survive. They become slaves to that 100 dollars they send back, slaves to their families back here, to the system.'

I wonder if this is the fault of the system they're in, or of the one they left behind where 100 dollars means so very much. Perhaps it's both.

'People are cared for here,' he says, 'you'll see.'

The hospital is a teaching hospital, part of the prestigious University of Havana. In a side entrance about a dozen people, relatives of patients upstairs, are already sleeping on benches or are rolled up in their coats on the floor.

'Doctors and nurses are the real heroes of the Revolution,' Simon says as we make our way through the silent, dark building. 'There are thousands of Cuban medical personnel in needy countries, particularly in the Third World – Latin America, Africa. The government sends them all over the world. You know that Che was a doctor?'

I nod.

'It's not easy – they all earn peanuts and work like dogs. Giolvis barely makes ends meet. He could easily steal medicine and sell it on the black market, or even more easily sell himself to foreigners, but he has a lot of self-respect and says he won't be a thief or a whore. Did I tell you that in his spare time he works as a volunteer HIV counsellor? He's a good man.'

Almost every door is barred, and we have to wait while someone comes to open up for us. I have a feeling that we're only allowed in because we are foreigners and, paradoxically, because Simon seems so at home. The lift attendant, a decrepit elderly man with few teeth and a pungent smell, has to be bribed to take us to the intensive care floor with one of the cans of soft drink that Simon has brought for Giolvis. It's all very clean, but as we walk down the low-lit, echoing corridors the place feels like a deserted spaceship. The corridors smell of disinfectant and more remotely of sickness. I wonder where the sick people are; there's no sign of them, no sign of wards. We stop in front of a darkened door and Simon rings a bell. After a few moments Giolvis' smiling face appears and we're let into yet another corridor as he bars the door behind us. I think what a trap this place would be if there were a fire, then put the vision from my mind. Giolvis explains the closed doors are for security – to prevent theft in a society where everyone is 'making do'.

'It's very quiet tonight,' Giolvis says, 'not much happening. I can show you something though. Come.'

Down yet more corridors, and in a small room packed with ultramodern Japanese machinery a swarthy man in a thick plaid jacket is smoking and staring at the television. A tired, harassed-looking doctor is adjusting the equipment and I don't at first notice the patient lying on the trolley bed, a young black man, naked under the sheet draped carelessly across his lower body. I suddenly feel very conspicuous and intrusive. Why am I standing in the middle of a hospital room watching a stranger being treated? But the young man doesn't know I'm here, his half-open eyes are stony and flat and he seems barely conscious.

'Look at the equipment,' Giolvis says, 'it's one of the most advanced haemodialysis machines – amazing isn't it?'

The television plays on, cigarette smoke drifts around the room. The man on the bed never moves. Outside in the corridor Giolvis tells us the patient is sixteen and dying of cancer, they know the treatment won't save him but they're trying the only thing they have.

Walking to meet Cecilia on our way to the midnight celebration outside the cathedral I mention how scary the whole place had seemed, with its mixture of prison-like security and offbeat care.

'Look at it this way,' Simon says stopping in his stride and turning to face me in the middle of the road, 'that guy was being given very expensive treatment, completely free, by a highly qualified man, very late at night. Tell me where else that's going to happen.'

I decide that I like Simon very much. He's an old-fashioned liberal socialist of the English type that almost became extinct several decades ago. There are contradictions, there would have to be, but he seems to me an honest man who lives as much as possible by what he believes. He knows the problems here – his comments often echo Martin's, though they are on different sides of the divide. But there's no question that both men love Cuba and love Cubans, literally and metaphorically, and walking past the busts of heroes I feel fortunate to have met them.

Inside the cathedral a large Christmas tree hung with white thread and silver glitter towers over an irreverent congregation. Confessional boxes buzz with sinners repenting a year's worth of un-Christian thoughts and deeds, purging themselves in readiness for rebirth and, if luck is with them, a whole new year of transgression. In the queue outside the confessionals, women in low-cut vests smoke fat cigars and chatter in rolling Spanish. Across the nave a Nativity scene, complete with ass, ox and Latino shepherds, is taking place inside a cardboard cave hung with real Spanish moss that's crisping in the heat. The shepherds observe the velvet-swathed Christ-child under a pea-green light, which reflects eerily in the faces of bright-eyed, sugar-drunk children sitting high in their fathers' arms to ogle the plaster child and each other.

Tonight the Plaza de la Catedral, former 'Swamp Square', is rapidly filling with a cross section of *habaneros*. Even the nonexistent middle classes are drawn here in order to see and be seen among the crowd gathering for a newly fashionable display of religion and campery, though not necessarily both together. The mood is courteous and, unlike the many British midnight masses surfacing in my memory, no-one jostles and no-one is raucously drunk.

Men, dressed in everything from checked shirts and leather jeans to full drag, cruise the aisles like a school of sharks. There are black men with bleached white hair, white men with dyed black hair, men with hungry eyes, and others who look surprised to find themselves here at all.

Seeing Cecilia, Simon and I, Joel leaves his flamboyant young friends and joins us briefly. This display by gay men is all part of recent tradition he says, like saying that if religion is back then so is homosexuality; though everyone knows that neither ever really went away.

The families climbing the cathedral steps as the bells start to ring are obliged to run the gauntlet of the gay men filling the balconies to each side of the main entrance. To the left are leather-clad men who use their elevated vantage point to eye the entire square with brazen unhesitancy; on the right are ordinary-looking chaps in jeans and tweed jackets. The *padres de familias*, well aware of the crossfire of catcalls and eyeballing cutting them off from the safety of the church, walk fast, eyes lowered, wives and children trailing. But even inside there's little sanctuary; Havana's social insurgents, already established in the aisles and pews, are claiming their place on this one night of the year. The air is dense with cigar smoke and electronic organ music, the temperature rising from the growing press of bodies wired to a tangible sense of expectation and the sheer joy of something different.

At a few minutes to midnight the bells ring out for the last time and a shrill, recorded voice starts singing a hymn. The cigar-smoking women sit down where they can admire the Christmas tree decorations and the gay men who intend to last out the mass stand around the walls, arms and legs nonchalantly crossed. There's an absence of any identifiable religious feeling; rather the place hums with a pagan casualness and lack of inhibition that is positively refreshing.

Later a group of us sit in another old square near the Princess Diana Memorial Garden and drink rum and eat fries until the early hours when I leave them still talking and laughing. My flight departs next morning for Santiago de Cuba – capital of the former province of Oriente – where, I'm told, everything is different.

'You must take care,' Maria told me after our last lesson together. 'I worry that you will be alone in those places where the people are not like us. They eat different food, speak differently, think like Africans, like Haitians . . . you will not understand them as you understand us and our city.'

Do I understand Havana? I don't think so. Perhaps decades wouldn't allow a grasp of this city's moods and shades. There's too much to understand and I'm already taking my first leave. Like every capital in the world, Havana is not Cuba. Tomorrow the real journey begins.

ORIENTE

Gothique Tropicale

> When the full moon rises
> I will go to Santiago de Cuba . . .
> The roofs of palms will sing
> I will go to Santiago . . .
> With the blond head of Fonseca
> I will go to Santiago
> And with the rosebush of Romeo y Julieta
> Oh Cuba! Oh rhythm of dry seeds!
> Oh warm waist and drop of wood! . . .
>
> Federico García Lorca, *Son de negros en Cuba*

It's said that Federico García Lorca talked so much about going to Santiago he almost didn't get there. Some people, even today, think he did not. He seemed hardly able to draw himself away from the pleasures of Havana, writing to his parents in Andalucia that if he ever disappeared, this was where he could be found. *Habaneras* were the most beautiful women in the world, he wrote, 'owing to the drops of black blood that all Cubans carry . . . The blacker the better', though women were not, of course, the reason for Lorca's love of the island. The poet seems to have become almost drunk on the humid hedonism of 1930s Cuba – who else could have made cigars, Fonseca and Romeo y Julieta, erotic with tasteful double entendre. Lorca experienced the earliest of those days described to me so ambivalently by Enrico Cirules under the soaring spires of the Hotel Nacional: days of growing U.S. control, of the dictator Machado, of the violent economic crisis caused by the country's ties to Wall Street, and of the plunging price of sugar. But Lorca, fêted and loved, seems to have seen little of these things, rather he appears to have been swept up in the beauty and the exotic richness of the music and literature around him. How unlike Hemingway, who sat in his hotel room in Old Havana and wrote stories of blood and violence between short walks to his favourite bars.

Some chance meetings have more significance than others, though at the time they often seem alike. The young Englishwoman with red-gold hair sitting next to me on the plane dislikes flying but hides it well. She tells me she works for the *Times* of London, that she's here with her mother but got bored of the tourist resort where they'd been staying and decided to head off alone. I ask if she's enjoying herself.

'I don't know to be honest. I feel I ought to be. Cuba is one of those places, isn't it, where you *ought* to have fun . . . but I don't think I am yet.' She grins apologetically.

Almost the entire length of Cuba passes below, a panorama of green and brown and red broken occasionally by a skin of creamy cloud. We touch down briefly at Holguín and, looking out at the dusty landscape, I think of Reinaldo Arenas who wrote about his childhood in this province, buggering his cousins and eating dirt to quell hunger. Thirty-five kilometres north-east of Holguín city is the Bahía de Bariay, Columbus' first landing point on this island which he named 'Juana' in honour of an heir to the Spanish throne, an heir who became mother to a Holy Roman Emperor, grandmother to a king of Spain, the Low Countries and the Americas, and who was known as Juana La Loca, the Mad, because she was foolish enough to adore her husband.

Columbus' first words to the local hunter-gatherer Indians were typical of the adventurer and his time, and précis roughly as, 'Do you know the place where the gold grows?' He imagined, optimistic with the weight and power of Spain, that this was the auriferous coast of Asia and these the first dry steps towards unimaginable riches for his masters and himself. He was disappointed. Cuba's importance would lie then, as now, in its strategic position rather than in any great intrinsic wealth.

Cubans still talk about Oriente. 'She is from Oriente,' they say, and, 'All the police in Havana come from Oriente . . . the government think they are too stupid to be corrupt.' Oriente hasn't existed as a province since 1975, but there remains a mysterious otherness to this easterly region of Cuba that I can feel even before arrival. The modern eastern provinces of Santiago de Cuba, Guantánamo, Granma, Holguín and Las Tunas just don't have the same appeal to the romantic imagination as 'Oriente'; even the word itself is tinged with exotic fancy.

We come in over El Cobre, the plane banking steeply above the great red wound of Cuba's largest copper mine . . . the oldest European-run mine in the western hemisphere. Close by and pale against the camouflage of the land is the Basílica de Nuestra Señora del Cobre, the country's holiest shrine and home to Hemingway's 1954 Nobel Prize medal for *The Old Man and the Sea*. There seems to be no escaping Hemingway on this island.

The one-storey house of the Hamera family looks insignificant from the outside, no different to any of the other properties in this dusty suburban street, but stepping through the front door into the cool, shuttered darkness I find the most varied collection of books I have seen anywhere in Cuba. *Moll Flanders* and *Jane Eyre* squeeze between Gorky, Turgenev and Dostoevsky.

Within minutes of my arrival, Rafael Hamera tells me that he has read them all, that the pretty plates and saucers hanging on the walls are his, that the engraved glass cups in the cabinet were a present to his mother on her birthday. He shows me a *faux* eighteenth-century vase locked in a cupboard, a gift, he says, from his gay uncle in New York.

'We like it very much. It's probably worth a lot of money,' he says. 'It's English; have you seen anything similar in England?'

I look at the bottom where it's clearly stated that the vase was made in Czechoslovakia.

'No, never,' I say truthfully.

Rafael is twenty-one, an architecture student at Santiago University and scion of a privileged middle-class family now reduced to dependency on relatives in America. His enthusiasm for kitsch is infectious, almost as infectious as his delight in having a stranger to talk to about his life, his family, his city, his eclectic interest in religion, his garden and his melancholy. He speaks very fast and with great intensity; large grey eyes wide in an olive face that looks more Nuristani than Cuban.

'You are not our only guest this evening,' he says, gleefully, 'we have two more ladies coming to dinner, English Quaker ladies.'

My introduction to the Hameras came from an English Quaker and I'd assumed the family were Quakers too. So it's with slight surprise that I see the Star of David hanging around Rafael's neck and the purple kippa he shows me among his 'things'.

'Our family name is Jewish,' he says, though when I ask how and when they came to Cuba, he doesn't know.

The visit from the English ladies is not a success; there's an all-round clash of cultural expectation and the atmosphere is stiff. As a newly arrived guest I hope to be fed; as guests at dinnertime – Christmas dinnertime – the English ladies also hope to be fed, but they too are disappointed. What our hosts expect is unclear as we sit in a circle of rocking chairs and Rafael translates for his mother and grandfather.

Olga Hamera, a sturdy woman and a former professor of linguistics, now has a part-time job as the director of one of the less-visited museums in the city and feels that she has come down in the world through no fault of her own.

'There isn't enough money for so many professors any more,' she says, 'and we have to live.'

Her father, Virgilio Domenico Hamera Jubal, is eighty-four years old and angry. I'd always assumed that, like teenagers, the elderly would find each other vaguely interesting or at least have things in common – like survival or piles. Virgilio makes a point of entirely avoiding the aged Amelia, one of those eccentric English ladies whom life has gifted with unconcerned forthrightness, and age with selective deafness. Amelia's travelling companion Laurel, a much younger woman who lives in mid-Wales but is neither Quaker nor eccentric, makes polite conversation. Olga hovers, courteous and anxious, then disappears into the kitchen.

'The old woman asked for something to eat . . .' Rafael whispers to me, ' is that usual in your country?'

'She's hungry, so she asks,' I whisper back. 'They probably thought they were being invited for dinner . . . that would be what an invite today, at this time, would mean in our country.'

'Oh . . . I never thought of that.'

The small plates of purée Olga puts before us suggest we've been given everything the family had in the larder – a few spoonfuls each of mashed *malanga*, a potato-like vegetable. I feel awkward, embarrassed by Amelia's lack of tact, but grateful for it too. It's a long time – twenty years ago on the India–Nepal border – since I was in a house with kind people who left me hungry because they had nothing to give.

West of Santiago de Cuba, the tree-clad Sierra Maestra rise steeply against a hard blue sky. East, the Cordillera de la Gran Piedra stretches towards Guantánamo and the furthest point of Cuba. Santiago lies between these high places, in a green continuation of the fertile lowlands of San Luis and Palma Soriano to the north and a turquoise inlet of the Caribbean to the south. When Diego Velázquez first set eyes on this land he reputedly murmured, '*Ah, la nueva Galicia.*' But he hadn't seen the mosquitoes.

Oriente has always been at the forefront of change. It was the first place in Cuba to receive African slaves and the first to free them. It was the birthplace of every revolutionary movement from the declaration of a Cuban republic by Carlos Manuel de Céspedes in 1868, which started the First War of Independence, to the *Granma* landing of 1956. Santiago was Cuba's first capital. Its first mayor, Hernán Cortés, made a career move in 1519 and became the scourge of Montezuma. The first place of higher education in Cuba, the Seminario de San Basilio Magno, was founded in 1722 and the archbishopric of Cuba was established here in 1804. But the city's meteoric rise preceded a rapid decline; natural resources, including the indigenous population, faded quickly. In the mid-1550s the city was violated by Lutheran privateer Jacques de Sores and the superbly named pirate Peg-Leg Leclerc. One hundred years later it was the Welshman Sir Henry Morgan who came to Santiago still looking for Montezuma's plundered gold on its way to Spain.

In 1607 Havana became Cuba's capital while Santiago was relegated to capital of the newly created province of Oriente. Despite this apparent diminution of its national role, Santiago remained significant in the imagination of Cuba and its people. Its isolation, due to its distance from Havana, allowed an entirely different cultural life to develop and this was one reason the region was at the forefront of change. Revolution thrived in the city's streets and heroes were born on farms and *estancias* throughout the province. In 1845 Antonio Maceo, hero of the Second War of Independence, was born in Santiago not far from the place where his and Cuba's hopes of final victory against the Spanish would die, when the United States intervened to remove the Spanish. Bullyboy and future U.S. president Theodore Roosevelt used the sinking of the USS *Maine* in Havana harbour to seize the long-coveted Spanish colony. Roosevelt's Rough Riders – which included former members of Butch Cassidy's Hole in the Wall Gang – rode up Santiago's San Juan Hill, over the Spanish defences and into history, trampling Cuba's hopes of freedom. Thirty years after de Céspedes began the long, bitter struggle for independence, Cubans weren't even invited to the peace talks that followed U.S. intervention; they had merely exchanged one colonial power for another far more vigorous one. José Martí, dead three years before Roosevelt's incursion, proved prophetic in his fears regarding U.S. intentions.

'Santiago is the most historic place in all Cuba,' Rafael tells me as we walk through the old heart of the city. 'I am very proud to have been born here.'

Discovering Santiago with a student of architecture is an unexpected pleasure. Rafael shows me how the narrow side steps leading from street level to high, wooden verandas indicate that a house is French and not Spanish in style.

'This old part of the city is as much French as Spanish,' he says. 'You can hear in the black people's accents that they are from Haiti, that their original language was French.'

He explains the pleated glass windows of the old cinema; the 400-hundred-year-old churches; the former Jesuit mission, a shell now, but still impressive. And the role of Freemasonry here.

'Santiago was built by Masons,' he says as we sit in one of the city's many small squares. 'Most of these plazas have a pattern to them; you will see a church, a lodge, a ceiba tree and probably, in the centre, a statue of one of our heroes who probably was a Mason too, like de Céspedes or José Martí. And Castro of course was a Mason, but when he became *comandante* he tried to reduce their influence because he understood from the inside how strong they are. But here in Santiago they are still strong and do good work for schools and hospitals. My grandfather was a Mason . . . he was a powerful man, a lawyer and a teacher, so it was right he was a Mason and helped people.'

Coming from a culture where liberals regard Freemasonry as 'boys' playing at secret gangs, or with suspicion as an arcane society of men who operate by rules outside law and democracy, I'm surprised to find that such a reactionary organisation is intimately connected with revolution and change in Cuba. The society was probably introduced into the country by the British during their brief sojourn as rulers of Havana in the 1760s when English merchants, flocking to sell into the new market, brought Masonic practice along with cotton stockings and tin buckets.

'Look,' Rafael points to the open compass symbol of the Masons. 'And there,' he turns towards a large, densely foliated tree. 'That's the ceiba tree . . . do you see what's on the ground?'

Among the dead leaves and dusty soil, a cockerel lies in a heap of black and red feathers surrounded by rotting fruit, boiled sweets and shrivelling gourds.

'The ceiba is a sacred tree in Santería,' Rafael says, 'the most sacred tree in Cuba. These things are offerings to the tree. You will find a lot of African religion here in Santiago, much more than in Havana. And not only Santería . . . we also have *vudú* because of the many people who came from Haiti 200 years ago – French people.'

The collapse of French power in Haiti in 1791, after the only successful anti-European slave revolt ever, had a profound effect on the culture and economy of eastern Cuba. The escaping French, black and white, brought superior technology for sugar milling, a distinctive folk culture and music, powdered wigs, and a form of African religion that was both darker and more secret than Santería.

Walking through the streets of Santiago's old French quarter, we pass houses that to me look all alike but to Rafael have tiny telltale signs of *vudú*: a bunch of leaves, an eye with what could be a bloody teardrop beneath, or a tongue pierced by a dagger. Either way it looks like a warning against gossip, a warning Rafael chooses to ignore in his conversations with me under the branches of Santiago's ceiba trees and whispered in the silent rooms of his house.

'Everything is ruined here,' he says, 'my beautiful city, my country, my life.'

Surprised by his vehemence, I ask what he means.

'Why do you think? It's this government, it has taken everything that was really Cuba and destroyed it. There are people here in Santiago who vowed never to leave their home while Castro lived . . . they are still there, shut inside for more than forty years now. That is what hate is. But you do not understand these things, I can see you do not. No-one from your world could know.'

Before I can reply he says, 'And what is worse, we are supposed to be grateful, to be happy that we have been *liberated*.' He almost chokes on the word. 'Our family was educated, we worked hard, now we have nothing . . . even to eat we must wait for relatives in Florida to send money to my grandfather. So, in turn, my mother and I are dependent on him. My grandfather hates me because my father is in Spain and has never contributed anything, because he is eighty-four and his life is over and I am young with my life in front of me, because he is too proud to go outside and let people see him walking with a frame. He hates me and treats my mother like a servant.'

He speaks so rapidly that despite the excellence of his English I can barely follow. But it doesn't matter. He isn't really talking to me, just unburdening himself to someone who will listen.

'My sisters both hate me because I live at home still and they fear when my grandfather dies I will take our house for myself, though they are both married and have their own homes, they do not want me to have anything.'

It's all far more interesting and unpleasant than anything 'La Fuerza del Deseo' could come up with. Now I understand why Virgilio has the flat whiteness of a vampire; why he shuffles from room to room stooped over his Zimmer frame chanting 'The old are ugly, the old are ugly'. Of course he couldn't acknowledge Amelia, with her wrinkled, sagging skin and white hair.

'Don't you think the old are ugly?' he demands of me. *'Don't* you?'

'Not particularly,' I say, 'people can be ugly or beautiful at any age.'

This isn't what he wants to hear and he shuffles off in angry silence. Perhaps I should have said 'Yes they are . . . *you* are.' Perhaps that's what he wants from me. And all the while Rafael sits with a copy of *Wuthering Heights* in his hands and says nothing, avoiding his grandfather's eye.

'I like melancholy,' he says later, 'I like the creativity of it.'

That night we walk again through the steep darkness of the old French quarter, its lines a web of eighteenth-century straightness. We pass the house of Frank País, a youthful leader of Castro's 26th of July Movement in Santiago, and continue along streets celebrating revolutionary heroes. The names have changed over the years, along with the revolutionary consciousness of the streets' inhabitants, but now few people appear to know the names of the roads around, or even their own address. I wonder how mail gets delivered, but perhaps few people get any.

There's music everywhere; different kinds of music, fleeting sounds that fade into one another, layering echoes between the pastel-coloured houses of long streets called General Máximo Gomez, Juan Bautista Sagorra (a.k.a. San Francisco) and Donato Mármol. Someone is playing 'Stormy Weather' on the saxophone to a rhythm I've never heard before, and a few houses down Elvis is revisiting 'Heartbreak Hotel'. *Son,* ancestor of salsa, whispers through the air accompanied by laughter and snatches of Spanish that's not Spanish at all, being so full of French words and sounds. The air is soft, warmer here than in Havana, and for the first time, in these old streets, I glimpse the Cuba so beloved of Lorca. Rafael has momentarily forgotten the horrors of his home life and, wearily boyish, is immersed in showing me columns, porches, windows and roofs that reach up to a busy, star-filled sky.

I pause outside a pair of heavy wooden doors. There's a new sound, arresting, insistent – drums throb and stutter until I imagine their vibration climbing my body through the soles of my feet. I start towards it. Rafael hangs back.

'Come on!' I say. 'It sounds great.'

He joins me reluctantly as I step inside an open-air school hall and see a dozen people gathered around the drums, watching and listening. Young women, black and white, are rehearsing what Rafael tells me is a sacred dance, a story of the African gods. The drummers are male and black, old and young, and all dressed in white. Drumming is not music, it's religion, a sacred task for which the drummer must be dressed appropriately. The instructor, a mulatto man with hips that swivel and jive with no relation to the upper part of his body, dances the role of the god, passing between the women with smiling sensuality, never touching.

The dancers are all different shapes and sizes. One woman is very large indeed; her bright pink Lyra haunches taper to slender calves and ankles with an unfortunate porcine effect, but she moves like an oiled blade, her pretty face alight with pleasure. I watch in wonder as she rotates, undulates and stretches her flesh. It's mesmerising

and I'm not the only one to find it so. Rafael thinks her unaesthetic
. . . but then he likes little plates and vases.

I saw drumming in Havana, attended the celebrated *rumba* in
the Callejon de Hamel and stood in the street outside the Casa de
Africa, but none of it was like this. That was Cuba; this, as Maria
told me . . . this is Africa.

At three in the morning I'm woken by a feculent smell that
invades my mouth and makes my eyes sting. In my hypnogogic
state Virgilio, Masons and *vudú* form a sinister amalgam. I have
never smelt evil, but now I have a pretty good idea of how it
would be. With a slight *frisson* of anxiety I start trying to locate
the source, knowing nothing human could make this scent, not
even dead. Beyond my bedroom door the house is open to the sky
and I hear the sharp plop of *cucarachas* falling into the tarpaulin
that covers the kitchen area. Walking up and down in darkness I
discover that the smell is outside my door and nowhere else. I still
don't know what it is but as I've not been cursed with rapid decay
and nothing is rotting among my possessions I do the only thing
I can and go back to sleep.

In the morning a tiny pink rose sits under my upturned teacup
at the breakfast table.

'It's beautiful,' I say to Rafael, who smiles with pleasure at the
romance of his gesture while Virgilio shuffles in the background
scowling.

'It's from my garden, over there . . .' Rafael points to a garden
of stones and roses, a small area between a door and a wall that he
has turned into something lovely. A single dark red rose lies across
a large, square stone. 'When I was in the army, up in the mountains, I carried that stone for many kilometres because I thought it
was beautiful. The rose is an offering to the spirit of the garden –
it came from a cutting given to me by a very old man I met in one
of the deserted mansions here. He was working in the garden,
which surprised me – mostly gardens are just left to rot because
no-one here sees beauty any more. Later, I went back to look for
him to tell him the cutting had grown well and had many flowers,

but I never found him and when I asked other people no-one had ever seen him. Now I wonder if he was a spirit . . .'

Virgilio snorts. 'Sit, eat,' he says, 'our nigger servant has just arrived. She is a good woman, one of the family. She will make coffee.'

'She's *not* a servant,' Rafael says under his breath. Then he whispers, 'Eat, or there will be nothing for you; he'll take all the bread and then in half an hour say we are trying to starve him.'

Left alone with the old man, I decide that I dislike him intensely. There's something sinister about his white skin, his ssh-ssh-shuffling walk. He has become the ugly thing he fears, but not because he's old. He ladles honey onto a large bowlful of toast, half the pot disappearing in moments. I wonder if he's already too old to get late-onset diabetes.

'*La miel es buena para los viejos*,' he says with relish, sticky crumbs hanging from his plump, fleshy mouth, and in halting English repeats, 'Honey is *good* for the old. Don't you think honey is good for the old?'

'Is it?' I say. 'I didn't know that.'

'Oh yes, all the doctors say so. It's very good indeed. Don't you agree?'

'I really don't know. I don't suppose anything is good in large quantities,' I say, knowing I'm being bloody. But it doesn't occur to me that his question isn't a question at all and I'm startled by his reaction.

'No!' he bellows, banging the table with a fist. 'Honey *is* good for the old!'

'Okay, okay,' I say quickly. 'Honey is good for the old.'

But it's not enough. Before my eyes Virgilio Domenico Hamera Jubal turns into a patriarch of Marquezian proportions. I realise too late that what I'd assumed to be a question was no such thing. I am meant to agree without thought, without deliberation of any kind. When he sees that I *am* thinking, even in order to agree with him, he rages on.

'*Honey is good for the old!*' he yells and when I hesitate, he drops his voice to a strangely cajoling and even more repugnant

tone and says, 'Do you understand me? *Do* you? You *must* understand me! *Please* understand me!'

But he isn't begging, not at all. It's an order, and I feel my hair
literally stand on end. I see his frustration at being old and inca-
pacitated, his fear of being misunderstood and invisible, but his
expectation of power is undiminished and I am shocked at how it
makes me feel, at my own refusal, finally, to back down to an
elderly man in whose home I am a guest. This is a culture clash
outside my personal experience, replete with the weight of Latin
machismo, the blind assumption of submission, however enfee-
bled the patriarch might be.

'Oh I understand you,' I say. 'I understand you very well.'

'No you don't,' he says, 'your Spanish isn't good enough. *La
miel es buena para los viejos!*' Behind him, the black woman giggles as she scrubs the pans. 'You have a hard head,' he says to me,
his expression a mixture of wonder and sneer, 'a very hard head
for a woman.' Then they are giggling together like children.

'Thank you Virgilio,' I say, 'so do you.'

Rafael is listening to the score of *Schindler's List* in the darkened
sitting room.

'I'm sorry,' he whispers, 'he's like this with everyone. He
spoils everything.'

'Don't worry,' I say, 'I wasn't too polite myself.'

'You see,' he says, 'you see what my mother and I must live
with . . .'

'Why do you stay?' I ask, knowing already that it's a stupid
question.

'I have no money and until I finish my studies, no job . . . and
even then no money to be independent. I have no choice, I am a
prisoner. I wish I could leave this place, this house, this country.
He hates Castro, but in this house *he* is Castro.'

His rocking chair moves back and forth, creaking gently over
the polished tiles. Every house in Cuba has a rocking chair, and
looking at Rafael I wonder if it's for their lulling, soothing-of-
pain motion.

'I'm sorry about the piss outside your room last night.'

'What?' I say, confused.

'Eva Luna, she pisses everywhere and her piss stinks – she's a pig. You're a pig aren't you . . .' he says affectionately, rubbing the ears of the fluffy blonde dog named after a novel about dreams.

'Rafael,' I say, 'I'm going to find a hotel today . . . I think it's best.'

He nods, sadly. 'I know, no-one can stand it here long. Another foreign woman stayed with us and left because of my grandfather. You see what my mother and I have to live with . . . and it's all because of Castro.'

★

The Horned Moon

The roof terrace of the Hotel Casa Grande overlooks Parque Céspedes, where earlier in the day hundreds of schoolchildren in their distinctive dark yellow uniforms gathered to mark some revolutionary happening. Now a horned moon, almost the same colour as the uniforms, hangs over the cathedral. I'm still surprised each time I see our nearest planet from a different part of the world – its new colours, sizes, and shapes. I was in my twenties before I realised that the upright British crescent was not an international standard; that at the equator and beyond there were other moons of blue and gold and red – moons like the horns of buffalo, like a matador's hat, like the face of Buddha. Once, in a town on the most southerly point of Burma where the moon was vast and very near, I lay for hours on a scrap of concrete examining its face through binoculars, unable to abandon craters, mountains and dry lakes – the wonders of another world. This Santiago moon supports a shadow moon within, as it sinks rapidly towards the cloud line above the Sierra Maestra, then lower into the slight haze of pollution from the chimneys along the bay. Overhead distant Jupiter dazzles despite a misty halo that far outshines the rapidly falling moon.

Down in the park a quartet is entertaining a small crowd. The music is pleasant, a light local jazz that shifts tempo abruptly as the singer's voice and the murmuring audience are drowned out by a trumpet blast – a cadence of pure Latin hyperbole. There's a reggae sound out there in the streets too, a reminder of the many Jamaicans here in Santiago. 'Drug dealers most of them,' Rafael had whispered as we passed a couple of Bob Marley lookalikes, their dreadlocks stuffed into distinctive red, green and gold tea-cosy hats. 'No-one likes them; they're too arrogant, too different.'

That almost-anthem of the Cuban elderly, Compay Segundo's 'Chan Chan' rises up from a nearby bar. I like the song very much; I like the mournful minor key which belies the subject matter of agriculture and women's backsides. I recall the posters advertising Segundo's end-of-year concert at the Hotel Nacional in Havana, and that I couldn't possibly have afforded to go.

Visiting the English ladies on the roof of their upmarket hotel is always entertaining and there are cocktails. Amelia explains loudly that despite the comforts of the Casa Granda she's not enjoying herself. There's no swimming pool here and, being unable to walk long distances, sunbathing beside a pool is all she really wants. The younger woman explains that her elderly charge makes do with frying her near-naked body on the roof terrace every day instead.

'I'm supposed to look after her,' Laurel whispers, glancing towards the old woman who's ordering a fourth piña colada from a confused-looking waiter with a medallion of the Virgin of Charity and a Star of David twined round the smooth expanse of his neck, 'but she's impossible. She says she's going to her room and next thing I know three or four local men are half-carrying her back to the hotel. She's lucky Cuban people are so honest.'

I don't tell her I'd met her charge earlier in the day wandering the streets, her purse hanging out of the basket of her wheeled Zimmer frame, clutching a copy of *Granma* which she'd been sold for three dollars instead of a few centavos. Instead I ask if she's enjoying herself. She thinks for a moment.

'Some of the time. Mostly I'm just glad to be here because if I were at home I'd have to go to work, and that means trudging three kilometres up and down a Welsh mountain in the snow, on foot.'

It's almost midnight. Up in the tower of the cathedral the bells ring out and between each peal a man strikes a single chime twice with a heavy wooden rod. Illuminated by a lantern his body casts a grotesque shadow on the wall, but there's nothing of Notre Dame here. His blows sound like someone beating an old boiler – a brazen, barbaric sound that has little to do with this 300-year-old Christian church and everything to do with Africa.

So many ways of seeing this world and the next in this one, infinitesimally small piece of the globe: Roman Catholic tradition represented by the fine cathedral; the young waiter hedging his spiritual bets or perhaps embracing a wider canon; the gathered crowds that stare longingly at the electronic goods and brightly coloured contents of cabinets in the 'dollar shops' on Victoriano Gorzan Road; schoolchildren celebrating the deeds of a revolutionary hero; and the moon itself, object of the most ancient of traditions.

Walking back to my down-market Cuban hotel I pause, listening in the darkness to voices speaking in spatially distorted unison. Not a political monologue, but the melodramatic sighs and whispers of 'La Fuerza del Deseo'. The sound echoes from almost every house in the street, the same eerie glow lighting every front room. I peer cautiously through an open window and find myself trying to work out what's happening in the plot – who has betrayed who and who has slept with their sister's husband.

The air of these narrow city streets is dense with smog that reflects the headlights of oncoming vehicles, making it almost impossible to see in the darkness. It catches at the back of the throat, irritating and impure. 'There isn't that much industry here,' I'd said to Rafael during one of our walks. 'Why is there pollution?'

'Castro says it's because we can't afford cleaner air. Perhaps about that at least he's telling the truth.'

Juan Jesús Ribéra is a masseur and a professor of zoology. A short, slender man in his fifties, Juan has something of the athlete about him as he shows me to the massage table wearing only trim shorts and a singlet. I feel strangely comfortable removing the majority of my clothing in front of this complete stranger, his manner is at once professional and reassuring, he must have been a remarkable teacher.

'I loved teaching,' he says, his Spanish crisp and easy to follow, 'but things are so difficult here. How can I teach young people a subject that is always changing when I have no access to new things myself? We have no new books, almost no books at all, and access to the Internet is very strictly limited. So then, we must ask, what is education? Is it being able to read and write and add figures? Or is it something more than these? We all worked with this situation for many years, my colleagues and I, though it was hard for us to exist on our salaries, then one day I went in to work and found I had no job. I'm still not quite sure why.' He slides his thumbs under my shoulder blades, pushing out tension. 'But now that I have time to read, there is another, similar problem: I have read Tolstoy, Dostoevsky, Victor Hugo and of course James Joyce – we Cubans are very fond of *Ulysses* –' he smiles, 'but I have read nothing written after 1960. There's a whole world of literature out there that I am ignorant of, written by authors from countries that did not even exist when our Revolution happened. We are so very far behind the rest of the educated world because of these things, these limitations.'

'Why do you think people accept these things?'

'Oh, that is very complicated. There are many reasons why we are tolerant of things we do not like, but I believe that one of the main reasons is that there are very many Cuban people outside our country, particularly in Florida, who feel sentimental about their homeland and send large sums of money to their families. I believe this has a great influence over how people feel here, both negatively and positively. But it means there is a huge external influence on how things operate . . . it's a paradox, but our government is undoubtedly supported by its enemies in Miami. The money that enters this country contains what would otherwise be a very difficult situation.'

He turns me on my side, and with a swift, painless motion adjusts my lumbar spine.

'I am a very fortunate man,' I can almost feel him smiling as he says this. 'I have my mother, my wife, my children and my dog, and thanks be to God, I have many, many friends. I write poetry and songs for musical groups. I exercise and I say my prayers.'

'Which God do you pray to?' I ask. 'There are so many here it's easy for an outsider to become confused.'

Juan laughs, a genuinely light-hearted sound. 'I'm Roman Catholic, that's it.'

'Just straight Catholic? No Santería, no syncretism?'

'There is truly a great overlap between Catholicism and African religion here in Cuba, but Santería is a black phenomenon; you will not find many white people who follow it, unless they are hoping for some kind of power over their lives, or maybe over their neighbours. Naturally, I believe they will be disappointed.' He grins and goes into the adjacent bathroom to wash his hands. As I dress his voice echoes from behind the door.

'The most important thing for anyone – whatever their colour or their religion, or absence of religion – the most important thing is to be strong in the spirit, even more than in the body. I can tell you are not strong in the body, but I feel that your spirit is strong, very strong . . . that is the most valuable thing. Keep hold of it.'

At the front door he presses something into my hand – a slip of paper. 'For you . . . something small but from the heart.'

His wife smiles and kisses me on the cheek, one hand in her husband's as they say goodbye. I walk away feeling lighter and more relaxed than in many weeks.

The courtyard of the old colonial mansion is galleried and hung with creepers that curtain the layered balconies like hanging gardens. It's a bar now, a place where *jiniteras* take tourists away from the public gaze. I take a corner seat and wait for Claire, the red-haired Englishwoman I met on the flight from Havana. Across the bar, a young black prostitute is entertaining a client. A waitress brings me a beer I didn't ask for and I unwrap Jesús' slip of paper as the young woman insinuates her tongue into the man's every facial orifice while grinding her pelvis against his thigh. I open the paper and lay it carefully on the table; inside are two small dried leaves, like scentless bay, and written on them in pink felt-tip pen, the words *Dios es amor* and *La fé salve*. Love and faith. God and salvation.

Palely handsome, the punter looks like an SS officer in mufti and grins like a mantis – no easy task with a tongue most of the way down his throat and a small, black hand where the air doesn't circulate. In the brief moments when they separate to breathe, the young woman's body writhes provocatively as if unable to keep still. They don't speak to each other and I realise it's very probable that they can't. There's something fascinating and repulsive in this scene; it's the first obvious expression of prostitution I've seen here and there's something oddly archetypal about it – the square-jawed Aryan male, the young, buxom black woman. As if aware of my gaze he glances towards me, pushing the woman away from him as he does so. He looks mildly uncomfortable, like a small boy caught with a finger in the honeypot. The young woman looks up and starts to giggle.

'God!' a voice says, 'Look at that!' Behind me, Claire is staring disgustedly at the couple. 'Sickening,' she says. 'I'm all for people enjoying themselves but that isn't about fun or even sex . . . it's about exploitation and being able to have all those things here that you could never have at home just because you have money. Ugh!'

I remember Simon Wollers explaining in one of our conversations that prostitution in Cuba has very little to do with economic need and everything to do with consumerism.

'If a kid wants a pair of Nike trainers,' he'd said, 'they'll fuck someone to get the money to pay for them. They aren't hungry, they aren't poor or uneducated in any Third World sense, they just want things.'

'Are they wrong?' I asked.

'Perhaps not,' he said, 'but it just makes me feel that the U.S. is winning here after all . . . still fucking Cubans over, persuading them to buy things no-one really needs.'

'Listen!' Claire says, turning away from the couple. 'I've been invited somewhere really brilliant tomorrow night . . . want to come?'

It's not easy finding a taxi driver who will divert even slightly from the tourist track in Santiago de Cuba. Money doesn't do it – two or three months salary for half a day's work and there are no takers. It's not that it's not wanted of course – several men say they don't have enough petrol to take me into the mountains because it's rationed unless you're in the army or are somebody important. Maybe it's true, or maybe they fear breaking down in the middle of nowhere without spare parts; maybe they know things about the mountains and the military stations there that I don't know. The feeling that nothing is ever what it seems here is particularly strong and I must be satisfied with El Cobre, twenty kilometres north and west of Santiago.

It's good to be out of the city, to see greenery and breathe clean air. The suburbs are brief, partly because the driver is going very fast indeed; then we're into scrubby, dry grassland, passing small huts with corrugated roofs. A thin man leads an even thinner brown pig into vegetation of a kind I've never seen before: tall, red-flowering plants jostle with palms and pines. It's attractive and somehow familiar despite the alien flora; the small scale and undulating hillside reminds me of the Welsh border country, but here mustachioed men with creased, brown faces and low straw hats lean on the backs of tethered horses. Overhead, vultures circle above fields of Spanish bulls.

The traffic is no more than a trickle, mostly trucks heavy with produce from the organic vegetable gardens that stretch back from the road in neat green stripes. Streams cut through pastureland grazed by mules and an occasional goat. Then the driver curses and swerves violently as the truck in front of us sheds a few hundred kilos of concrete and planking. The people travelling among the building materials are laughing, banging on the driver's cab and pointing to the mess.

There has been a copper mine at El Cobre since pre-Colombian times and a shrine to the Virgin of Charity since the early seventeenth century. The original shrine was little more than a hermitage, now there's a tropical Art-Deco church. Why here, I wonder, as the shiny basilica appears through great stands of palm trees and small children run shouting into the road waving medallions and drooping flowers.

The answer lies in a glass case: a small, 400-year-old statue of Cuba's patron saint. 'Cachita' the people call her, because she's *their* saint. Found floating among the waves by three fishermen off the island's north-east coast in 1606, the message around her neck read '*Soy la Virgen de la Caridad*'. Looking at the statue, crowned and robed among banks of fresh flowers, there's little of the simple, wooden woman to be seen. I wonder who wrote that anonymous label; was it tied lovingly around her neck by some devout nun in Granada or Seville, or perhaps by a youthful apprentice in a mass-production workshop in Madrid? Perhaps she was lost from some great Spanish galleon attacked by French or British pirates, the Virgin of Charity on her way to colonies where charity was in desperately short supply. Two years after the discovery she was brought here to the mine, no-one can tell me how or why. Maybe one of the fishermen, tired of the sea, decided to try his luck in the great copper gash of El Cobre and brought her with him.

Most interesting of all in this holy of Cuban holies is a large cabinet that contains some of the many hundreds of thousands of promises and petitions; mementos left here by the satisfied or hopeful faithful – medallions, a crutch, a dagger, photographs and letters, locks of hair, spectacles and military decorations. Two things, neither obvious in themselves, draw my attention. One is a small handwritten piece of paper dated 1994: *To our Lady of Charity, in the hope that she will help me leave this my country and never return*. The other is gold and quite small – the figure of a guerrilla fighter given to the church by a mother asking protection for her children fighting the government in the Sierra Maestra. The prayers of Lina Ruiz were surely answered in full; today her sons, Fidel and Raúl, are among the most famous survivors of the age.

★

'This is Dulce,' Claire says, when we meet that evening. 'She's going to take us to the ceremony, we'll be her guests.'

Dulce, a small, well-dressed black woman in her early forties, smiles reassuringly. 'I speak a little English,' she says, 'if you need anything please let me know. Now we must look for a taxi, we must not be late . . . it's important not to be late.'

We seem to have been driving for some time through a maze of narrow streets when I ask Claire if she knows where we are going.

'Vaguely, it's the Haitian quarter of the city I think. I was there earlier today watching the preparations. Apparently it's all part of a three-day festival to honour some saint – this is the second day. It looks really fascinating . . . and the people, they're really friendly. '

The house is open to the street, the drums are already set up and a few people dance casually. But we are not late. Dulce sighs with relief as she guides us towards the small, windowless room where the *madrina* Elena, 'queen' of the ceremony, sits like a large, friendly spider awaiting the two foreign women. The introductions are almost formal – we are guests, honoured guests, it would seem, but she is the queen. The room's focal point is a shelf used as an altar. It's stuck with knives and machetes and beside the blades is the plaster head of a cartoon black man, his straw boater set at a jaunty angle. Candles of different colours have spilled their wax in brittle rivulets along the stone of the altar; bottles of hand cream rest against twigs and sticks beside a photograph of a baby that Elena says is one of her great-grandchildren. She speaks in a patois almost impossible to follow, the words are mostly Spanish but the accent is the singsong up-lilt of Haiti. There's a powerful stink of animal decay and a bitter scent rises from partly crushed herbs in what looks like an African mortar and pestle.

'You can take photographs,' she says, 'you can write what you want.'

I've passed some kind of test and wonder what would have happened if I had not.

Elena reads playing cards to tell my future while a coconut cockroach as big as my hand clambers along the wall behind her head. Claire translates much of what is being said including the card reading, the gist of which is that I don't have much luck with the *pantalón*. Claire wrestles with the patois, uncertain if this means I don't have much luck with men, or if I don't have much luck with men because I wear *pantalón*.

'*I'd* fancy you if it weren't for the *pantalón*,' a man giggles drunkenly behind me. Elena withers him with a glance and he slinks from the room.

'We came to Cuba from Haiti in 1925,' Elena says, 'my parents never returned to their home. When my family first came here we lived in Holguín. I sold food on the streets and the roads. There were animals everywhere and my parents had many children.'

I ask where in Haiti her family came from but she knows only that it wasn't Port au Prince – the name of her ancestral village she knows only in patois. She says she would like to return to Haiti one day but she's getting old. She smiles showing strong, white teeth. Her cheekbones are high and her faded eyes almond. She must have been beautiful when she was young. Like many here tonight she looks very different to the black people of Cuba's west. Her face is not a Yoruba face.

'I have three children and eight grandchildren – this is my oldest grandson, Niolvis.'

She points to a silent, heavyset young man in a panama hat who had been dancing as we came in. He sucks intently on a small cigar, blowing cloud rings of incense towards the saint identified with the moon and sea goddess, Yemayá, daughter of Obatalá.

At first only a few people dance, the rest of the guests sit politely on chairs around the walls, like at a church-hall disco – everyone waiting for something to happen. By ten there must be at least 100 people crammed into Elena's long, narrow house: old men with grey against the dark of their jaws, plump women smoking pipes, nubile girls in brief dresses, muscular young men already wearing a sheen of sweat, and small children wide-eyed and excited. In a corner of this main room, a semitransparent white curtain hides a large, white-draped table laden with white food and drink. Chicken, bananas, white rum, white bread and rice are interspersed with perfumes in white-labelled bottles and white flowers, all surrounded by white-draped chairs. As I wonder what this represents the curtain is whipped aside and I'm propelled into the sacred space by a man dressed mostly in red, the colour of Changó. He attempts to explain the symbolism of the table, the food, but the drumming is so loud that I make out only one word in every five. Beside the image of a female saint is a saint on horseback who looks just like Saint George – but he can't be Saint George because his flag is plain white and his horse is not trampling a dragon, but screaming human beings.

'Obatalá,' the man beside me whispers, 'the father of all, the father of whiteness.'

The *batâ* dominate everything: space, sound, motion. There are three drummers. One is tall, slender and light brown, he wears a woollen hat and smiles a great deal. The second looks Jamaican with his pushed-up sunglasses, heavy silver earrings, dreadlocks and denim shirt. But the chief drummer is something different. Short, heavily muscled and naked from the waist up, he's already soaked in the sweat running in glossy streams down his shoulders, chest and belly. Like a snake charmer he watches each dancer who comes forward to dance alone with the drum; watches each move, each twist and jerk, his wide, fixed eyes never leaving theirs, his long full lips compressed. He strikes the drum that's almost as tall as himself with a mixture of violence and lust. I stare, fascinated by the synchronous relationship of drummer and dancer. I wish I understood it better; I wish I could drum like that; I wish I could dance at all.

'They are dancing the animals of their personal *orishas*,' Claire whispers to me, 'that's what the guy in red said anyway. His name's Joaquin. He's like . . . Elena's consort, male counterpart. God the dialect's a nightmare!'

In the open-air kitchen – which is cluttered with partly washed bowls, drying herbs, squeezed limes and desiccated orange peel – three roosters, a small black goat and a piglet are dozing fitfully. Asleep in its trough the piglet twitches its way through porcine dreams. It's nearly midnight and with the exception of the pig, all these animals will soon be dead, sacrificed. A doll's body parts are scattered around like on the set of a cheap murder mystery. The head – jammed onto a spike of the wire that separates the pig from the goat – looks oddly like me: pale skin, grey eyes and dark curly hair. I feel a momentary stirring of something primitive and neurotic.

The drums are set up in the sloping back garden – a patch of rough grass and bushes divided from the neighbours by small palms and clumps of banana plants. A pole, about ten metres high, reaches into the star-filled sky. A couple of bottles of rum and Yemayá's blue-and-white flag hang from its highest point. Someone whispers that it's Joaquin's task, at the end of the night, to climb this pole and retrieve the rum and the flag. I wonder what this has to do with the Christian saint who I seem to have lost somewhere, but the noise is loud now and serious questions and answers have become impossible. Later I remember that such poles and the act of climbing them are the remnants of universal traditions; the shaman climbing the Tree of Life, linking earth and the spirit world above and below.

There are people in the narrow darkened passageways that link the rooms together, in the kitchen and in the garden. Walking is a constant brush of bodies, of shapes and scents and the hot breath of others. The main room is crowded with people on stools and rocking chairs; they fill the entrance to the house, the brief veranda and the dirt street beyond.

Elena presses something hard and sweet into my mouth; it tastes of sugar cane. It's meant to give energy to the proceedings – sugar, and the bottles of *aguardiente* that are passing from hand-to-hand. It's twelve hours now since I last ate or drank anything and when I see a bottle coming past me I reach out eagerly. After initial surprise that I drink alcohol, bottles are pressed on me from all sides.

I lift one that at least twenty people have drunk from and pour without touching my mouth. The clear white spirit eats its way over my tongue and down my throat; it looks innocent as water and burns like the fires of hell. Not long after, I'm dancing stiffly over the uneven, sloping ground of the garden, and grinning. No-one is rude enough to laugh and I begin to believe I'm doing okay. Not sober, hungry and thirsty, my property scattered among hundreds of strangers, I am entirely happy.

At about two, Elena's silent grandson Niolvis makes his way to the foot of the pole. Over the course of the night he has changed, becoming even more withdrawn. Close to, the changes are eerily obvious: his mouth has taken on the shape of a beak, his head and neck move with abrupt stabbing motions while his hands flutter at his sides.

'Look!' Claire hisses. 'He's turned into a chicken!'

'Maybe he's possessed by a chicken spirit,' I say.

'Fantastic!' Claire says and giggles under her breath.

Niolvis stands at the foot of the pole, a pickaxe dangling from one relaxed hand, then he starts turning over the ground, loosening it into clods. He drags heavily on his cigar as he digs, the clouds of pungent smoke around him illuminated by bright white light. The rhythm of the drums intensifies. The neighbours peer over the fence with folded arms, some swaying and dancing themselves.

When he stands upright at the foot of the pole, a plump black woman in shorts appears at Niolvis' side. He takes off the straw hat he has been wearing all night and places it on her head. As he walks away all eyes turn to the woman who stands motionless under the fluttering flags. After only a few seconds she shudders, arms and legs waving disjointedly. Her eyes glaze as she presses the hat more firmly on her head, and I wonder if she's being possessed by the hat or the chicken spirit of its former wearer. Coming suddenly to life, she charges round the garden, snatches a bottle of rum from an unsuspecting onlooker and lights up a fat cigar. Fascinated, I see her turning into a man, a very badly behaved man.

This spectacle is the kind of thing writers long for – the bizarre meeting the unexpected – and the writer-me is hugging herself. But the me that studies shamanism and knows we are not alone is observing with a curious eye. The woman's expression is glazed and dead, whatever she's experiencing it isn't conscious. For the next few minutes she chugs the drink and puffs the smoke, swaying conspicuously and farting loudly. I'm finally convinced that she truly is a man, when she drags up her singlet and starts scratching her belly in an archetypal gesture of Cuban macho. I can see the silver lines of pregnancy criss-crossing her skin, but at this moment it's easy to believe the unbelievable.

It's almost half past three in the morning and the air of expectancy is thick around us, the drumming constant and accompanied now by the ringing of a small bell. Joaquin has changed into little black shorts and a vest and is flapping his hands camply at every opportunity. His change of clothing marks a shift of gender related to the dual nature of some of the Yoruba deities. More men have joined the core group now, among them a *brujo* with water-grey eyes that seem to see into whatever they look at. He's respected, even by Elena and Joaquin, and I wonder what a man must do to earn that respect – fear and intimidation are two words that spring to mind as I watch his red-clad figure move sinuously through the crowd that parts before him.

'He is a great *brujo*,' Dulce whispers, 'a son of Changó . . . he can do many things.'

'What kind of things?' I ask, but at that moment Elena and Joaquin appear carrying a vast platter of iced cakes which they lay on the newly turned earth at the foot of the pole.

'Oh God,' Claire says, 'I'm starving but I can't eat any of *that* . . . I saw cockroaches climbing all over it earlier.'

From the kitchen comes the shrill squawking of irritated roosters. At this moment Claire turns to me and mutters, 'I've never actually seen anything dead.'

'You mean anything dead, or anything being killed?'

'Both . . . neither, not even a roadkill.'

I'm surprised, given her very practical, almost gung ho, attitude to the entire evening. 'What about funerals?' I ask, trying to be helpful. 'No elderly relatives, no pets?'

'Nothing.'

She looks at me anxiously. 'D'you think it'll be all right? I mean, I won't pass out or anything?'

'Of course not, you'll be great . . . just remember, stiff upper lip and all that.'

Oh God! I actually *said* that; I said 'Stiff upper lip'! It must be the drink and lack of food. But it seems to have done the trick; Claire's face takes on a determined expression, which is good because at that moment they start killing the birds.

It's not a quick business – not a twist and crack – more a slow, sawing motion with a blunt-looking knife. Squatting in the dirt and using the pole against my shoulder to steady the camera, I catch the blood midair as it sprays over the tray of cake; thick scarlet puddles forming among the raised curls and ridges of icing sugar. I've always known that looking through a lens is a kind of protection, a veil of glass between the observer and reality, so when the *brujo* puts his mouth to the pulsing gash in the bird's neck and sucks, my finger keeps on pressing; keeps on until Elena and Joaquin kill the second and third birds and the lens suddenly needs to be cleaned. There's blood everywhere: like Lady Macbeth I'm surprised at the quantity. What isn't on my lens, the ground, the cakes, the mouths of the officiators, is drained into a cup that passes round the rapt audience. I glance at Claire who looks pallid but unshaken, then at the pale-eyed *brujo* who is red and wet from throat to eyes. A few moments later, when he thinks himself unobserved, he carefully wipes the blood from his face with a neatly folded handkerchief. There's a distaste and delicacy in the gesture that is fascinating in this silent, sinister man.

Like the birds, the goat is fed at the killing-ground. Its sense of self-preservation overcomes fear and the smell of blood; its willingness to eat is a symbol of general good fortune. Then its head is gripped firmly between the chubby knees of the possessed man–woman who holds its jaws clamped shut in one hand, machete in the other. She slices; the animal screams and bucks and again I catch the moment as blood jets between the camera and the sea of faces looking on. The woman stoops and literally sucks the life out of the still-struggling creature before turning it on its back and castrating it in a single motion. In the photographs her eyes are half-closed, rolled back into her head making her look like a discarded doll as she sucks the bloody testicles. The camera captured moments *I* missed: horrified glances from the crowd, mouths twisted with revulsion.

I turn at a sudden roar behind me and see Claire, hands out in front of her defensively, and the man–woman flying backwards.

'What . . .' Claire yells, 'was that?'

Her face is streaked with pink slime from the warm testes. Dulce and the other women gather protectively around her, tutting and casting dark looks at the possessed one.

'It's horrible, horrible . . .' Dulce says soothingly, 'but it's very good luck you know, it means you will be fortunate.'

'Are you okay?' I ask, because now she's very pale and looking decidedly shaky.

She nods, 'I'm fine, they're just going to take me and clean me up a bit.'

She disappears inside the house, surrounded by concern. The perpetrator is still dancing around, sucking the balls like a lollipop.

It's almost six and I'm suddenly very tired. They are just lighting the fire to cook the goat and it will be at least another hour before Joaquin has to climb the pole for his rum and flag. The goat's sticky red skin is already hanging beside its moth-eaten predecessors on a wall in the kitchen. The carcass gleams, pinkly opalescent in the harsh electric light. I would have liked to taste freshly killed goat; I would have liked to see Joaquin shinning drunkenly up a completely smooth ten-metre pole, but in three hours time I have a flight to catch. My last memory of Elena's house is of Joaquin posing for final photographs in his third change of clothing – a short pleated skirt and clashing sailor top. He's standing beside a pretty young man, also in a skirt. The transformation from serious macho man to camp hermaphrodite is in its final stages – all part of an unfolding story of the Yoruba gods of which this night is only a fraction. We say our goodbyes, shaking hands and kissing. I've been here almost twelve hours and would stay another twelve if I could.

At seven I look out at the roofs of Santiago de Cuba and at the Sierra Maestra for the last time. A woman is sweeping the backyard of a house just below my hotel window; she must have some kind of sixth sense because as I look down she looks up at me, her figure framed by white and blue convolvulus hanging from the Spanish tiles. Nothing else moves and I realise how much I enjoy urban landscapes before they wake, the potential for noise and movement still arrested in sleep. Thick, pearly mist rolls down out of the mountains, much as Lina Ruiz' sons did in 1958; it moves into the deep cracks in the face of the Sierra Maestra, smoothing and caressing. And overhead the sky is blue – absolutely, immaculately blue.

★

Baracoa

> . . . Then felt I like some watcher of the skies
> When a new planet swims into his ken;
> Or like stout Cortez, when with eagle eyes
> He stared at the Pacific and all his men
> Look'd at each other with a wild surmise
> Silent, upon a peak in Darien.
>
> John Keats, 'On First Looking into Chapman's Homer'

The flight from Santiago to Baracoa is short and frightening. The blue sky of Santiago slips behind a screen of cumulus to the west of Guantánamo; dense cloud obscures everything as if the entire world is shrouded with moisture. This is the Caribbean and there's something incongruous about the grey half-light and spiteful rain. As we drop altitude, vapour enters the cabin from somewhere behind the luggage racks to drift around passengers' heads like Tennysonian wraiths. Leaving the cloud I notice we're descending too steeply over the sea and that the land seems very far away. Forewarned is not necessarily forearmed, and I wish I didn't know that a few years earlier this same flight crashed into the sea close to here. None of the bodies were ever found; the sharks smiled for days. Our wheels hit the water and spray flies up, striking the large, porthole windows: I imagine looking out at the waiting marine life as the aircraft turns into a submersible. But the pilot is only flirting humorously with disaster and then we're climbing steeply and swinging round for a second attempt. Across the aisle Claire is talking animatedly to a young English man and seems not to have noticed our near-death experience. Perhaps the testicle face wash brought good fortune after all.

'Never again! Never, I'd rather crawl!' she says as we walk from the plane into Baracoa's tiny airport terminal. 'I just kept talking and talking to stop myself thinking about what was happening. Oh God . . . did you see the smoke coming into the cabin?'

'I thought it was cloud,' I say. Now I can tell her about the crash and the sharks.

At the outbreak of the Russian Revolution, Magdalena Rovienskya, daughter of an aristocratic family that was reputedly one of the wealthiest in Russia, left her country for ever. She became a performer in Paris at a time when educated, respectable women didn't. But she was a success and her husband didn't seem to mind travelling through Europe from capital to capital in his wife's footsteps. Like Hemingway a decade later, Magdalena left Paris for Cuba; it was, after all, *the* place to be if you were young, beautiful and looking for fun. Like Hemingway, she stayed; first in Havana, then, hearing a description of Baracoa, she moved in the thirties to this most remote of places. In the fifties she built a small hotel on the edge of town and sea and lived there with her fox furs and beaded shoes, a displaced diva, until the Revolution, which seems to have given her a new lease of life. She became a radical Fidelista and founding member of a network of revolutionary organisations, including the Comités de Defensa de la Revolución. Cuban writer Alejo Carpentier wrote a novel based on her life, and today her face gazes down at guests entering the lobby of her hotel, which was named 'La Rusa' after her death in 1978.

Looking at the pretty blonde aristocrat in the photographs, I wonder why a woman who fled one left-wing revolution in her youth should so keenly support another in later life. Perhaps a bit of Parisian slumming showed her the other side, or maybe it was Cuba that changed her. But the hotel manager doesn't know the answer – I hardly expected that he would. A plump man, he stares like a frightened rabbit, exuding sweat and anxiety. He clearly thinks I'm some kind of visiting dignitary because I have a press pass and a letter from the director of the chain of Cuban hotels which owns the La Rusa. Remembering Martin di Giovanni's comment on jobs and government control I feel sorry for him. He really is afraid of me (I must be a spy after all) and of being watched and reported on.

'You can have Che's room . . .' he says, gasping his way up the narrow staircase under the weight of my bag, 'it's our best one.'

Alone I flop exhausted onto a narrow bed and look up at the classic image of Che Guevara printed on cardboard and finished off with a red tassle. But this is no ordinary revolutionary symbol, this states: *Che Guevara slept here*, as did Castro, Cuban prima ballerina Alicia Alonso and Errol Flynn – not necessarily all in this room and almost certainly not at the same time (what a picture *that* conjures . . .). Looking up at the handsome fanatic's face, I wonder who Che stayed here with, and if he slept at all.

'Oh my God! You're in the same room as *Che*!' Claire says when she stops by the hotel later in the morning.

'Jealous?' I ask jokingly.

'Of course! He's so bloody gorgeous and there's that thing about him, that hero thing . . . don't you fancy him?'

'Not really, though I can see the attraction. Beards and extremism never really did it for me.'

'I know what you mean, but it's like something we grew up with isn't it, even though he was dead before I was born . . . it's just that face, that photograph I suppose.'

'Well, if it is any consolation, the manager told me the room is completely changed since he stayed here and the mattresses are definitely not the same.'

Cuba's first town and original capital is very small, little more than a narrow strip of habitation between the Bahía de Baracoa and the Bahía de Miel, between sea and dense highland forest. Landing here in 1492 Columbus thought he'd discovered the coast of Asia and named the place Porto Santo.

What was it like to first see new land, a new continent? Was it a matter of awe and excitement for those early adventurers?

Or, in the absence of context and scale, was it just another pragmatic venture towards Mammon? We will never know their experience, never feel like Keats' Cortés – we would have to travel in dimensions beyond the physical to grasp that enormity, or be an astronaut facing the final frontier.

But it's not hard to imagine Baracoa as it would have been at the time of Diego Velázquez' first venture in Cuba. The town is small and slow enough to have changed relatively little since 1511. Until the 1960s it was virtually cut off from the rest of the country by an absence of roads through the encircling mountains. After three years here Velázquez realised that remote, rainswept and harbourless Porto Santo didn't have the potential for a capital and he moved on to found Santiago de Cuba, and more distant Trinidad, in 1514. Baracoa clung to its pre-eminence for a few more years then fell into a decline when Santiago became the capital.

It's New Year's Eve and Claire and I decide on an end-of-millennium lunch at a restaurant in the old Spanish fort at the end of the Malecón; but the place has no food, just cans of soft drink. It's bizarre and depressing being in a place where food grows all around you but it's not possible to buy a meal. Food distribution is rigidly controlled in Cuba, much of what's produced being siphoned into the tourist industry. Even in Havana, conversation overheard in the streets centred around food – what was available, where and how much.

Fortunately Claire is staying at a *casa particular* run by a plump family with an abundance of illicit produce.

'You must eat with us too,' the owner says. 'What would you like? Every evening we have lobster, crab, flying fish, chicken . . .'

After many weeks of poor food and no variety I want to shout, 'Yes, yes all of it, anything.' At least I'll get one decent meal a day. But where to eat before eight?

Hungry and still tired from the night before, I leave Claire with her hosts and set off to look for Baracoa's two main food outlets – a pizza restaurant and the Casa de Chocolat. The words 'pizza' and 'chocolate' create delightful visions of gastronomic debauchery, but these poignant hopes are quickly dashed when I find the pizza restaurant.

Like McDonald's in Minneapolis or Tampa, this is where Baracoa's larger inhabitants spend their pesos. I guess at once that it's government-owned because it's ghastly. Old people, workmen and several indigenous-looking families sit at large round tables and wait. No-one serves them and no-one asks to be served. Customers don't speak to each other, giving the place a funeral-home atmosphere. Occasionally a waitress runs out of the kitchen laden with plates, dumps them and rushes back inside. There's no obvious logic to the ordering and delivery of food: people who arrive after me are served before those who have probably been here twice as long. Perhaps there's some invisible hierarchy? But it's worth the wait; in fact it's quite an education watching Baracoans eat pizza. First the crust is cut away and discarded like a doughy halo. Only the soggy, six-centimetre core is deemed edible, which surprises me until I realise it's not about food or hunger, but a financial statement: 'Look at what I can afford to throw away'. While this gesture may satisfy the ego, it doesn't fill the belly, so several pizzas are ordered at one time, and though the menu suggests the toppings vary, they are all a brown-grey mass indistinguishable from each other. When mine finally arrives – after twenty minutes I took the bold step of attracting a waitress' attention and placed an order – it's virtually inedible. I've never tasted sour pizza base before but it pales in comparison with the topping. After eating two, crust and all – as a foreigner my finances require no statement – I have no idea what I've just put into my mouth.

Still hungry, I head to the 'House of Chocolate'. For almost thirty minutes the queue for a table doesn't move. On the point of giving up I'm squeezed in to sit among silent customers. It's all rather Stephen King as the motionless men and women around me stare at the Formica table tops without speaking. But unlike the pizza, it's worth the wait. The hot chocolate is of the

Mexican variety and undrinkable, but the coconut ice cream is the finest I've tasted anywhere and *cucuruchu*, a sticky local delicacy that is a mix of dried and sugared fruit, is perfect for delivering pancreatic shock.

Sugar is a matter of pride in Cuba. In the monthly ration quota that all Cubans receive, the sugar is demerara brown, which implies that brown sugar is cheap and therefore inferior. Everyone wants white sugar, white bread – white, the symbol of purity, of spirituality. The sugar here in Baracoa is neither brown nor white, but a humid pearly grey. As I finish the last of my *cucuruchu*, digging it out of its banana-leaf container with glazed fingers, a fly lands on the plastic flowers in front of me, looking for something that isn't there.

Every important town in Cuba has a Casa de la Trova, a house of song where traditional Cuban music is played to a very high standard. Cubans know how to play and how to listen, and Casas de la Trova are not just places of entertainment for tourists.

The Casa in Baracoa is warm after the damp chill of the streets, and full of light and the smells of cigars, rum and dancing people. It's New Year's Eve; locals of all ages are shimmying vigorously and a few tourists are trying to show that white people can move too. Local men in patterned shirts stand like wallflowers, waiting to dance with foreign ladies.

'I can't dance,' Claire says, 'no sense of rhythm at all.'

'Have a few drinks and you won't care . . .'

So we order the mojitos and find that we are paying the same in U.S. dollars as the Cuban customers are paying in pesos, a difference of 86 per cent. I discover that I mind this very much and wonder if it's about the money or the way I'm being classified as 'different' from the man at the bar beside me, and being made to pay for that difference. My reaction is gut, not head. The head says, 'But surely you can afford to subsidise, even if the distinction is artificial and undignified?' The gut says, 'Bugger off and let me pay in pesos too!'

A man in a too-tight brown suit makes a grab at me and is turned down; after that no-one comes near. Claire is a big hit, despite her misgivings, and seems to enjoy salsaing with a young man who immediately tells her he's in love with her and wants to make love to her. He's leaning in close, whispering in her ear. I wonder if he charges.

Deciding the old guys will probably have given up on the romantic chitchat and are the best dancers anyway, I smile at a dark-skinned man with greying curls who smiles back and holds out his hand. As we move together he is patient and gracious with my inadequacies: he knows foreigners can't dance for shit but he's going to have fun anyway. There are wide gaps between all his teeth and the palm and fingers holding mine are rough and thickly calloused. I've never felt the hand of a man who has worked manually all his life, not as intimately as this anyway, and it's a strange realisation: this man *really* works. I can feel the bones of his spine and shoulder through the cheap material of his striped shirt and wonder where his wife is and how many children he has.

The music never seems to stop; the guitarist is unflagging and the trumpeter doesn't need to pause for breath. The smallish room is a whirl of colour and sound. Everyone is laughing and spinning in the small space between couples. The doors are open wide onto the night and the misty rain that's drifted in from the sea. I'm exhausted, but I've done it, done the Cuban thing – the mojitos, the salsa. I've done it.

It's still raining when Claire and I huddle under my small umbrella and head along straight colonial streets towards the New Year celebrations. Cycle rickshaws hiss past and we walk on liquid patchwork as water turns the dimly lit street to black and gold. At midnight we're standing with two English teenagers we met in a rum bar, waiting for the fun to start. The youngsters at least seem bent on having a good time. Claire asks if they are enjoying their holiday.

'There are good days and bad days I guess,' Atlanta says, 'but on the whole we'd prefer to be here.'

She's sixteen and back home what's there to do but just more clubs and drugs?

'Yeah, I mean, what'd we do if were back in Somerset?' her brother adds. 'It's even colder and there's only *so* much television you can watch!'

I've heard this answer somewhere before. No-one wants to say they aren't having a good time here; after all, this is Cuba.

On a stage in the middle of Antonio Maceo Street a man and two girls are doing a half-hearted imitation of Ricky Martin under an awning advertising Cristal beer that sways and drips in the rain. I look at it for several minutes before realising I'm seeing a commercial advertisement. The crowd of about 1500 people is very quiet. In comparison with New Year's celebrations in Anglo-Saxon countries this is a sober and sobering affair. A few people hold half-empty bottles of rum and one or two people are drunk. A lone woman seizes me by the neck, tangling me in her arms.

'My friend,' she slurs, 'my friend! You are my friend, no?'

She staggers, giggling, as the crowd looks on disapprovingly.

Midnight comes and goes and the political speeches continue, words washing away in the watery air. Eight minutes into the new millennium the speaker finally stops referring to the Revolution, the struggle, the enemies of the people and says, 'Now it is the New Year.' But even with permission the crowd does nothing, as if no-one knows quite what to do, what's allowed. The faces around us are shut off and silent, looking with a mixture of boredom and anxiety towards the stage. Only the drunken woman shouts and wishes everyone '*Felize Año Nuevo*'. Her kisses slide off my face with her beery breath; but at least she's warm.

The entertainment is a kind of singing competition. The crowd listens silently, politely to the first singer, a young man with a dreadful voice which he obviously thinks quite lovely. By his fourth or fifth false note we've all had enough. I watch, delighted, as people start shouting and waving their arms. Cries of 'You're crap!' and 'Get off!' echo in the narrow street. It's one thing to put up with political mumbo jumbo and allow it to hijack your millennium moment, but being forced to listen to bad music is clearly unacceptable.

Leaving Claire with the youngsters I head back to the La Rusa and bed, past darkened shop windows hung with what look like eighties fashions (in daylight I realise they *are* eighties fashions – donations from some distant country.) In a dark alleyway a group of small boys are banging a large, wet drum with a hole torn in its skin and smacking an old metal bucket with a bent spanner. The cacophony gets louder as they surge forward grinning and asking for a dollar. One of the boys is wearing a plastic tablecloth tied around his head; he looks like a small, wet Lawrence of Arabia.

Two days later we meet Dulce again, looking very different to when last seen at five in the morning, dancing with Joaquin, eyes closed, hips swaying. She tells us that she's on holiday, staying at a *casa particular* in the town, but when we ask more she clams up. Cuban women don't take holidays alone in places where they don't know anyone. But she seems glad to see us and to reminisce over coffee in an outdoor bar filled with men hung around with gold and silent young women.

'Can you tell us more about Elena?' Claire asks. 'It was all so fascinating and there was so little time to really ask anything.'

'Elena is our *madrina*,' Dulce says, 'the godmother of everyone who comes to her house'.

'And the *brujo*, the guy in red?' I ask. 'What about him?'

'Is he a good witch?' Claire asks ingenuously.

Dulce laughs, a harsh sound, more surprise than humour. 'There are no good witches in Cuba. Shall I tell you what kind of things witches make here?'

We both nod eagerly.

'A man will go to a witch, he will say "I want you to break my enemy's foot with magic." Then the witch will go to the man's enemy and say, "So-and-so has paid me to break your foot, but if you pay me double I won't do it."'

She shakes her head disgustedly.

'Perhaps extortion is marginally better than actually breaking the foot?' I suggest.

'But we have a government of *brujos*,' Dulce says. 'Fidel has a *padrino* in Haiti, a godfather who looks out for him, who protects him with talismans and casts spells around him. Our government has learnt this *extortion* from a Haitian *brujo*.'

'How do people know these things, know what goes on?' I ask.

'Because we don't hear about what happens outside our country doesn't mean we don't know the inside; maybe it just seems like that because nobody says anything. But I can tell you that when Fidel goes to Haiti he always wears white . . . though they say he is a son of Changó.' She pauses for a moment, her eyes flickering to the tables around us. Then she leans forward and says, 'You have heard of zombies . . . the dead who are living?'

We nod again.

'That is how we are, we Cubans, like the dead who walk.'

'Why do you say that?' I ask, surprised by her vehemence.

'Because it is true . . . nothing ever changes here, it is like the grave, people are dead, everything here is dead. But the worst is that it can never change, it will always be like this . . .'

'That's not possible,' I say, 'everything changes. Look at Russia, East Germany, even North Korea . . .'

'But not here,' she interrupts, 'not here.'

'Cubans awake!' Many of the clarion calls to revolution shouted across this country over the centuries have included those few words. Now they seem to have another meaning.

We walk the short distance to the cathedral to see the bust of Hatuey, a local Indian chief burnt alive by the Spanish in 1512. The bronze gleams in the afternoon light, the powerful shoulders and strong, idealised face of the long-dead man look almost alive as he appears to lunge forward off his pedestal. In contrast the cathedral behind him is closed up and falling down, damp and rot slowly eating it away. Offered repentance and baptism while standing on the faggots, Hatuey asked if agreeing to be baptised meant he would go to heaven. Told that he assuredly would, he refused, saying he could think of nothing worse than eternity in the company of Spaniards.

The taxi driver seems to know everyone in Baracoa, even people who don't know him. He waves and calls at passers-by, many of whom stare back, bemused. We pass Peters Chocolate Factory, the same army-run company that owns the House of Chocolate. There's something bizarre in the idea of soldiers and chocolate, but this is business not pleasure. I made inquiries in Santiago about visiting the factory, only to be told that no-one can visit without permission from 'the ministry' in Havana. The taxi driver waves violently at the guards on the factory gates; he seems so happy and jolly that I suspect he doesn't have the complete set, but he's such fun that Claire and I go willingly along with his sunny, upbeat manner and end up on a farm in the forest beyond Baracoa.

The Finca Duaba is a showplace for tourists, but it's none the less charming for that. Tropical vegetation grows in verdant profusion: mango, orange and cocoa trees hang thick with fruit and giant spiderwebs. Rats scuttle in the undergrowth. I touch a banana plant, drawn by the dark red flower that hangs like an eviscerated heart at the end of a long stalk. Banana flowers open one dense, waxy segment at a time. I pick up a fallen petal wondering at the corrugated thickness of it.

Juan, the young mulatto farm hand who shows us around, seems glad of our questions: yes, the work is very labour intensive; each stem of the plant carries a single bunch of bananas and then dies back. He cannot believe that we have never seen a cocoa tree before and leads us across squelching duckboards to where the hard fruit spring directly from the trunks of small, wiry trees. There are different varieties, he says, with different colours and qualities. His machete slices down, splitting a long, bright yellow pod, revealing the purple-grey seeds in their beds of sweet, white mucous. I bite into a seed and find that like coffee, cocoa fruit gives no hint of what the final product will taste like. Juan tells us that some of the *finca*'s produce makes chocolate and some makes body cream. He smiles slowly and says the women of Baracoa have the smoothest skin in Cuba. There's something marvellous about seeing the origin of things, particularly those common things most taken for granted. I never knew bananas were the offspring of such sensuousness, nor that cocoa swells within an amniotic slime.

Returning to the *finca* complex, we're hustled into a van full of craggy men with guitars. Squashed between large vats of cooked food and trays of shredded white cabbage, the staple of Cuban salad, we bounce out of the gate and into the unknown. It feels quite normal, being expected to go along with things without question or explanation. There is going to be some kind of a party, but it can't be on our account. No-one has asked if we want to join in, or if there is somewhere else we need to be. No-one has asked if we have money to pay for whatever is about to happen. Oddest of all, we've just gone along with it. The cooks and musicians beam and hum and say nothing. The van chugs on, down twisting roads lined with lianas and lichen-covered tree trunks. The potholes get deeper, the trees bend further over the road until we're in a gradually steepening tunnel. Then the van stops in sand and we emerge onto a beach at the mouth of the River Toa.

There's an open-air kitchen, a thatched bar, even a thatched toilet with woven baskets for used toilet paper in this ecological seaside spot for tourists. On a beach awash with the dead stems and husks of coconut palms, small, semi-naked boys play among the organic litter that stretches as far as I can see and looks like an elephants' graveyard. The children squat on their haunches, dropping pebbles from one hand into the other and staring out at waves grey-brown from the merging of sea and river. There are children everywhere – all ages, various colours and in differing degrees of dress. I wonder where they live as there's only one house nearby.

The sky is heavily overcast, giving the landscape an unreflecting quality that is oddly beautiful. The river is shallow here, with a syrupy flow that snags on tree stumps and the rotting vegetation protruding from its opaque surface. It's very quiet, the only sound an occasional human voice and the flop-flop of breaking waves. Something is missing and I realise there are no sea birds here, no screaming gulls.

It starts to rain just as two buses draw up and discharge a large number of Europeans, mostly Belgian, a few Dutch and French. They have been flown to Baracoa from the northern tourist resort of Guardalavaca then bussed here. The food and music make sense now but as the newcomers file into the restaurant hut and sit on the narrow benches the atmosphere is almost as chilly as the weather closing in around us. All look thoroughly disgruntled – who knows what they have been promised as a change from margaritas and sunbathing? The weather-beaten musicians play their guitars quietly and sing in low, pleasant voices as the *finca* men serve the food and a uniformed chef carves a small roast pig into chunks of succulent flesh and crisp, perfectly brittle skin. Claire and I are thrilled at the unexpected feast but the others merely look depressed, not acknowledging the locals and barely speaking to each other. What must they have paid for this trip to make them so thoroughly unable to enjoy it? I catch a glimpse of the plastic, hospital-style bracelets around their wrists – they must be staying in one of those resorts where you pay upfront for everything you might need then never venture beyond the walls of the complex. Perhaps they are suffering separation anxiety? The rain lifts briefly, but none of the visitors look at the beach or venture to the river.

They finish their meal and trudge back onto the buses as we stroll to the little bar and join two elderly local men – two brothers with piercing light blue eyes. They tell us that they are seventy-two and seventy-six years old, that their grandfather was pure Spanish from Galicia, that the older man has three wives. They look like retired *vaqueros* with their deeply lined faces, denim trousers and straw hats. The younger brother asks if we would like to go up the river in his rowing boat.

As we walk to the pretty thatched jetty I'm excited at the thought of seeing what lies beyond the upstream bend in the river. Our boatman, who seems livelier without his brother, pulls out a Peter's chocolate bar as he talks about rain and fish, and hands us some. I've never before eaten chocolate I was unable to swallow, and a struggle between politeness and reflex ensues as the man prepares the boat. Oblivious, he tells us that most of the locals live on the beach and that one woman has twenty-four children. Maybe it's true or just a story he tells to shock prudish Westerners, but there's a wicked glint in those blue eyes.

As we're about to set off it starts to rain again, lightly at first, small splashes roughening the smooth surface of the Toa. Within a few minutes it's a tropical storm, water needling through the air, churning the river, filling the boat. People appear as if from the ether and join us under the thatch. Looking around the huddled group I wonder which of the women has twenty-four children and try not to think what her insides must be like. Sunlight slices intermittently through the clouds touching the sepia landscape with blurred gold. The hiss of water striking water is like a chorus of deep-fat fryers, loud enough to make conversation impossible. The old man shakes his head, he knows this isn't going to stop for a long time and his attention is focussed on preventing the boat sinking. The people around us take off into the rain, their heads covered with plastic bags and palm fronds which are about as useful as an umbrella in a swimming pool. Just as we think there's nowhere for us to go, the older brother appears and invites us to his nearby house for coffee.

'You will meet my wife,' he says, grinning and showing clean, white teeth, 'my main wife – she is a very good woman and a powerful *bruja*. I am Fernando. Please, come.'

The stone-built bungalow is quite grand for its surroundings; Fernando is evidently a man of some means. As we trot under the protecting spread of palm trees our host lets us know that he has had 288 women. It's said in a conversational tone with only the mildest hint of pride as if it's important for us to have this information. I assume he means girlfriends, lovers, one-night stands – but who knows.

Most historical information on Cuba states that the indigenous populations were wiped out within half a century of Velázquez' governorship, from disease, exhaustion or interbreeding. How then to explain the large numbers of indigenous-looking people in and around Baracoa? 'Mexican,' someone muttered when I asked about this, 'immigrants who came here looking for work.' But Fernando's wife, Caridad, has a face like Hatuey and the quiet immobility of a small mountain.

Showing us into his sitting room, Fernando repeats the number of his sexual conquests and his wife nods in agreement, her face expressionless. I glance around wondering where the other two wives are, but there's no sign of them – maybe he meant three wives one after another rather than all at once? He treats this large, silent wife with the utmost deference and respect, holding her hand gently as they sit side-by-side in matching rocking chairs in a room that's a monument to surreal kitsch. The long wooden bench is buried under sixties and seventies rubber dolls of varying sizes. There must be at least thirty dolls, all dressed and sitting comfortably, hands by their sides. I ask who they belong to and Fernando says he has had many children and that these dolls belonged to them. There's something almost eerie about the blank, white faces and messed-up nylon hair. The children are gone, grown up, with children of their own, but their alter egos remain, sharing space with various kinds of revolutionary symbolism – images of Che, Camilo Cienfuegos, Fidel and Raúl Castro. Statuettes, plaques and medals hang from ribbons and nails in the wall.

'I love the Revolution,' Fernando says. 'Before the Revolution I didn't have twenty-five centavos in my pocket nor did my brother. We had no money and no prospects. Everything I have now is because of the Revolution and I love it and I love Fidel.' He grins. 'We are almost the same age, me and Fidel, he is like another brother. I fought for the Revolution and it has repaid me . . . all of this land is mine, the company that brings tourists here has to pay me, so though I am retired and no longer young, I still make money . . . I am happy, my wife is happy, my children are happy. This is all because of the Revolution.'

With his slight figure, white hair and brilliant blue eyes, Fernando looks nothing like his beloved *comandante*, but perhaps they are brothers as he suggests, survivors and more than survivors of a difficult past. Fernando says he's comfortable and satisfied, his only problem age. Even Castro cannot hold back the tide of time and these two men who have never met are linked by age and shared memories of the past. Fernando belongs to that generation which has benefited most from the changes since 1959 – those men and women who *were* the Revolution and who, today, still believe.

Outside the rain falls even more heavily, the beach and palms almost invisible behind a veil of water.

Fernando says, 'I am sorry it is raining because you would like to see my wife's garden . . . I told you she is very wise and knows many things. Out there she grows plants for healing – people come from far away to be helped by her power.' He smiles and raises Caridad's hands to his lips. 'She is a great *bruja*.'

I mention that I have severe pain in my knees and would be very glad if she would look at them. I suspect I'm getting arthritis. Having lived on a damp, north-west European island all my life, it's ironic that I should develop arthritis within a month of arriving in the Caribbean. The pain started in Havana and worsened dramatically on arriving in Baracoa with its extreme humidity and sharp chill. The town's high pavements are agony and I'm only able to climb La Rusa's stairs by hanging onto the walls. I don't really believe Caridad can help me, but anything is worth a try.

Getting to her feet with surprising speed, she leads me into the bedroom and tells me to drop my trousers; as I hesitate, she hands me a clean towel to drape across my hips. Modestly covered, I lie back across the bed, clothes round my ankles, while she proceeds to massage my knees with a herbal ointment of her own making. She hardly speaks, and her silent solidity gives me growing confidence. She seems to know exactly where to touch, exactly where my pain is, and kneads and soothes with warm, powerful hands. To my enormous surprise the pain lessens almost immediately; I don't know if it's the ointment, the massage, or the warmth, but I don't really care. (I'm even more surprised to find that the relief lasts many days.)

I don't know whether to offer Caridad money, my Spanish still isn't up to delicate negotiations, but I offer anyway and am refused.

Pulling my trousers up I ask, 'What are your origins?'

'I am Taíno.'

'But I thought there were no native peoples left . . .' I blurt. 'I read that you were all wiped out or assimilated.'

'But here I am.' She smiles slowly. 'This healing is something I learn from my people. There are many of us, all across the islands. Taíno people were everywhere in the Caribbean, not just in Cuba. You should not believe everything you read.'

The rain continues to sheet down and we are starting to wonder if the jolly taxi man will remember to come and pick us up as promised when a horn sounds over the thunder and there he is, grinning from under a large, striped umbrella. Caridad surrenders up her smooth, broad cheek to be kissed and Fernando his lined one. Then we're running to the car, the driver's giggles in our ears.

Driving towards town we realise his effort in coming to get us is more a rescue than a pick-up. Most of the road is now deeply under yellow, surging water and the gutters and ditches are invisible. Water cascades from the roofs of houses and a waterfall has formed over a set of high steps, bringing down the surrounding soil and shrubs in a foaming torrent. Conversation in the car is impossible as the drumming of water drowns out even the noise of the engine. Undeterred, the driver waves to every face that peers out from behind half-closed shutters and looking at us in the rear-view mirror, chatters on as he drives into the oncoming flood, laughing cheerfully.

★

Guantanamera

> Yo soy un hombre sincero
> De donde cresen las palmas
> Y antes de morirme quiero
> Echar mis versos del alma
> Guantanamera
> Guajira Guantanamera
> Guantanamera
> Guajira Guantanamera
>
> From *Versos Sencillos* by José Martí

A man lies in the running gutter of Baracoa's Plaza Martí. He's fully dressed, wide awake and doesn't look drunk. Nobody pays the least attention to him, just as if this were London or New York. He sits up suddenly, smiling to himself, and collecting handfuls of water starts pouring them over his head and shoulders like a baptism.

Claire leaves for Trinidad and Havana two days later; she would have gone before, worn down by cold and rain, but leaving Baracoa is more difficult than arriving. I learn a new Spanish word, a wonderful word that ought to be onomatopoeic, but isn't. *Madrugada* means that time of night between midnight and six; it is an important word in Cuba because that's when things like reserving and buying tickets and setting off on journeys happen.

'I'm having an okay time,' Claire says as we say goodbye, 'but I don't want to spend all my annual holiday here – it's partly about the weather of course and there's nothing to be done about that, but . . . it's just all a bit depressing really, not at all like I thought it would be.'

The relentless rain, the limitations of my Spanish and the slow return of pain are combining to wear me down too. Then I find a lump in my right breast and quite suddenly I really don't want to be here. Over the next few days frantic transatlantic phone calls ensue to the doctor who saw me through cancer in my left breast eight years earlier; recent mammogram results are declared okay and the panic passes.

I start reading *In Siberia* by Colin Thubron for something to do. I find myself enormously cheered by the beauty of Thubron's writing, but more importantly by Siberia itself, a nightmare landscape that makes Cuba seem like Eden. Siberia reminds me that I *can* write about Cuba, it will be all right. The next realisation, however, is that no-one expects Siberia to be anything other than a nightmare, while expectations of Cuba, my own included, are very different. Cleaning my teeth in Che's bathroom I tell myself that this is not a problem but a point of interest – this relation between image and reality. I'm beginning to wonder how much of Europe and Canada's current love affair with Cuba is actually about a delight in snubbing the United States. As I digest this thought there's a tremendous crash in the bedroom. Rushing in I find the sea has come through the window: the bed is soaked and there's an object moving feebly on it. Squatting in brine I find a very small crab about the size of a fingernail. I look at it and it appears to look back. Death throes follow and to my surprise I see the life disappearing from its eyes as it expires, leaving a strange, inky outline on the bedsheet, rather like the Turin shroud.

Writer Jorge Hernández is irritable and wary. The first time we met, on New Year's Day, he was drunk and very affable; he's now utterly sober, hence the wariness. I know he only agreed to see me at all because some distant relative in Santiago put me in touch, but I don't understand his rancour. Perhaps it's a hangover, he does look pink around the eyes. It's hard to tell how old he is, as flesh and large black spectacles obscure most of his face. His Spanish is almost impenetrable, I don't know whether he has a strange accent or a speech impediment but I understand about 30 per cent of his conversation and he clearly finds my feeble Spanish aggravating. I ask some general questions about Baracoa, its history, its people, but barely grasp the answers. I hoped he'd be generous with me but he isn't, which is okay . . . he's probably tired of ignorant foreigners asking foolish questions. After twenty embarrassing minutes the doorbell rings and another visitor arrives, a tall, grey-haired European with perfect Spanish and English. The atmosphere changes immediately – with a translator present Hernández cannot answer enough questions and makes all kinds of suggestions; he even asks if I like Cuba.

'Naturally,' I say, 'but not the weather, it's too much like England.'

'Then you should be here in the summertime,' he says, 'then it is too hot.'

The new visitor, Pieter, is a photojournalist and an old friend of Hernández. He tells me he's been coming to Cuba for many years, that he lived here in the eighties, that he adores it, that it's the most photogenic place on earth. 'I drove down from Havana,' he says. 'I love driving in Cuba . . . people complain about the roads, but generally they're okay and there are no other vehicles, just long, straight, empty space. Fantastic! I came down through Holguín and Moa and I'll go back a different way tomorrow, get some variety.'

'Which way will you go?' I ask, my next question already forming.

'Via Guantánamo – I'm taking Señora Hernández to see her daughter who's at school there. Then it's straight up to Havana.'

'Do you have room for another person?'

'Sure, why not . . . it's a long drive and I'm always glad of more company. Where are you going?'

'Camagüey.'

'Great, I've never been there . . . it will be an adventure.'

Leaving, I ask Hernández what the song title 'Guantanamera' means.

'It's a woman of Guantánamo,' he replies, 'maybe a woman from the city or from the province, like here. You could say my wife is 'guantanamera'. He looks at Pieter, a complicit, masculine glance. 'You will meet my wife tomorrow,' he says to me, and grins.

Leaving Jorge Hernández' house, I take a final walk through Baracoa's quaint colonial streets. It really is a pleasant place and probably wonderful in the sunshine. The food turned out in the end to be some of the very best in Cuba; it was just a question of finding *paladares*, with their great seafood and fruit salads. Eating in these places is given added piquancy by the air of intrigue and daring at every meal. The majority of *paladares* serve restricted produce – only government-run hotels, I'm told again and again, are allowed to serve lobster, crab, certain fish. Which doesn't explain why breakfast at the La Rusa is invariably two pieces of dry bread and Spam. When I ask for fruit I'm told there is none, though I can see it growing on the trees around me, and no milk or other dairy produce because, I'm told, that all went into making cakes for New Year. After several breakfasts of Spam I remember Monty Python and start to hum.

Things that seemed bizarre at the time now take on different colours; like Rebeca Corazón's dramatics over the neighbours seeing her guests eating. I remember Juan Pérez telling me that the seas around Cuba are fished out, but there doesn't seem to be a shortage here, not if you know where to look and are prepared to pay. I wonder if I've been trying to understand things the wrong way round. Maybe at last I'm beginning to have a tiny glimmer of how things work here. But the risk is not mine, it's the person feeding me who will be punished. Even the Spam starts to make some kind of sense.

Near the Plaza Martí a large young man in a red tracksuit sits in a rocking chair on the veranda of his house, feet up on the balustrade. On the wall beside the front door is a plaque that reads: *This is an Olympic home*. When I ask if I can take a photograph of him he puts his feet down, sits straight in the chair and gazes into the lens, large, black face solemn. From behind the door come the whispered voices and giggles of young girls. Sitting here in his national colours he's still representing his country, and why not?

Cuba, one of the world's poorest nations, has one of the proudest per capita Olympic medal records. There's something touching about the plaque, the way that pride and success are shared. The door opens a crack and a young girl's face peers out – she puts out her tongue at the man in the chair, whose solemnity disappears into a broad, white smile.

The south road out of Baracoa is lined with children walking, sitting in horse carts, on the backs of tractors: small, uniformed people. Ahead, two small peaks that look like tree-covered breasts dominate the skyline. The gentle roundedness is an illusion created by the creepers that grow through the trees, giving a dense, rainforest appearance. The rain has ceased, but water-filled ditches and profuse greenery are its legacy. The fields lining the road are thick with orange trees, banana groves and stands of royal palms; the bushes are gay with pink, yellow and white flowers. The spaces between children are shared with oxen, dogs and pigs. Water buffaloes wade in mud, pristine white tick-birds clinging to their dirty backs. The neat, straight lines and raised, bamboo-edged beds of the organic vegetable gardens contradict the curving landscape.

We pass several schools, each with their bust of Martí, their Cuban flag and political slogans: *Revolución y Combativos*, one sign reads, but no-one here is looking very revolutionary or combative. They look like what they are, *campesinos*, *vaqueros*: thin men in mud-caked Wellington boots; horsemen in white straw hats, their legs straight in the wide, Latin stirrups.

In the front of the car, Señora Hernández is talking rapidly in a high, whining voice that sounds like the buzzing of an insect. I switch off after a while and don't try to follow the conversation. I wonder how Pieter copes, but he seems perfectly happy.

'You want me to translate?' he asks after a little while.

'If you don't mind,' I say, 'if it's not too distracting.'

'Not at all, and you should hear what she is saying, it's very interesting. She was telling me her daughter went to a school near here, a boarding school, and that out of school hours the kids were made to work in the fields. When she came home at the end of term she was always very thin and debilitated and she says it was because they were underfed and overworked.'

Glancing at Señora Hernández I suspect 'thin' is a highly relative term.

She continues talking and I wish I could understand her without Pieter's help. I grasp that she's complaining about Cuba, about her life which is filled with '*nada, nada, nada*'. The more she talks, the faster she talks and the more angry and distressed she becomes.

'There are four classes of people in Cuba,' Pieter translates. 'There is the lowest class, the *comemierdas*, the shit-eaters, the people like herself and her husband, who work for around 300 pesos a month, roughly fifteen dollars . . .'

'She understands "shit-eaters"?' Señora Hernández interjects.

I say that I do and she nods, satisfied.

Pieter continues. 'Then there are the people who own *paladares* and *casas particulares*, the people who work at the bottom of the dollar tourist market. They have some problems, pay expensive licences, get into trouble over nothing, get closed down . . . but mostly they are comfortable. Then there are the people who work for the government, maybe in tourism or other business. These people travel abroad, they have holidays in Varadero, they are very comfortable. And at the top of this heap of shit, is the army . . . the *chupadores*, the bloodsuckers, the exploiters who own everything and have everything in their control.'

We climb steeply. The hills of the Chuchillas de Baracoa are behind us now, the near horizon filled with the serrated spires and sheer walls of the Sierra del Purial, Cuba's most easterly range. To reach the southern coast and the road to Guantánamo we must climb on a road that is a feat of engineering: one side sheer cliff, the other sheer nothingness. The sun is shining but the streams and small waterfalls cascading over rock and bright ferns are a memory of rain. It is all so clear and fresh. My spirits lift looking at the dense green of the high forest, the stark beauty of the mountains – and the sun. The sun!

Small towns and villages – Paso de Cuba, Alto de Cotilla – speed by unremarked. On a high mountain bend, a lone man sweeps the road slowly without looking up as we pass. Pieter was right: there is almost no other traffic and it feels as if we are alone in this beautiful place. Alone with Señora Hernández' voice, as she gives her version of the televised meeting between Castro and President Flores of El Salvador a few months earlier.

'Flores hammered Castro,' she says with relish, 'accused him of damaging El Salvador, of training and sending guerillas to kill people. It was wonderful! Castro didn't know what to say. For the first time someone was standing up to him publicly . . . and Flores is so young! The programme was live on television and people were delighted to see this young *Latin* president standing up to the old man and accusing him – no-one has ever done that in this part of the world. There was a great deal of discussion afterwards. People were fascinated – seeing our great leader being put in the shade and openly criticised.' She looks at Pieter and myself as if checking our reaction to her words. 'It's hard for you to imagine what that's like, coming from your countries where such things are normal. ' She pauses briefly for breath before changing direction and starting again.

'Did you know,' she asks Pieter, 'about that man in Baracoa and those foreign journalists?'

'You mean the *Colors* thing? Yes, Hernández told me . . .'

Undeterred, Señora Hernández presses on, perhaps wanting me to hear the story from her. 'There's a man in my town who has received death threats and threats against his job from the local Communist Party because he helped foreign journalists from some magazine make an article about our town.'

'The Benetton photo-magazine *Colors*,' Pieter adds in his translation. 'Do you know it?'

'Yes'.

'There was a photo in this magazine,' she says, 'of a man lying in a coffin; he had a beard and looked a little like Fidel. Of course, the man wasn't really dead and he only looked a little like Fidel – he was *much* younger – but it was the words that made people angry, the words with the picture.'

Pieter laughs. 'It was a joke,' he says, 'that's all. The *Colors* guys find this man who looks like Castro and photograph him pretending to be dead. The caption read *Cuba Libre* – quite humorous – though not, as the Señora says, for the poor guy who helped them put the piece together. It seems his life has been a misery ever since the magazine came out.'

She shakes her head, 'People call him a traitor and say he works for tourists and foreigners and not for Cuba. How did he know what they were going to do with the picture? He couldn't know that. He's a friend of Hernández' and that's not good. I'm afraid for my husband now, but he won't stop seeing this man.'

My last encounter with Hernández and his anxious irritability with me, a foreigner, is becoming understandable. As his wife chatters on, I wonder if it's usual in Cuba for women to refer to their husband in this Jane Austen-ish way and decided it probably isn't.

Too soon we start to descend. Emerald ferns turn to brown scrubby bushes and the clear mountain water disappears. The change is abrupt. Where there were trees and grass now there are stands of giant cacti. We hit the coast at Cajobabo and start the drive west towards Guantánamo on a road lying casually between turquoise sea and high pink cliffs. José Martí and Dominican general Máximo Gómez landed here in 1895 to begin the final drive towards independence from Spain. Martí had done all he could as an exiled activist with his journalism, essays, poetry and anticolonial statements, now it was time for direct action. Soon after their arrival the president-in-waiting and his general linked up with Antonio Maceo's rebel army and it looked as if this Second War of Independence would succeed. But within a month Martí was dead, killed in a brief skirmish that hardly qualified as military action, his body seized by the Spanish.

The cliffs resemble membranous flesh; caves pit them like giant pores. Once the sea reached up to these high places, forming deep holes by its incessant action. Now it has retreated leaving the rock unwashed, the caves barred by slender stalactites that fill their mouths like teeth. Between the road and the shore, black lava spreads in sharp swathes of sea-cooled rock millions of years old. Cacti rise like spined pillars from the harsh ground and rock skulls and vertebrae lie scattered by the movement of the earth. The view along the coast we've just travelled is of stark mountains and volcanic beaches. I can see where the walls of lava broke through and hurtled, glowing, towards the sea, depositing great basalt boulders, concealing the true, warm orange of the land beneath.

This coast road is dotted with occasional campsites and broken-down motels; one place has an air of post-Soviet Bulgaria, with its bent beach umbrellas and dismantled, roofless chalets. A former army resort, Señora Hernández says. Maybe the military too have fallen on hard times, or perhaps they've moved up in the world and want five-star luxury now.

The handful of towns we pass through are small, nondescript places. Yacabo Abajo, Macambo, Imías: the names sound alien, pre-Colombian, but their pretty, whitewashed schools have names like 'Los Héroes de Gíron' and celebrate more recent martyrs than the Taínos. There are gardens of giant cacti, gardens larger and more beautiful than the small wooden houses they surround. Spiny hedges grow between dry, gravelled tracks that lead from the only road into nowhere.

At Glorieta we are ten kilometres from Caimanera; ten kilometres from the bottleneck that cuts the Bahía Guantánamo in two and the U.S. naval base that occupies the southern half. The presence of many thousands of U.S. military and their families living in considerable affluence along the shores of this bay in the twenty-first century can be traced back to José Martí's death at the end of the nineteenth. What would Martí have thought of the presence of the 'monster' in his own country? Martí's death obliged Generals Maceo and Gómez to continue the fight without the political leader who had inspired them and Cubans everywhere. The absence of his voice, or any Cuban voice, in the subsequent American-Spanish negotiations resulted in Cuba being governed by the United States, though by that date 90 per cent of Cuban land had already been liberated by Cubans themselves. When the Treaty of Paris was signed in 1898 Spain ceded control of the Philippines, Guam, Puerto Rico and Cuba to the United States. Though Cuba was officially granted independence, it was the U.S. flag, not the Cuban, which flew over Havana that day. This indignity was followed by the 1901 Platt Amendment, which, like the governorship, the United States thrust on Cuba as the price of the independence it had already achieved for itself. The amendment gave Washington the right, among other things, to intervene militarily in Cuban affairs. The only choice the Cuban people had in this matter was to accept the Amendment or remain indefinitely under U.S. occupation. Had it not been for the anti-American uprising in the Philippines which drew U.S. military attention to the other side of the world, it's possible that Cuba would not have been given even this choice. In 1903 Washington applied the Amendment to obtain two naval bases, one at Guantánamo, with no expiry date on the lease. A hundred years later, the base, the 'Americans', their yacht clubs, golf courses, supermarkets, hospitals and cinemas are all still there. So are the trenches, security fences, guard-towers and 75,000 mines – the largest mined area in the Western Hemisphere.

Within a year the world's eyes would be focussed on Guantánamo Naval Base and its 'Islamic' prisoners, transported here from across the globe. Even Martí would surely have been rendered dumb by this use of his homeland.

Señora Hernández is telling Pieter about her husband's twenty-three-year-old mulatto mistress. There's no rancour or distress in her voice. Monogamy seems as unusual a concept here as three nutritious meals a day. I don't even wonder why she tolerates adultery, it doesn't seem relevant. I glance at her stout, unwaisted body in its too-tight orange dress; her orange-brown skin and orange-painted nails. Her hair is dyed orange, though the roots are dark and streaked with grey.

Her voice drones on, then she says to me, 'Normally this journey would take me many, many hours on a crowded bus . . . they
often break down you know and then you stand at the side of the
road all day.' She sighs happily. 'This is so wonderful, to be
driven quickly in a car, it will take less than half the time and I
will be able to spend much longer with my daughter.'

I feel guilty for wishing her whining gone, for being irritated by
the way she cuts across conversation because she's not speaking.
Then there are suddenly a lot more vehicles, and we're negotiating
a large roundabout ringed with people trying to flag down passing
cars and trucks. I notice that the people are all black; black in the
way that central Africans are black, and it's odd to notice this after
many weeks in Cuba, where all skin colours seem to merge. We're
on the outskirts of Guantánamo and Señora Hernández is clam-
bering stiffly out of the car and bustling across the busy road
towards the college on the other side, bags of food and clothes for
her child clutched tightly in both hands.

Between Guantánamo and Palma Soriano the land changes once
more, into a mix of green, river-filled plains and the northern edge
of the Cordillera de la Gran Piedra which seem mere hills after the
eastern ranges. North of Santiago we join a brief stretch of freeway
which expires beside a river. Pieter is an excellent driver, taking
the holes and sudden, knee-high drops in road level with aplomb.
He has been everywhere, or so it seems, taking photographs for
Paris Match, *Elle*, *marie claire*, *Le Figaro*. I notice that he's an
urban man whose work takes him to the capitals and coastlines of
the world. When I ask him about this he laughs and says he hates
nature, describing an assignment in the Amazon with horror. He
talks about living in Cuba during the eighties, and how he was
thrown out very suddenly after complaining about the treatment of
a Cuban friend by the authorities.

'This friend was a great artist and he and his wife had been
invited abroad to receive some award. Everything was organised
– tickets, luggage. The night before they were due to leave there

was a group of us at his house for a good luck party, when there was a knock at the door. It was the authorities, telling him that his passport had been withdrawn, that he was not allowed to leave after all. That was it – no explanation, nothing. After the bad guys left my friends were so upset, crying and shaking, but no-one said anything at all except me. I asked why this was happening, what had he done? I started saying things about the government, about Castro . . . I never thought it would be a problem . . . I thought I was among friends.' He shrugs. 'But in a situation like Cuba there is always envy, always someone who is happy to undermine, and I think – no, I am certain – that this is what happened to my friend. Some jealous, small-minded competitor said one word into an ear and ruined him.'

'And what happened to you?'

'The same . . . I was betrayed and I know who by. There was a man at the party, Alberto Korda, he took that photograph of Che. We'd been friends for a long time, or so I thought. It never occurred to me that he might envy me. But he's not a good photographer, his work – and he hasn't done much in years – was opportunistic. He's also a turncoat. Under Batista he was a fashion photographer, taking images of the rich and famous and then suddenly under Castro he's a revolutionary!'

'But what made you think that it was Korda who betrayed you? Surely he had enough prestige of his own?'

'That's what I thought too. However, not long before this party, I'd exhibited my work for a group of foreign and Cuban artists and photographers. Everything was in colour, which raised a lot of comment. Remember this was the eighties and most Cubans had never seen serious colour photography before; even today it's almost impossible to get good colour film here, and harder to process it. So, most people loved the work, loved my images of their country and were really excited to see that documentary kind of work in colour. But Alberto was angry. He and a few others argued that black and white is the only way to portray Cuba, the only way to capture the essence of the nation. Of course, you have to say this when you have no choice, but I was shocked at the way he attacked my work – and me.' He shakes his head as if still dazed. 'It might have been all right even then, except there was a Czech artist in the audience who stood up and said that mine were the best images of Cuba he'd ever seen, that you can't convey a land of colour without colour, that black-and-white photography was a thing of the past, that Cuban artists were living in the past and that they should be grateful to me for revealing new aspects of their country.'

'Oh dear!' I say.

'Exactly. That was it. That one, well-meant declaration was the beginning of the end of my honeymoon with Cuba, though I didn't know it until after my friend's party. I was given three weeks to pack up and leave the country. It was eight years before I was given a visa again.'

We stop for lunch at a *mirador* near Palma Soriano. From this high point the land is fertile, organised; there are small herds of cattle, fields of sugar cane and maize. It is hard to believe that food is rationed here. We eat fried chicken on a table crawling with flies, and Pieter shows me some of his photographs. There are interiors: the homes of the urban poor, surreal images of an elderly man living in an American car parked in his eighteenth-century front room. There are the former rich: elderly ladies living in faded palaces surrounded by fabulous antiques they could never sell. All dead now, he tells me, their property confiscated by the State. But most remarkable of all are images of cane cutters – exhausted, filthy men, machetes dangling from fingers barely able to grip any longer. He lived beside these men, he says, getting up with them at five each morning and going to bed when it got dark. He tells me how they would burn the ground each night to make the cutting easier in the morning, that not all the men were black, though all look black from ash and sweat. But the colour! The colour is painterly, unreal and not at all like a photograph. I try to work out how it's done, what printing tricks he employs, but soon give up. I can see it would be easy to envy this man's work. I envy it myself, and I'm not even a photographer.

Near Contramaestre a *vaquero* leads a string of pack mules across a shallow river far below the bridge we're travelling on. This is cowboy country and from here on there are horsemen everywhere – brown, thin men with heavily lined faces. Even the young look experienced. They ride on the roads, on the verges and in the fields alongside us, and the sight is foreign and exciting. Everyone seems to carry small cloth bags held together with string and when they meet on the road, men and women hand each other packages whose contents I can only guess at. Barter perhaps, in a place where even if you have money there's little to buy. There's no Lycra or American cars here. These are the rural people of Cuba, the *campesinos*, a world away from their Havana brethren – much more so than New Yorkers from Idaho farmers, or Londoners from Hebridean crofters.

It was here, twenty kilometres north of Contramaestre, at Dos Ríos, that José Martí and his companions met a small party of Spanish soldiers. There are those who find what happened next mysterious, inexplicable. Gabriel Cabrera Infante, who has an interesting thesis on Cuba and suicide, suggests that what happened to Martí on that fateful day in May was not a military error on the part of the Cubans, nor even of Martí's own bodyguard, a man with the name of Angel de la Guardia. Cabrera Infante believes that Martí committed an act of Romantic suicide, a 'self-immolation that was a will to martyrdom', comparing the Cuban writer with Byron and the Hungarian Sandor Petöfi. Like the two European poets, Martí, according to Cabrera Infante, longed for a battlefield death even if he didn't know as much himself, and seized it at the first opportunity. His aide, the son of General Gómez, also perished in the skirmish, possibly by his own hand after seeing Martí fall. Whatever the truth of Martí's end, his loss to his country is incalculable even today. How different might this road, this near-empty countryside, be had he lived to take the presidency he already held in name. Martí still lives in his poems and essays, his liberationist writings, his children's stories, but his beloved country looks as if it has lived less because he died too soon. More than a century after his death,

Cubans still mourn José Martí. Entering Cuba's heartland, I wonder if it's the Cuba they were promised but never had that they really grieve for.

We enter Granma Province skirting its capital, Bayamo – Diego Velázquez' next urban venture after Baracoa. There are occasional palms, tall and solitary, but this is a landscape of cattle and of open ground divided by drying rivers and muddy lakes. Strung like tiny, semiprecious stones along this road that leads into the heart of Cuba are pretty, homogenous, stone-built villages and towns. The road continues to stretch ahead of us straight and open and edged with green. It cuts through the cluster of rivers between Embalse Cauto del Paso and the swampy coast, before running north into the fertile lowlands of the Peniplano de Florida–Camagüey–Tunas and the heart of Cuba.

HEARTLANDS

★

Puerto Principe

> Another time I went to the Military Museum in Retiro
> Park [Madrid]. I went up to the top floor, and just as
> you had asked me to, I found Antonio Maceo's sad-
> dle. I caressed it for you . . . His saddle is no different
> from any other, assuming that the saddle really *is* his.
> These Spaniards have complexes that haven't even
> been invented yet. They are the only people I know
> who can fart higher than their asshole . . . I know this
> will upset you, but I have to say it anyway, so you
> don't have any great illusions about the Spaniards.
> Below the General's saddle is a little card that reads:
> Saddle Once Belonging to the Cuban General
> Antonio Maceo. Spanish War Trophy. That "War
> Trophy" hit me like a ton of bricks.
>
> Zoe Valdés, *Yocandra in the Paradise of Nada*

There are manicurists everywhere in Cuba. Like letter-writers or
street portraitists, they set up their table and chairs in front rooms,
streets and market places, and wait for business. Here in Camagüey
the world passes by the doorstep where I wait my turn. The road
beside me is divided by disused tramlines and busy with workers
pushing barrows of coiled wire and soiled, empty baskets. A man
sweeps the cobbles with a wide, thin brush; Cuba's streets seem
fanatically clean after London. Camagüey is a colonial town that
seems at ease with itself, with peeling paint and crumbling pillars.
What in Havana can seem tired and soiled, here is faded and
romantic. From my seat on the front step of the manicurist's apartment block I count eight layers of different coloured paint on the
eighteenth-century door and there are clearly more beneath. If each

layer lasted only twenty years then the long-concealed green and yellow would have seen the First War of Independence, the struggles of de Céspedes and local hero Ignacio Agramonte. This door is black now, cracked with age and sun like the skin of an elephant, but its hidden colours trace the history of Camagüey and those other lives that passed through a differently coloured door when this town was known as Santa Maria del Puerto Principe.

The well-dressed young woman before me is having her fingernails painted with one layer of dark mauve followed by a clear varnish heavy with silver speckles. This is a particularly Cuban style of decoration: in Santiago I had gold on blue, in Baracoa gold on red. The manicurist is heavy-set, with thick glasses and pink lips. Finishing her client's hands she turns to her feet which have been soaking in a bowl of water under the table. The young woman drops a slender, aristocratic foot into the other's lap and winces, as the sharp tools dig into her cuticle. I decide to limit the manicurist's efforts on myself. An old man walks by, a fat cigar butt in one hand and a few brightly coloured zips for sale in the other. Women and men eat ice cream and hold their children's hands loosely. I haven't seen another foreigner in the streets since arriving here, though my hotel is full of them, and the difference between this place and the coastal cities like Havana, Santiago and even Baracoa is striking. Camagüey is a Cuban city, the heart of cattle and cane country. Its life does not centre around tourism and there is a sense of slow contentment here.

Pieter and I arrived in the evening when the stones of the town were still warm and flushed with the sun. We walked and ate and found a bar rich with a provincial bohemianism which I later realised was not typical of Camagüey. Over a large, seven-year-old rum I looked at the many death masks set into the plaster of the walls: closed, chalk white faces, some with blindfolded eyes and names beneath – Gato, Nino, Mariposa. I asked the barman about them, but he just shook his head. Pieter headed for the Wurlitzer standing forlornly in a corner of the room. Close up it looked new, the 45-rpm records gleaming. But it was silent, waiting for that necessary part, needle or surge of power to belt out the 1960s Latin music it held like a secret.

'It will work again one day,' the old man sitting beside it said. 'I used to listen to it years ago, and I will listen to it again.' He stroked the glass cover lovingly. 'Such beautiful music.'

Walking through the streets earlier, Pieter was surprised by Camagüey. 'I always thought there was nothing here,' he said, 'that it must be boring. But it's not, not at all. I mean, look at the inside of these houses, they're just wonderful . . . wonderful to photograph.'

The narrow, winding streets were lined with small, single-storey houses – lines of muted pastel homes. Air ferns sprouted from beneath rotting wooden balconies. We stood together peering through open, grilled windows into rooms so vast they disappeared into shadow. No one interior was the same as the next. Rooms of neogothic arches and pillars filled with seventies Russian furniture and plastic nick-nacks nestled comfortably between a neighbour with an arch straight from the Alhambra and a bright green room with a shiny sixties lamp and fast club music. But all this diversity and difference was inside, hidden from all but the most curious eye.

'Night is best,' I whispered, 'for seeing without being seen.'

'But not much good for photographs.'

The interior spaces beyond the wrought-iron grilles were often like scenes from a Murillo or a domestic Goya: still lifes, untouched for generations. There were empty houses too, façades without roofs, palms and bananas growing in the space where people once fought and cooked. Dense gardens, their emerald colours a shade of night-time black, rustled with nocturnal life. There were *tinajones,* large earthenware water jars, lying half in and half out of the ground. These jars once symbolised Camagüeyano prosperity – the larger a family's wealth, the larger its *tinajones* – now they held air and nests.

'There's so much here,' Pieter said and smiled. 'Just shows it's never good to make assumptions.'

In the morning he was gone. I could have gone with him, north and west, some way towards Trinidad. But Camagüey had already exerted its charm and I wanted to see the 'real' Cuba – whatever that meant. Maybe it meant the Cuba Cubans have constructed for themselves, regardless of people like me.

The town of Puerto Príncipe was founded in 1514 near Punto de Guincho on the north coast not far from Nuevitas. It was another of Diego Velázquez' creations and another that had to relocate. The town's first move was due to 'adverse geographical conditions' – swamp, mosquitoes and the terrifying *jején*, midges. The second move also failed because of what Cuban tourist information refers to as 'aborigine resistance' – the locals weren't happy about arrogant, unwashed whites living on their doorstep.

I seem to be following in Velázquez' footsteps and wonder at his energy – at the energy of all those earliest adventurers – faced with the hazards of conquest: sickness, lack of information, the 'aborigines', and of course, bad urban planning. In 1903 Puerto Príncipe was renamed Camagüey, a word from that aboriginal past, though as with many aspects of Cuban history there is flexibility over its origin. Maybe the word derives from *camagua*, a local plant, or was it from Camagüebax, a local Indian chieftain, or *cacique*?

It was to a Cacique of Camagüey that Columbus sent an embassy during his voyage of 1492, in the belief that he was the Great Khan or the Emperor of China – perhaps Columbus hadn't read the writings, fictional or otherwise, of his fellow Italian, Marco Polo. In Sebastiano del Piombo's portrait of him, Colombus is frowning, vertical lines creasing the space between over-large eyes and arching eyebrows. He's dressed with the understated simplicity of the very wealthy, a brown hat on his dust brown hair. Only his hands are beautiful, slender and tapering, the hands that wrote those first words about the Western Hemisphere. Looking at his anxious, unhealthy face, I find a peculiar satisfaction in knowing that having led an expedition which changed the world, to the continuing detriment of the inhabitants of the new-found land, Columbus died still believing Cuba to be the Indies, and that ultimately his ignorance was almost as great as his arrogance. Cuba's island nature was only revealed in 1508 with Sebastian de Ocampo's circumnavigation.

Camagüey reached its final location in 1528. Its town planners deliberately eschewed the grid system favoured in the rest of Cuba with the specific intention of deterring pirates – a strange notion in a town more than thirty kilometres from the sea – and the streets were built narrow and tortuous. But the riches of Puerto Príncipe were such that determined filibusters like the Welshman Sir Henry Morgan considered extra travel worth the effort. In 1668 the town was stormed by Morgan and held for several days while it was stripped of everything worth taking. The British reportedly committed atrocities, which included locking the town's Spanish elders in the cathedral and starving them into surrendering their gold and jewels. Morgan's report of the raid was somewhat different:

> We marched twenty leagues to Porto Principe [*sic*] and with little resistance possessed ourselves of the same . . . On the Spaniards entreaty we forbore to fire the town or to bring away prisoners, but on delivery of 1,000 beeves released them all.

What appeared an act of piracy was actually part of the larger war between Spain and England then waging over control of the Caribbean and the incalculable wealth of Spain's American territories. Morgan, a privateer who terrified the Caribbean's Spanish settlers with recitations of Christian prayers inserting the word devil in place of God, was rewarded for his efforts, above and beyond loot, with the acting governorship of Jamaica. The scourge of the Indies died in Kingston, far from the Welsh border country of his youth, of liver failure and venereal disease after a life of diabolical fun. Having grown up in the same Welsh-English county – beautiful as it is – Morgan's desire for wide vistas and vast oceans makes perfect sense.

It took many years for Camagüey to recover from Morgan's visit, just enough time for buccaneering Frenchman Francois de Granmont to repeat the indignity in 1679.

There's major restoration going on in the town's main square, though everyone ignores the Keep Out signs, slipping behind the corrugated boards to get where they want to go. In the middle of piles of earth and rebars, the statue of one of Cuba's earliest revolutionary heroes, Ignacio Agramonte, looks lost, out of place. Two hundred years after Morgan hammered the Spanish in Camagüey, the province's *criollo* aristocracy, led by the twenty-seven-year-old Agramonte, did the same thing, though for quite different reasons. Today, Agramonte sits astride his horse, sword raised, surrounded by faded colonial mansions and builders' rubble. He died in the First War of Independence, his body captured, mutilated and secretly burnt by the Spanish. In my imagination, Agramonte is a more romantic figure than his great compatriot Martí, perhaps because he was a cattle rancher rather than a man of letters. Brash, gung ho and old enough at thirty-two to have known better than to pursue personal glory over national wellbeing, he epitomised the physical energy that so characterises Cuba – unlike Martí, whose rarefied energy was of the intellect.

In one of those encounters that only seem to happen in distant places, I walk into the library named after revolutionary student–martyr Juan Antonio Mello and find an Italian exhibition of the life and work of Italo Calvino. I ask the receptionist about the display but she shrugs and tells me she has no idea why it's here. A very handsome young man with pale eyes and the febrile intensity of Rafael Hamera approaches and tells me his name is Eric. Together we look at the Calvino family – at photos of the agricultural experiment station at Santiago Las Vegas in 1923; of San Remo in Italy; of the young Calvino, slight and potent. I peer in the semidarkness at sepia images of Santiago's unrecognisable streets. All the while Eric talks rapidly in good English.

'My two favourite Englishmen are Shakespeare and Freddie Mercury . . . actually not just Freddie Mercury, but all of Queen.

Do you like Queen?' Before I can reply, he goes on, 'I love their music, the way it talks about freedom and expressing yourself however you want . . . that is very important, don't you think?'

'And Shakespeare? Why do you like him?'

'Because he writes about the same things, about expressing yourself or being unable to . . . like in Romeo y Julieta, or Hamlet . . .'

Then he's gone, disappeared into Camagüey's cold sunlight and I am alone with Calvino and surrounded with things I recognise: quotes from R. L. Stevenson, Jonathan Swift, Kipling and Lewis Carroll – just a few of the Italian writer's many influences, a part of that eclecticism he absorbed with Cuban air. I consider that Shakespeare–Cuba connection made by cigars and wonder what the Bard would have thought of smoke-sticks named after his plays rising to heaven as incense to strange gods.

In a remote corner of the library I find a book on Diego Velázquez. The Spanish is complex, possibly old-fashioned, but I learn that in the year he founded Santiago de Cuba and Camagüey he was already an old man in sixteenth-century terms. Fifty-four years old and struggling with ambitious younger men like Diego Columbus, son of the adventurer, and Hernán Cortés, whom he sent to Mexico and whose exploits there he tried but failed to contain. At the age of sixty-one, after ten years as *adelantado* – civil and military governor of Cuba – he was replaced. I run my fingers across the words and wonder how it felt to a man like Velázquez – to be 'replaced'. What did he do, where did he go? The book doesn't tell me. It only says that in 1523 he was governor once more and held the post until his death the following year. The energy never deserted him – the ambition, the desire for power.

Next door to the library the Casa de Trova is closed for business but the door is open and music drifts out like perfume. A local *son* band is practising among the arches and pillars of a restored colonial mansion and, not for the first time, I am struck by the professionalism and skill of Cuba's musicians. The Buena Vista Social Club, which seemed so remarkable to Western listeners, is only remarkable out of its context. Here, everyone seems to be able to play that well, that movingly. No-one appears to notice me and my camera, and when I finish taking photos I leave money on the bar for the musicians to have a drink. But it's too much of course, no Cuban in a place like this spends five dollars on drink. The barman hands the money over to the band leader and suddenly they seem aware of me for the first time. A chair is placed in the middle of the courtyard, I'm urged to sit, and then they really start to play. They are playing for me and I squirm in my seat, moved by their generosity and embarrassed by my gesture of money which now seems paltry and inappropriate, though it was money that made this happen.

'*Besa me . . . besa meeee*' – ' Kiss me . . . kiss me' – the elderly mulatto singer croons above the sound of the double bass, the guitars, the drums, the flute and a woman in a red beret who bangs two sticks together and sways her hips in perfect time. I've never been serenaded by seven people before, and there's something about the candour of the music that pricks the back of my eyes. And it's not just one song, but piece after piece as each musician takes a turn to dazzle. I leave at last, humbled by virtuosity that seems so easily taken for granted here.

That first night with Pieter I glimpsed how the living live and now decide to visit the dead. Walking towards Camagüey's oldest and most picturesque square beside the Church of San Juan de Dios, I pass a house which advertises the teaching of *mecanográfica* and *taquigráfica*. I don't know what these are, it all seems impossibly antique, but from somewhere in the dim interior I can hear the clatter of a machine still doing its 'graphic' thing long past its allotted time.

In 1875, during the First War of Independence, Joseph Alden Springer, a consular clerk at the U.S. embassy in Havana, spent time in Puerto Príncipe and recorded his visit with some wit and a clear eye:

> We next visited the Plaza San Juan de Dios, where
> is situated the Church and Hospital of the same

name, built in 1728. Here, in May 1873, at the door
of the hospital as shown in [my] sketch, the body of
the Cuban hero, Ignacio Agramonte – slain in battle
– was deposited as a trophy of war and exposed to
the gaze of the populace for two days. A rumour
was current at the time that the body was not
interred, but burned in secret on the night of the 15th
of May, being first saturated with petroleum and
placed on a funeral pyre of wood. But I could not,
and dared not, ascertain if the story was true. The
Colonel, however, admitted that the Spanish soldiers are practical cremationists and had on various
occasions burned bodies of the dead, but added that
it had always been done for sanitary reasons."

The plaza was already old when Agramonte's battered body lay
in it. Apart from a few tasteful craft stalls, there's little sign of
the twenty-first century or even the twentieth. Under a brilliant,
cloudless sky, the restored square's pastel colours look clean and
gay. The old hospital is now a museum and the directorate for the
restoration of Camagüey's historic monuments. Beyond its open
double doors there's a courtyard of potted ferns and delicate
fountains, but it's not impossible to imagine the chaos after that
May battle – Spanish soldiers, dirty, wounded but exhilarated by
success, moving across the torch-lit square towards food, water
and the sanctuary of the hospital, while their senior officers
argue and gesticulate over what to do with their prize, the corpse
at their feet.

From the plaza, I walk through some of the town's oldest streets
to the necropolis beside the Church of Santo Cristo del Bien Viaje.
It's beautiful, or seems so in the red and gold of the afternoon sun.
At the entrance I'm asked for a dollar but refuse. This is a graveyard,
open freely to the public, and I keep walking. The tombs are vast
and grand, evidence of Camagüey's former wealth, its ranchers and
sugar growers. The stones are warm from the sun; ivory-coloured
marble illuminated by the low light. Emerald lizards bask on the
smooth surface of tombs, their tails drooping across the inlay of

famous names. Here lie the leaders of the First War of Independence – Agramonte, Betancourt, Cisneros, Varona – whose names echo, like those of their revolutionary descendants Maceo and Martí, in street names across Cuba.

The American Springer paid a visit here too and was relieved at the absence of bad taste:

> We also strolled into the Cemetery and I was agreeably surprised to see the elegant and tasteful resting places of the dead, so different from the repulsive tiers of 'ovens' – or niches, as they are called – of the Havana cemetery . . . Monuments, marble figures, carved gravestones, tombs in shape of domed mosques . . . and other mementos of the dead, all in good taste; and the melancholy sound of the wind through the tall pines made a pleasant impression in one who expected to meet again the formal and stereotypical form of 'ovens'.

I get thrown out of the necropolis by a man with an eye disease. The lids and whites of his eyes are red and angry-looking, which make the irises an eerie shade of green. He points to my camera bag and holds out his hand for money. I show him my expensive press pass, which he seems not to understand. He demands again. I refuse again. He is ruthless and so am I. I leave, both of us defeated.

Saturday night is party night in Camagüey, *La Noche Camagüeyano*. At least that's what I'm told. República Street is the place to be and I head there around half past eight. But it's winter and the only life is in the still-open shops and perfectly preserved sixties hair salon, filled with old-fashioned hairdryers, red plush and plastic. A sign on the door states *Viva la Revolución, victoriosa en el nuevo milenio!*

Camagüey's stores are a fascinating glimpse of pre-revolutionary design. Nothing has been changed; fittings and cabinets gleam with long polishing. The interiors are lit, brightening the dusk and it's easy to be lured by the feeling of normality that temporary brightness gives, but close up the windows and shelves contain little more than bottles of cooking oil and elderly boiler parts. The internal mechanisms of machines seem particularly fascinating to the people of socialist and former socialist countries and looking at these Cuban nuts and bolts, elements and coils, I sense a shopkeeper's delight in creating an almost pornographic display of things normally invisible to the eye.

The smell of bread draws me into a bright, modern bakery. Five men between eighteen and forty years of age are cutting, weighing and kneading dough at incredible speed. I ask if I can take photographs and the youngest disappears off to ask permission. He returns, grinning, and takes his place again in the bread-roll chain. The man cutting the dough does so by eye only and continues without pause as I raise the camera; but colour creeps up his face and then all the men are affected, blushing and trying not to smile. Crop-headed, presumably because of their work, they are extremely attractive; the most attractive men I have seen in Cuba, all here in this one room, blushing in their white overalls and white rubber boots. When I leave, one of them hands me a warm roll and I hold it to my nose all the way along the street.

By nine o'clock 100 or so young people have gathered in República, but there is none of the promised dancing or stalls. Boys stand around holding their bikes, looking longingly into a bar where well-dressed black and white people are drinking to non-Cuban music. Young, ponytailed men prowl the street with plastic roses in their hands and faint moustaches on their upper lips. They look innocent and menacing and every few steps they pause to shoot a stream of saliva carefully between their feet, avoiding their polished shoes. Older men pass by mumbling strange nothings into the air, sometimes in English. 'Where would you like to go today?' someone asks, and it takes a few minutes to realise I'm hearing an advert for computer software.

In a side street I pass a notice nailed to a door: *Danza Cuba! Tonight at the Teatro Nacional – 20.30.* I look at my watch; it's almost ten but maybe something is still happening. After a few blocks the rich throbbing of Cuban drums is in the air; closer still and it's in the pavement underfoot, bouncing off the walls of the surrounding houses. Then I'm walking up the steps of the freshly painted colonial theatre and into the darkened auditorium. Nobody stops me, nobody notices as I drop into an aisle seat. All eyes are on the stage, which is filled with movement, colour and sound in a display of dance and costume that would grace any Broadway or West End theatre in its professionalism and vibrancy. Within moments, I'm as rapt as anyone in the audience.

The dancers spin and jump, faster and faster, to the sounds of a traditional band in nineteenth-century costume. The set is the colonial streets of Camagüey and all the various inhabitants are on display here. Ladies in long silk dresses of iridescent primary colours flutter their way round the stage like exotic birds, supported by beaux wearing breeches and silk waistcoats. There are *santeros* dressed in the white of Obatalá and shamanic figures in pointed hats, some invisible under zebra costumes. One character in a grass skirt and horned headdress is all Africa. Two male dancers cavort, holding poles topped with puppet figures, another has a hobbyhorse attached to his body. A short, broad man is hung with strips of coloured fabric and looks like a displaced Morris dancer.

Just as the performance seems to be reaching a climax and about to end, it starts again, surging and building to yet another high, until the women in coloured silks lift their dresses over their heads and show their black underwear.

When it's over everyone stands up and claps. My only regret, as I clap until my palms hurt, is not having seen the entire show, but even now it's still going on. The dancers sway and shimmy up the aisles, singing their way out of the auditorium, out of the theatre and into the courtyard beyond with its fountain of naked women. As they head around the side of the building to their dressing rooms, I think how unlike Western theatre and dance this is, how unlike the separateness of art and audience in Europe or North America. It's innocent, unquestioning entertainment; but as performers and audience merge I'm swept along on the feeling that this really is *popular* entertainment.

The audience flooding the courtyard is mostly black, middle class and provincial. Most are fashionably well-dressed, with the air of artists, musicians or intellectuals. There are black men in dark glasses carrying pretty children on their shoulders; elegant and beautiful women of every shade of brown; children of all ages, laughing, running and re-enacting the show. As I walk through the crowd, camera in hand, I'm greeted by confident faces that smile into my lens. Cubans are gracious about being photographed: even when the camera isn't turned on them a person will rearrange and beautify their neighbour so everyone is seen to best advantage. Outside the theatre someone actually thanks me for taking their picture, or perhaps for finding them interesting enough, attractive enough, to want to photograph.

It's late when I pass the pizza restaurant at the end of República, but the place is crowded and there's a queue outside. Men in checked shirts and straw hats are buying small, doughy pizzas, ten or fifteen at a time, folding them in half and stuffing them into carrier bags. This is Cuban takeaway, the most commonly eaten fast food in the country. The pizzas look appalling and even though I'm hungry, I don't want one. I know what they taste like.

The Gran Hotel is the only place I've stayed in Cuba upmarket enough to have a television in the room. Foreigners get to see international news here, and it is strange, looking through the window of the small television at the world I know. Everything on CNN looks shiny and brittle: the newscasters, their computers, the studio furniture. Strangest are the between-news adverts, all about food, money and fear of death and disease, with no sense of irony anywhere. 'Were you strip-searched by the New York Police Department between 1998 and 1999? If so you could be entitled to $ . . .'. I watch the screen like a rabbit in headlights, fascinated and repulsed. Next, a fat man sweats hard on an exercise bike as a voice-over croons, 'You've got to the rest of the year to keep your New Year's resolutions, so why not order a FatArse pizza now!' I stare, incredulous, but it can always get worse. And it does. 'I didn't want my diabetic father to develop wounds [cut to close-up of suppurating diabetic ulcers] so I took out health insurance because I love my Dad. If you love your father, you'll make sure he stays healthy too!' Quite suddenly I find myself a fervent Fidelista. It takes a few more minutes for me to remember that contrasts are invidious and invariably untrue, but I am left with a sense that Cuban pizza, however bad, would be less likely to choke me than FatArse.

The north road out of Camagüey is dead straight and lined with small, pollarded trees. The earth is red here, red as the coats of the horses tethered by the wayside, and the stark flatness of the land contrasts with its lush greenery and vivid colours. The openness is exhilarating after days in Camagüey's narrow streets and I wind down the windows of the car to bring that space inside. The driver, Conrado, has a Spanish–Indian face the same sienna as the earth. He's a good driver, avoiding the potholes, stopping cautiously at every rail crossing, even ones overgrown with disuse. For a while we follow the lilac bumper of a vintage car, its rear end as plump as the thighs of Camagüeyano women. Everything is neat, the clapboard houses newly painted, porches clean and swept, gardens cared for. Soldiers, guarding nothing, huddle around twig fires sheltered from the wind by bits of rusted metal. Overhead the ubiquitous vultures swoop hopefully above the thin dogs, goats and pigs that cluster round the village perimeters. The land is fat here, but people and animals are not. This is the road taken by Henry Morgan and every other buccaneer with his heart set on Puerto Príncipe, the road to Nuevitas and the sea.

Deeper into the countryside the houses are made from wood and thatch, the roads lined with sugar cane and deep ditches. The traffic now is mostly horse carts and oxen; if it weren't for the nature of the crop and the telephone wires this could be an ancient Roman road almost anywhere warm in the Empire. Multicoloured cattle graze the fields with their accompanying flea-picking birds. Driving on, the vegetation slowly becomes more sparse, palms fade away. Train lines continue to crisscross the land and Conrado tells me that they feed the chimney stacks of Nuevitas with fuel. After an hour, a power station appears at the distant end of the road, like a monument at the end of a sacred way. White steam rises from thin chimneys to merge with cloud.

At the junction of the Nuevitas–Santa Lucia road we turn sharply left and continue north through high scrub and into marsh. At the first police checkpoint the official doesn't even bother to look at my passport. From this point on the road surface is a brilliant, white gravel which Conrado seems not to notice, though wearing my darkest sunglasses I am almost blinded – then deafened as it strikes the car like giant hailstones.

In the middle of nowhere a Russian tractor is cutting down trees and bush, opening up the already very wide road as if to make way for some oncoming change that will require great leeway. Great craters of greasy, yellowish mud have been created by machinery. In places the ruts are dried hard and lie like discarded ropes or the corpses of crocodiles. Piles of rebars lie around in rusting heaps, but it's all deserted except for the tractor and a wild-looking, bearded driver who flags us down to ask for a light for his cooking fire. He looks alone and confused, as if this were a desert island and we the first people he's seen in years. As the road worsens I think of remote Celtic Britain, with its bad roads and high hedges. But the flowers here are orange and black and I recognise none of them.

The final checkpoint is a more serious business than the last: these are military police, their live-in hut flanked by a tall radio aerial and a freshwater river. Conrado beeps the horn and a man walks very slowly out of the hut and up the slope towards us. I get out of the car and stand in front of the high, closed gate with the sign: *Cuerpo de Guardia de los Bosques de Cuba*. Below in nutmeg water, two of the guardians of Cuba's woodland are swimming naked, their buttocks gleaming white as the road. Then the gate opens and the bridge to the cays is before us.

Dense forest turns abruptly to salt swamp and the road narrows to a hard line across open water. A skein of flamingos turns the horizon a mobile pink. Pelicans and other waterfowl dart low over the mirror surface of the cay that reflects a sky streaked with high, mackerel cloud. Yellow scum has crusted like scabs on a wound around bleached tree stumps that thrust out of the water like the bones of long-dead sea creatures.

Playa los Pinos on Cayo Sabinal has the shifting contrasts of a Jack Vettriano painting. Knee-deep warm water stretches half a kilometre out to a sandbank that shimmers turquoise green and blue against the cerulean sky. The pale, powder beach is dotted with thatch sunshades and plastic deck chairs, all empty. I am here with a bony pig and the two men who run this little place for foreigners who want something other than spreading hotels and chemical swimming pools. Right now it seems I'm alone in wanting that. Alone, with the biggest, most vampiric mosquitoes I have ever seen.

The huts along the beach are spartan but comfortable with unexpected white-tiled bathrooms. I hunt for arachnids under the bed and hang my mosquito net from the slender tree trunk that supports the thatched roof. Within hours and in broad daylight I'm bitten through two layers of repellent – one on my skin, the other on my clothing. I eat a meal of chicken and chips followed by mango in the open-air dining room. The afternoon sun hits low, striking through the horsehide chairs until they glow like finest vellum in candlelight. A mozzie coil burns between my thighs, but it does no good – the whining bastards are desperate and foolish enough to brave anything for a taste of fresh blood. When they start on the chicken I feel almost relieved.

For three days I write and walk along the beach. At first I walk in the sun and laze in the shallow water. I find a conch graveyard, a mini reef of sea-stained shells and learn to spot the perfect, pink-lined ones buried in the sand by a single, jutting whorl. Stink leads me to a turtle carcass. Thrown there perhaps by the soldiers who live in an outpost along the beach, it's little more than white ribs and bits of membrane dancing in the water. I paddle closer and a small crab nips my ankle, warning me off its catch with upraised claws and ballerina steps.

A kilometre along the beach, a handful of young soldiers cavort on the flat roof of the military post. An aerial reaches into the sky picking up or maybe blocking signals from the United States, and looking at the place I feel both guest and enemy. Beyond the post a wide stockade for trapping fish stretches out into deep water. Gulls perch like weather vanes on its wooden posts and a young pelican stares fixedly into the limpid water, occasionally diving and re-emerging, swallowing tail. A small, yellow boat sways at anchor on a sea of striated blue–gold, a variety of shades almost too great for my eye to detect. I walk out to the sandbar and find grey starfish stranded there – from the shore it would seem I walked on water, a halo of light around my feet. Beyond the bar I swim in cooler, deeper sea, past manta rays that glide silent as ghosts through thin veils of weed. Overhead the sky is divided between bright blue and a single, vast cloud, dark and purple as a fresh bruise.

The second day I burn badly, despite sun cream, and after that walk only at night when the beach is silver and the pines along its edge are black under the full moon. In the dark the tram lines of weed and detritus that mark the high tide lose their individuality, no longer layer on layer of single shoes, plastic containers, parts of dolls, empty cosmetic and medical packaging. There is no mainland between here and Cape Hatteras in North Carolina, but I know nothing of tides and currents and this stuff could have come from passing ships, or the tourist resorts up and down this coast. I stroll naked in the silver froth of waves, letting the wind cool the burns on my arms and back. Overhead the moon races across the space between clouds and Orion lies on his side, as if relaxing on an elbow.

This is World's End – ahead water and behind, hours of pale road. The manager told me a big development is planned here, as if there weren't enough already. This represents a kind of tourism that's already disappearing, rapidly replaced by the all-inclusive, plastic-braceleted kind where everyone does the same thing and no-one asks questions about Cuba, or Cubans, because they aren't interested in anything beyond diving, sun and sex. The manager looks tense as he talks. What will happen to these little men when the big boys move in, to the thin pig and people like me? Now I understand why palms fronds are missing off the roofs of the sunshades, the corrugate rusting. Everyone know Playa Pinos can't last, that soon it will be filled with concrete, laughing Italians and sunburnt British. At night I hear the men laughing with the soldiers who walk along the beach for a drink and a change of company. They play cards and when they're drunk I hear them arguing distantly, their voices high-pitched and petulant as children.

The last evening my hut is a charnel house, stuffed with things picked up along the beach: dead starfish, bones, the toothy jaw of some long-dead sea creature, sheets of turtle shell, a perfect conch. Opening the door the smell is meaty and heavy. These are not just treasures but things that once lived and I wrap them carefully, hoping they'll survive the long journey home.

I walk for the last time along the water's edge. The cold wind means a welcome absence of mosquitoes. The full moon is a vivid yellow that changes to silver as it rises. High overhead the sky has at least three dimensions as layered vapour makes a ribcage for the stars hanging like scattered diamonds among bones. The light is stark, all the colours of the day vanished into a beautiful, unforgiving black and white. There was an eclipse over Europe today; witches cast spells to stave off evil influences, but there's nothing like that here.

★

Adelante!

> There is a story that characterises the situation in
> Cuba and Castro's role at that time: The leaders of
> the Cuba revolution go up to heaven: Saint Peter
> comes out to meet them as God's official represen-
> tative and orders them to line up. Then he says, "All
> Communists, three steps forward!" Guevara steps
> forward, Raúl steps forward: so does someone else.
> But all the rest, including Fidel, stay in line. Peter
> glares at Fidel and shouts, "Hey you, the tall one
> with the beard! What's wrong. Didn't you hear what
> I said? All Communists three steps forward."
>
> Nikita Khrushchev, *Khrushchev Remembers*

There's a communist shrine in the main bus station of Camagüey
with photos of Fidel's recent visit; Fidel with the station manager;
Fidel alone, looking pensive. This collage of photographs is
approached through an avenue of silk flower arrangements almost
as tall as myself. Most striking is a large, moody oil painting of the
most romantic of all Cuba's revolutionary leaders, Camilo
Cienfuegos, the man Che Guevara called '*la imagen del pueblo*' –
the mirror of the people. Che had the charisma, Fidel the bullish
rhetoric, but the boyish charm and the people's hearts belonged to
the humble Havana boy who became a tailor because he couldn't
afford art school. Much of Cienfuegos' continuing aura of
romance probably lies in the fact that he died before he could tar-
nish his image. His plane disappeared in mysterious circumstances
over Cuba's northern coast less than a year after the Triumph of
the Revolution. Detractors of the Castro brothers, then and since,
claim he was murdered – because of his prominence and because

his politics were populist rather than communist – but no evidence of this has ever been found. Pictures of Cienfuegos show a young, thin man with a frank, even naïve, smile, white teeth prominent in a dark, bushy beard. For me, the most enduring image, taken by Cuban photographer Raúl Corràles in January 1959, is of Cienfuegos entering Havana in triumph at the head of his troop of *barbudos* – wild, bearded men in sombreros waving guns and flags. At the heart of the group is an almost delicate figure on a white horse, bugle resting on his thigh, clean-shaven face palely naked under a straw hat.

It's two in the *madrugada* and waiting for the bus to Trinidad I pass the time watching shadows flickering behind louvres in the block of flats behind the station. Two East European buses pull in and sleepy people pile off to smoke, find coffee and relieve themselves. Men spit copiously into the gutters and one man carries his small, sleeping son off the bus to piss. Keeping him upright he takes the child's penis from his pants with thumb and forefinger, holds him steady, then just as delicately returns it to his shorts and puts him over his shoulder, still asleep.

Cuba is one of the few places in the world where one sees more travelling by air than by land. Most long-distance public transport in Cuba moves at night, the result being that the traveller sees almost nothing. I arrive after a comfortable journey, ignorant of everything between Trinidad and Camagüey more than 250 kilometres away. Ciego de Ávila and Sancti Spíritus are behind me as if they never existed.

Diego Velázquez founded his third settlement in Cuba at La Villa de la Santísima Trinidad in 1514. It's claimed that the town's first Catholic mass was celebrated by Dominican friar Bartolomé de las Casas, 'Father of the Indians' – the man who could not save Hatuey from burning in Baracoa. As chaplain to the colonising forces in Cuba, de las Casas lived and worked closely with Diego Velázquez and reportedly influenced his dealings with the native populations. Velázquez would have seen a man with ambition to equal his own; but unlike Velázquez, the Dominican's energies were directed to the cause of the hapless, desperate indigenous peoples whom he watched being trampled by his compatriots' colonising zeal. De las Casas' humanity and charity were atypical of his time, though his drive was not. He never gave up his humanitarian efforts in the face of continuous setbacks, snubs and threats to his own life, just as Velázquez knew no-one could govern Cuba better than himself and pushed to maintain power until the end of his life. Despite numerous transatlantic voyages to petition the Church and the king of Spain on behalf of all the Indians of the New World, de las Casas never succeeded in reducing Spanish brutality and carelessness towards the native populations. (What did he feel when Cortés recruited here in Trinidad for his 1519 expedition to Mexico?) But of the countless Europeans who gave their lives to the New World, de las Casas was the greatest survivor. His last essay in defence of indigenous peoples was written at the age of ninety, in the quiet Spanish monastery where he spent the last twenty years of his life. Did he ever wish himself back among his Indians? Did he regret living long enough to see the loss of almost everything he'd worked for?

Standing in the beautiful Plaza Mayor in the heart of Trinidad's old town, I imagine how this place would have looked to Bartolomé de las Casas if and when he celebrated mass here: it would have been nothing like this elegant, pastel reminder of the bygone age of French sugar planters, Spanish ranchers and assorted pirates. Massive palms dominate a paved garden in front of the town's main church, the Iglesia Parroquial, and tourists drift slowly in and out of the restored museums that line this beautiful, colonial square. Tomorrow, the Trinidad Festival opens and workers are busily putting up a stage, watched by a madman who shouts and roars at the air.

Walking across the plaza it seems that the days of Velázquez and de las Casas are not wholly dead, as sword-fighting commands echo around the restored buildings, bouncing off tiled roofs. Under the trees beside the Museum of Archaeology, a group of young children is being taught to fence. No-one has a sword of course, not even the teacher, a large black woman who sits comfortably on a bench and directs with a stick and a powerful bass voice.

'*Guardia!*' she shouts and the line of children shifts as one. '*Adelante!*' . . . '*Adelante!*' and they all lunge forward, sword arm straight, rear arm raised like a scorpion's tail.

The children's ancestry is there in their faces and bodies: slender dark Spanish, tall Africans, blonde French. These descendants of colonialism are learning the skills of their ancestors, though I imagine few females ever picked up a sword in this country before the Revolution. They can't be more than eight or ten years old but they know what they're doing and I wonder if I'm looking at a future Olympic champion or two.

It's cool under the trees, soon it will be chill. Beyond the enclosing walls of the restored homes and churches of the Plaza Mayor, I glimpse the Pico de San Juan, a high point of the Sierra de Escambray, and vultures, circling below little puffy clouds. The fencing class breaks up and the children drift away in groups to play with wooden tops that look like rotten parsnips and require the greatest skill to spin. *Son* drifts casually from a side street: a polished sound, I assume it must be a recording playing in one of the many shops selling music to tourists here, until I find the musicians sitting on a pile of rubble in an unrestored road. There's no audience for the remarkable music the five black men make and they seem unaware of me as I sit on a doorstep and let the sound of Cuba flow through me.

After a day or so I know that Trinidad has many faces. The pretty colonial town is a tourist trap, probably the biggest in Cuba. The sunken, cobbled streets around the Plaza Mayor are crammed with women crocheting tablecloths and pants, men carving wood, and stalls covered with gleaming trinkets made from rare and endangered black coral. The stallholders are ruthless – they can afford to be – there are plenty of tourists here, day-trippers from the nearby beach resorts of Playa Ancón and María Aquilar. On the pavements, on corners, emerging from buildings I am besieged by beggars demanding *jabon* and making scrubbing gestures with their hands and arms as if to wash any colour from their skin. Groups of women prowl the poorer streets of the old town asking for the clothes off my back.

'Look, look we have no good clothes, only these . . .' pointing to leggings full of holes.

'You have many clothes, no? Give us your blouse. See . . .' pointing to another member of the gang, 'it would be very good for her.'

'But we're not even the same size,' I say, astonished.

'No problem, no problem, we can make it smaller, easy.'

Down in the new town, among the night-time stalls selling roast suckling pig, I'm asked for money each time my flash goes off.

'No fusion . . . no fusion!' one stall-holder bellows. 'One dollar for fusion.'

The dead piglets wear sunglasses and have cigars thrust between stiff, shiny lips in a peculiarly Cuban mix of humour and postmortem indignity.

After the calm of Camagüey, it feels like a return to the real world of need and greed. From curiosity rather than charity I put ten pesos into the grubby outstretched palm of a small girl. She gazes at the money.

'That's Cuban,' she says in disgust, 'that's nothing.'

'You're right,' I say and take it back.

'They don't really *need* things,' Simon Woller had said, 'they just *want* them.' Looking around at Trinidad's professional beggars it's impossible to decipher rights and wrongs. And then a glance at the foreign visitors to the town makes graft and daylight robbery almost understandable. Most give the impression of being rich, even if they're not. Bloated and pale with good-living and cholesterol, they pad around the town, buying without looking, hunting for bargains and food they can eat without choking. There are no villains here.

★

There's something going on; I sense but can't grasp it. Everywhere I've stayed there's been friendliness, a desire to assist, but since arriving in Trinidad I've noticed a change in the atmosphere, in the way government-run hotel staff look at me. It doesn't feel personal, but it's quickly becoming so. After two days I'm asked to leave the hotel, despite having a confirmed booking.

'No, your booking is not confirmed,' the attractive young woman with the overblown title of public relations officer announces, 'This room is promised to a government minister arriving here for the festival. It is not possible to refuse a minister.'

I say that if they can find me a place with equal amenities for the same money, I'll go, otherwise I expect them to honour my booking. Later, as I eat my breakfast of dry bread and fruit, I hear the manager shouting and the woman remonstrating feebly. Do they, like the manager of La Rusa, imagine I'm a spy for the company?

On television that night I learn about the two young men who died escaping Cuba in the undercarriage of a British aeroplane. They thought they were on a brief, low-level flight to Florida and instead fell to their deaths – if they weren't already dead of hypothermia – over the English countryside. Talking heads in ill-fitting suits read from prepared statements in a parody of a round-table discussion. There are no women present and there's no debate at all. In the background a lot of men in shell suits sit around to no obvious purpose. The footage from security cameras at José Martí airport could be anywhere. A man self-consciously delivers minute details of one of the dead youths' last conversations with his father. It's very bad journalism, very bad reporting and inconclusive about anything other than the fact that the *yanquis* are to blame. Much later I discover the young men had died in late December, more than two weeks earlier. Their deaths were kept from the public while the government prepared its response.

The next programme shows a student solidarity meeting. Castro addresses the young people in a soft voice, little of the firebrand of forty years ago visible now. He pauses often as if lost in thought or forgetful of what to say next, his head tipped to the left, one knuckle to his lips in a contemplative gesture.

His plain green uniform gives him both anonymity and force, which seems a kind of metaphor for how Cuba is run. There's something affected, almost womanish, about his style of speaking. He has that quietness that forces the listener's attention. He's followed by a young man in a T-shirt decorated with Che Guevara smoking a cigar. The youth tries to talk forcefully, waving a vigorous arm in imitation of the young Fidel, but despite the beret pulled low over his forehead he's an unconvincing orator, reading from scraps of paper. He talks a lot about '*compadres*' and '*Patria o muerte!*' No-one mentions democracy, but listening to him I remember sitting in the dirt outside the Rangoon house of Aung San Suu Kyi among a crowd of monks, foreigners and Burma's most downtrodden, listening to the voice of democracy suppressed. We were surrounded by military and police, the forces of tyranny. The only word I understood was repeated throughout Daw Suu Kyi's speech, the same in Burmese and English: 'Deemo-kracy'. This rally ends with music. Castro stands stiffly, listing slightly to the left, waving a small flag, a stiff smile on his teeth. There's something intensely dated about the scene. The young speaker and many of the crowd look like late 1960s throwbacks: the rhetoric, the clothing, the hairstyles, the gestures, the language, the ideology – everything's passé.

Watching as Trinidad's street life flows to and fro below my small balcony overhanging José Martí Street, contradictions seem highlighted in this 'museum town' where Cuba and the outside world meet and clash over expectations. I'm continuously surprised by a lack of curiosity about the world in the people I meet, by their very clear and fixed ideas about that world. There seems to be an easy spread of disinformation regarding peoples and nations beyond the shores of Cuba and the absence of accurate information for anyone about almost anything is startling in a country that prides itself on its education system. Perhaps I am naïve in my surprise – what else could there be after forty years of non-democratic socialism? And then the rest of the world has an equally strange and contradictory vision of Cuba, that place where people are so happy they dance and sing all the day long. Two worlds exist side-by-side, often anxiously, as locals and tourists meet. Surely, none but the thickest-skinned visitor could feel wholly comfortable, yet each day proves me wrong.

Gazing up at the cloudless, moonless night sky, I notice as if for the first time that the low level of electric light here makes the stars seem brighter.

The anteroom of the best restaurant in Trinidad has a gilded Christ figure beside a Christmas tree still heavily decorated in mid-January. The seventeenth-century building is filled to bursting with antiques, religious artefacts and paintings darkened with age and nicotine. I wait an hour and a half for a table, not a testament to the excellence of the food here – though its not bad at all – but to the dreadfulness elsewhere. This is one of the town's rare non-government eateries and there's an air of bonhomie, tinged with nervousness. Too many foreigners here means too few elsewhere, which could mean being closed down at any moment. The fact that foreigners want to come here – can actually eat the food here – is irrelevant.

Over coffee with a hint of nail varnish remover, I listen as the youthful Englishman at the next table reads to his partner from the guidebook open before him.

'"This led to the Cuban Missile Crisis, which brought the world closer to the brink of nuclear war that it has ever been. Only after receiving a secret assurance from Kennedy that Cuba would not be invaded did Khrushchev defuse the crisis on October 28th by ordering the missiles dismantled. The crisis had a sobering . . ."'

'Who's Khrushchev?' the woman asks.

'President of the Soviet Union in the sixties.'

'Oh.'

When we speak I discover that Michael and Pebbles truly enjoy Cuba and are amazed that others don't, though they admit freely to being cushioned by money and a four-wheel drive.

'It's great having a vehicle,' Michael says. 'We give lifts to everyone and they always seem so happy to be travelling with us. Yesterday we picked up three conscripts who asked us to play their tape of 'Hotel California' on the car stereo over and over again so they could sing along with it. It was great fun!'

They both work in the film industry, Michael as a producer and Pebbles in make-up. They have just become engaged and are clearly delighted with each other.

'The people are so generous and spontaneous,' Pebbles says. 'Even though they have so little, no-one ever complains. I can't believe you don't enjoy it as much as we do. You must be terribly cynical.'

I wonder if they have been travelling through a different country to me and ask where they enjoyed themselves the most.

'Oh, Maria La Gorda, definitely,' they both agree. 'The diving there is fantastic, some of the best in the world probably.'

'So it was great because of the diving?'

'Yeah, definitely,' Michael says, then pauses as he hears what he said. 'Yeah, I suppose it could have been almost anywhere really.'

'You should come out with us for the day, see what fun we have!' Pebbles chirps.

Looking at her slim, tanned body and Michael's athletic frame I doubt if I'd be able to keep up with them for a whole day.

'Absolutely,' Michael says, 'why don't we do something tomorrow? Go out in a boat somewhere . . .'

'Okay,' I say, 'I like boats.'

At ten the next morning, Ms Public Relations says she has found a *casa particular* for me and will I please leave immediately.

'But I'm going out for the day in fifteen minutes,' I say irritably, 'why didn't you tell me this before? I can't possible do anything about it now.'

'I couldn't tell you about the room last night, I only found it this morning. I have a fifteen-month-old baby and I was up until eleven last night looking for a room for you. I spent two hours this morning looking for new lights for this room, but there aren't any anywhere. Sorry . . . sorry.'

Fat tears roll down her flawless face as chambermaids gather around her protectively . . . or maybe they scent blood?

'Okay, okay, I'll clear the room now if someone will help me, and thanks for the *casa* but I'll find somewhere myself.'

'You can have breakfast here every day completely free,' she says, sagging with relief in her stilettos. Then she disappears to let everyone know the minister won't be on the street after all.

The boat swings in a wide arc out into the deep blue and white of the sea between the arm of Playa Ancón and Cayo Blanco, a tiny uninhabited island twenty-five kilometres off the coast south of Trinidad. It's a small boat on this big piece of water, just large enough for three foreigners and Alberto, our driver and fishing guide, who looks much as I imagine Gregorio Fuentes must have looked fifty years ago when he fished with Hemingway – hawk's face deeply brown and creased with the sun, dark hair and moustache bleached and greying. The fishing rods stand like slender bamboo against the boat's small roof; mine has a heavy brass reel stamped with the word 'Tallahassee'.

Alberto shows us how to cast our lines backwards along the white, churning wake. I run my line out and watch the heavy, metal bait fish flash and dance with each strike and swell of the water, feeling it drag against the current. Michael and Pebbles take off most of their clothing and relax with practised ease at the back of the boat, a rod nonchalantly clasped in one hand, a beer in the other. We talk about London, our favourite films, Michael's project on King Arthur and the Round Table and what Brad Pitt looks like close-up first thing in the morning. We find we know someone who knows someone in the way that strangers always do in a foreign place.

After thirty minutes we're out of sight of land and Alberto tells us to let out more line, let the bait fish drop to where the bigger, slower fish feed. I don't believe we'll catch anything: no fishing expedition of mine has ever produced as much as a sprat and Alberto is going through the motions as if the rods were toys and we overgrown children with more money than sense. But I'm happy just to sit and feel the sun and the rush of air and sizzling spray. There are no other boats on the water, which sparkles a blinding gold and turquoise in the midday sun. Light catches the foaming wake, turning it to ropes of great, creamy pearls.

Then I feel it – a twitch on the end of the line. I tell myself it's just an undulation of the water but when it comes again I know it isn't that.

'I've got something!' I say excitedly. 'It feels heavy.'

Alberto glances at me casually. 'Sure?'

'No . . .'

At that moment the rods jerks visibly and Alberto, all attention now, is immediately at my side muttering rapid instructions in Spanish. 'Careful! Don't pull too hard,' he says, his hands flapping as he stops himself grabbing the rod off me. 'No! Not like that . . . slowly, slowly!'

The end of the rod is digging painfully into the top of my thigh. My left hand holds steady while the right winds the reel fast. Fearful of losing the invisible creature whose struggles I can feel, I'm unaware of anyone else on the boat now. Even the sound of Alberto's voice is far away and I don't care if I'm doing it all wrong, I just want to do it myself. A narrow head that gleams like polished armour breaks the skin of the water. Alberto leaps forward, gaff in his hands, and the fish is in the boat, thumping its way across the floor, great needle-filled jaws snapping in fury.

'Barracuda,' Alberto says with satisfaction.

Even with the gaff lodged firmly in its side and my hook in its gill, the creature continues to fight. There's something viperish about the unblinking eyes, the sinuous, metre-long body, the silver markings dark against the pure white of its throat and underbelly.

In the photographs I hold the rod and the barracuda hanging from it and grin like a cat.

'Very good to eat,' Alberto says cheerfully, as he jerks his hand clear of the teeth that are still trying to exact revenge and throws the fish in the under-floor locker where it bangs and thuds for the next twenty minutes.

'Why didn't you kill it?' Pebbles asks, distressed by the creature's distress.

'*Mira* . . .' Alberto starts. 'Look . . .'

When I first arrived in Cuba that word, *mira*, seemed on everyone's lips and I wondered who Mira was and if she was really as popular as she appeared. I soon learned that it's a sign of mild impatience, of politely forcing a listener's attention.

'*Mira*,' Alberto says, 'all *extranjeros* ask me that question. I don't see why foreigners feel so sorry for a fish . . . it doesn't feel, it doesn't suffer. You eat them in your country don't you? Anyway, it *is* dead, it's just muscles twitching.'

'I hope I'll catch something too,' Michael says, listening to the banging of my prize.

'No,' Alberto says, matter-of-factly, 'you will not catch anything today – you wished yourself good luck as we left the harbour.'

'What?' Michael looks confused and crestfallen.

'It is very bad luck to say *buena suerte* when you set off to do something, particularly fishing. It brings the opposite to what you ask for.'

'Oh shit!' Michael says. 'I *did* say that, didn't I! Does that mean I'll catch nothing?'

Alberto nods. 'Nothing . . . today at least.'

The brief coast of Cayo Blanco appears ahead. Tourists cavort in the waves and along the beach, carried here by the gleaming white boats tied up along the rickety wooden jetty.

'I will cook the fish for you,' Alberto says. 'Go onto the shore now and I will call you when it is ready.'

The tourists on the beach are French: beefy men with attitude and necklaces tight around the base of their throats and well-oiled women in modish swimwear. There are also two giant iguanas which the French pursue in order to force-feed, and a great many mosquitoes. For once I am ignored as they dive on Michael, stabbing mercilessly. Then Alberto is waving us back to the boat and a lunch of Cuban salad, rice, lobster tails in salsa and grilled barracuda, followed by papaya and oranges. It's one of the best meals I've eaten since arriving in this country.

I'm not a good snorkeller, but the pleasure of propelling myself through the water surrounded by a new, silent world is uniquely exciting. My hands are ghostly against the green water. Michael and Pebbles swim far below me, so white and graceful, their hands touching. There are fish all around me: purple and yellow, black, iridescent blue ones, green, spotted. I swim in a slow circle above the brain coral before diving down for a closer look. Fan coral spreads lacy, dust-coloured wings beside me and then Michael is close by jabbing his finger upward. A large barracuda hovers overhead. Can it scent a dead relative on us? Michael gestures, territorial – avoid, and we swim slowly away. I feel the sting of invisible sea creatures and see a long red welt appear along Michael's cheek beside his face mask. He really shouldn't have said *buena suerte*.

The sun is setting as we walk along Playa Ancon, a clean white beach with a few overpriced bars and plastic lounges. A dark red sun liquefies into the sea, its reflection spreading across the burning water.

'Well?' Pebbles asks. 'Did you enjoy your tourist day out?'

'Very much,' I say, 'thanks for suggesting it.'

'You see, you *can* enjoy yourself here,' Michael says. 'It's not cheap, but what you get is really great value, at least we think so.'

'You're right,' I say, 'it is. But you know, it was like a marvellous dream, it didn't feel real somehow . . . it's so separated from the rest of life here. How many Cubans get to do the things we did today?'

I sound like a heckler at Hyde Park Corner and I don't want to seem unappreciative. My enjoyment of the experience has just the slightest tinge of guilt, which I tell myself is ridiculous – but I've been here for weeks now and today is the first I've spent without someone describing the problems of their life in response to learning I'm a writer.

'It's different for you,' Pebbles says. 'You're here to dig out the misery, we just want to have a good time . . . we work hard forty-eight weeks of the year and want to relax on holiday, doing what we did today. Is that wrong?'

I shake my head. Cuba needs tourism after all.

A man with a large, dirty blond moustache is waiting for me in the hotel lobby when I return to pick up my bags and move on. His eyes are sky blue and his uniform the green of the Immigration Police. He's been waiting for me all day. He says he wants to talk to me alone and tries to usher me into a small room beside the reception. Instead I ask him to help carry my bags to Michael's waiting car where my passport and documents are.

We must make a strange couple – the foreigner and the policeman with the luggage – because passers-by stop to stare. I give him the passport which has the visa extension clearly stamped inside but he seems confused by it.

'This isn't correct,' he says, 'it should look different from this.'

'It's a journalist's visa,' I say patiently.

'You are a writer?'

I whip out my international press pass, which only deepens his confusion. Luckily he fails to notice it's already out of date. I watch him make the decision not to pursue his ignorance any further.

'Okay,' he says and relaxes for the first time. 'Okay, no problem. You can go.'

'What was all that about?' Michael asks as we drive to their *casa particular*.

'Who knows,' I say. 'There's something going on, I just wish I knew what.'

I find a place in the *casa* where Michael and Pebbles have a comfortable suite. Miriam, a young, plump woman, shows me to a smallish room between the kitchen and a living room filled with rocking chairs.

'One night is okay . . .'

'No problem,' I say. 'I'm going to Santa Clara tomorrow.'

We eat illegal lobster on the pleasant roof terrace and drink Cuban beer before walking up to the old town and the open-air Casa de la Trova where *son*, *rumba* and jazz are all on stage as part of the Trinidad Festival. The music is excellent, the musicians colourful. Down on the Plaza Mayor the shades of Bartolomé de las Casas and Diego Velázquez listen with me, before shrinking back into the dark. People are dancing all around us, in one corner six fat men salsa happily with six fat women, their faces beatific as they sway, wrapped in each other's arms. The great and famous of Trinidad, or perhaps even of Cuba, appear among the tables of invited guests and kiss-kiss the air just like Oscar night. One woman draws all eyes: her silver sheath dress clings to her short, perfectly proportioned body as she dances with a succession of older, important-looking men, her backside wiggling like a pair of cats in a bag.

'It's a wig,' Pebbles hisses in my ear. 'Look how it sits on her head – and the hair, it's just dreadful . . .'

'How can you tell?' I whisper back.

'I've put make-up on enough faces under enough wigs, believe me! *That's* a rug.'

'She's a great dancer though . . .'

'Hmph!' Pebbles says, and getting up grabs the nearest Cuban and starts showing Trinidad how it should be done. When Michael reappears with the mojitos it's to find his fiancée embedded in the muscular arms of a fifty-something Trinidad wide-boy, her backside grinding with the best of them.

That night I am extremely ill. Something has happened to my legs and my lungs start to work in an unusual and haphazard way. Then I start to vomit and have diarrhoea all at once. At four I wake Miriam and ask for a bucket because my legs won't carry me to the bathroom any longer.

In the morning I wake unable to breathe and sit up in blind panic. Dehydrated and fevered, I realise I won't be leaving for

Santa Clara today, or even tomorrow. Miriam looks anxious and I ask if the room is booked but she says not. Michael and Pebbles leave for Baracoa. I fall into a fevered sleep, listening to the bubbling, tearing sound in my lungs and hallucinating that the heavy tartan fabric across my window is Rob Roy Macgregor's kilt, dropped in passing and turned into a curtain.

Three days later I'm still listening and trying to remember the ceiling in Keats' room in Rome, the room where he gasped his last from lung disease, begging his friend Severn to let him overdose on laudanum. Severn refused for fear of damning Keats and himself to hell and watched his friend suffocate on blood and mucus. Poor Keats. Thinking of him I feel less sorry for myself, with my massive bag of modern medication and freedom to use it. Something few Cubans have, I realise, as Miriam asks about every bottle and pill, what it does and how much it cost me. When I tell her it was free at home in England she seems not to believe me. Nothing in the world is free outside Cuba, her face seems to say – and what is free here isn't always worth having.

I've learnt the crowing routines of the many local roosters – most prefer the *madrugada* – and Miriam's pretty green-and-pink parrot has learnt to imitate my cough, which it seems to find sniggeringly funny, alternating gentle hacking sounds with giggles. Large doses of penicillin have improved matters but I'm still feeble. Miriam has looked after me with tea and soup and only occasional hints about Santa Clara. When my brain clears it dawns on me that this room is unlicensed and that she's afraid of being caught and fined by the tourism police.

'Yes,' she admits when I ask her. 'I have only two licensed rooms so this is not legal. We've already been fined once, it was $1000, we couldn't afford that again.'

'I'm so sorry,' I say. 'I really will go tomorrow.'

'It's no problem,' she says, 'you were very ill, there's nothing anyone can do about that.'

Listening to my short-wave radio that afternoon I learn that Laurent Kabila has been assassinated by one of his own bodyguards.

Congo is blaming Uganda and Rwanda. Miriam's much older husband, Rodrigo, is in the front room reading *Granma*. I ask if there's much foreign news in it. He laughs and points to a small, boxed column running down one side.

'That's our international news. Kabila is dead? I only know this because you tell me, maybe I would never know it otherwise . . . and he was a friend of Cuba, a friend of Che in the Congo.'

Once again I realise how very differently Cubans see the world – Kabila as a friend, a friend of socialism. My first thought on the assassination had been 'Live by the sword and die …'.

That evening I help Miriam pound garlic and salt to a paste in her comfortable modern kitchen. I ask for her thoughts on her homeland and admire the way she deflects my questions. Just as I feel we're getting somewhere all the lights fail. In the darkness she tells me about Rodrigo and his wife and children whom he left for her. He is an older man, fifty-eight, but a better man for that. She would like children herself one day, but first they must be more secure and have more money. Her voice is soft in the shadows, the voice of a hard-working and tenacious young woman determined on a better life, unwilling to accept the restrictions of authority. Listening to her I realise that she's the first person I've met who has revealed material hopes and dreams.

'Talk to Rodrigo,' she says when the lights come back on, 'he has more to say than I do, he has lived in different times.'

'What would you like to know?' Rodrigo asks that night as we sit in the kitchen together over a beer. Miriam is lying on the bed in the little room beyond the kitchen watching 'La Fuerza del Deseo'.

'How you see your country. What you remember from before the Revolution . . .'

Rodrigo begins his story as if it's been waiting to be told.

'I was eighteen when the Revolution happened. Things were very different then. Mostly things were cheaper and there was always food and medicine. My family were poor but I went to school and university and became a lawyer. Now things are very bad – they were worse but they are still bad.'

'Why is that?'

'Castro of course – he is like Stalin, a dictator. The prisons are full of people who oppose him. If you complain enough . . .' he clamps one wrist tightly on top of the other. 'In our one newspaper and on television there's nothing but Castro, from the *circulo* upwards our children have this thrust on them.' His laugh is cold. 'No-one is fooled by all that talk you know. Do not think we are such stupid people that we believe everything that man says. We have elections, but it's all a sham. Now there are elections coming up Castro is saying that soon he may not be president. Shit! Who else is going to be! And he lies: "Our economy is coffee and nickel etcetera etcetera" he says, but it's not true, our economy is immigrant dollars. Between eight and nine hundred million dollars come into this country every year. It's ironic – the people who most hate Castro, those Cubans in America, they are the ones supporting his government, keeping him in control. No-one can bank this money because there's no confidentiality here – so it's spent on televisions, clothes, food ... and who owns all those things? The government . . . the army.'

He talks about the army's separate existence, their superior rations, different lifestyle, and I recall Señora Hernández and the *chupadores*.

'But our leader has no idea of economics, he never did have. All his government have ever seen is political ideology and you cannot run a country on political ideology. Look at Angola, Congo, Tanzania . . . all those Cubans killed and injured, fighting for ideology.'

'But someone must support him, agree with him,' I say, 'otherwise no amount of money would keep him in power.'

'Those who support him are educated not to think, the rural people, the *campesinos*, they are his support and they are like perfect robots, working too hard to consider such a thing as politics. Anyone with education cannot accept this life – but we must, we have no choice.' He looks at his hands, pale fingers with wrinkled knuckles clasped in front of him on the table where a few hours earlier I mashed garlic in the dark.

'When the Revolution began I was as excited as anybody. I remember when we heard the *Granma* had landed, it was wonderful. There's no doubt that Castro is a highly intelligent man, particularly in the way he politicised the *campesinos* and created the possibility of revolution, something no other Latin country was able to do.' He shakes his head. 'But it hasn't worked and now Castro can blame everything on the U.S. embargo – nothing is ever his fault. But the U.S.A. is not the only country in the world or even in this region and we have trade with Japan, Venezuela, Canada and many more. The U.S. gets the blame for everything and there's no doubt it has done some very terrible things to my country, but that business with those two boys falling from the aeroplane – Castro says this is the fault of the U.S. Shit! It is the fault of *this* government. How could it be anyone else's fault? This government is to blame if people don't want to be here. Blame the U.S. for many things, but not that.'

His voice is raw, as if anger and frustration have scarred his throat, and I remember the passion in Martin di Giovanni's voice as he told me that Castro's dream had become the nightmare of eleven million people.

'How do you manage?' I ask. It seems a foolish question.

'I am marginalised of course. Because I do not shout "*Patria o muerte!*" all the time like an idiot, I am marginalised. All those people shouting "Fidel!" or "Elián!" at rallies, they don't know why they're there . . . they are schoolkids and peasants bussed in under obligation, everyone knows this,' he draws his thumb and forefinger across his lips in a zipping motion, 'and no-one speaks. You can get up to four years in prison for one comment. It is just like the Soviet Union or East Germany in the 1960s – everyone is afraid.'

'What do you think will happen when Castro dies?' I ask.

He shrugs. 'Raúl will take over – he is the military man and was always the successor. But he is old now too. So who knows, maybe things will change when they are both dead. They say Raúl is involved with communists across Latin America, that he's involved with drug cartels too, but I can't say if any of that is true or no.' He pauses. 'There was only ever room for the Castro brothers – Che was a foreigner so he didn't really count; Camilo was too popular, he smiled too much and he disappeared.' He grins unpleasantly. 'Have you ever noticed how people around them just die, while they go on and on?'

I tell Rodrigo how many foreigners see Cuba, how Michael and Pebbles see it, filled with happy, dancing, rum-drinking people. His lip curls.

'Prisoners dance, caged birds sing. We are very good at making the best of what we have. Russians sing and drink to forget. Cubans sing and dance – we also drink of course. Why do you think rum is so much cheaper than cooking oil?'

'But there are people out there in the world who really think Cuba is a kind of Utopia of the poor,' I say. 'Everyone wants to believe that there is somewhere in the world where it's possible to be poor and happy.'

He looks at me for a moment, surprise clear on his face. 'Why would people want to believe that?' He stands up, cracking the bones in his hands. 'And even if it were true, even if there were such a place, it isn't here, it isn't in Cuba.'

At half past one in the *madrugada* I get into bed and write up my conversation with Rodrigo. At a quarter past two there's a great knocking at the door and without thinking I hide my notes under the bed. But it's not the tourist police looking for illegally occupied rooms, only a fat Cuban-American couple in baseball caps and too much gold jewellery, staggering back to their rooms after a night of rum and dancing.

★

Los Cantos de los Hombres

Sobrevivientes somos
y aún nos aterra la aparición
el misterio que nos habita.
Puedo prescindir del equilibrio
de un falsa cuerda,
No me entusiasma el juego
porque mi ojo es de cristal
y un país es todo cuanto refleja.

Aristides Vega Chapú, from 'Hora Final', *El riesgo de la sabiduría,*

The road to Topes de Collantes rises steeply through a close, grey green landscape of small pastures and lumps of rock. The air is already cooler than in Trinidad – cooler and damper as we enter the rainforest zone. A backward glance shows the curving line of Trinidad's coast and the limb of Ancón, reaching along the shore like a hand tossing a pebble.

Approaching Topes, the quiet, pastoral atmosphere is disturbed by dozens of men and women in red tracksuits jogging towards us like a swarm of plump, angry ants.

'Who are they?' I ask the taxi driver.

'Army,' he replies, 'mostly high-ups and their families.' He grins. His name is Pedro and he has a picture of the Virgén de la Regla and his blonde baby daughter on the dashboard. 'They come here to Topes to get fit and lose weight, because they eat too much and work too little.'

'But where do they all stay?'

'Up there . . . you will see.'

With its strangely modern buildings nestling between slender dark pines, Topes reminds me of Twin Peaks. The sense of surrealism gets stronger as we approach the tourist cabins above the village. Then we turn a corner and I'm staring up a long, sloping road at the largest building I've seen since leaving Havana.

The Kurhotel is open to those who can afford it and to the army, trade unionists, certain students and government personnel who can all avail themselves of the spa's treatment regime and communist package holiday.

The spa dominates Topes – its architecture pure Eastern bloc grown rampant in the humid fastness of the Sierra Escambray. Somewhere in all that mass of brick and concrete, Pedro says, there's a helipad for the transport of flabby dignitaries. The architecture reminds me of the Hotel Nacional in Havana, so I'm not surprised to learn that it was the brainchild of Batista who opened it as a TB sanatorium in 1954. The style is not Eastern bloc at all, but Mafia. It's becoming hard to tell the difference.

While Pedro drinks coffee with his aunt, who runs a little refreshment stall for hikers, I walk through the most beautiful countryside I've seen in Cuba. The distant view is of a lush, jade valley and mossy forest canopy. Far below I can hear the rush of the Rio Caburní as it flows east and south from its source in these mountains, to the Valle de los Ingenios where it once powered some of the region's early sugar-mills. Giant stalactites droop like elephants' trunks from the surrounding crags and fresh water drips off the tiny, perfect ferns sprouting from smaller rock formations. Lichens clamber over the sandstone cliff that rises above me, and below vast tree ferns open, umbrella-like, over coffee bushes and lianas hung with yellow and red blooms. Aerial orchids cling to branches and trunks, pretty parasites that will eventually kill their hosts, as the grey, strangled trees scattered among the living testify.

Sandy soil turns to mud as the path drops steeply and pieces of limestone and white quartz glisten underfoot. Ants carry leaf fragments many times bigger than their own bodies in a busy line from who-knows-where to who-knows-where and a troop of wild pigs forage for fallen fruit, crashing and grunting through the undergrowth. The place is alive with bird sound, and the sense of being alone in a vibrant forest world is powerful, particularly after days of enforced rest. A tocororo, Cuba's national bird, opens its wings and displays the red, white and blue of the Cuban flag, but then I'm startled by something flashing past me and hovering, wings whirring too fast for the human eye. I know what it is and laugh with delight as the zunzuncito perches and stares at me. I'm looking back at a bee hummingbird, the world's smallest avian, no longer than my thumb and almost spherical as it fluffs its iridescent green blue body on a branch just above my head. I cough and it's gone, darting too quickly for my eyes to follow.

It is journeys like this one from Trinidad to Santa Clara that remind me of what it is I most enjoy about travelling – movement, the actual physical motion from one place to another, the constantly changing view. Arrival is almost always less pleasurable than the getting there, but today, surrounded by beauty and blue sky, there's nowhere else I want to be.

Fields of young tobacco, tender and emerald green, slope away from the road towards tall, triangular drying houses. Humped-back cattle tethered by the nose sit in water-filled ditches. Bright yellow chicks roam freely alongside horses, dogs and goats. Open ground quickly gives way to dense vegetation. Orange flowers with black hearts smother the roadside hedges and flamboyant trees, imported from the Far East, send their flame-coloured foliage into the sky. Under the big-bellied palms, banana plants and women are almost concealed by hanging vines. The *campesinas* sit under coffee bushes looking for fallen fruit in the dirt. *Vaqueros* clatter past, square machete scabbards bouncing against their thighs. Men and women walk together down long, empty roads in apparently uninhabited countryside, babies on their backs and the ubiquitous cloth bundles under their arms. One red-cheeked couple hold hands smiling: they look young, healthy, happy and I remember Juan Pérez telling me proudly how, forty years ago, he taught people like these to read.

Che Guevara and his men approached Santa Clara through the Sierra Escambray. The parents or grandparents of these *campesinos* might have provided food for the rebels, or joined their surge towards victory. I am following Che's footsteps with a sense of retrospection, towards his greatest hour and his final resting place.

By Cuban standards, Santa Clara is a modern town. Settled in 1689 its birth, like that of Camagüey, was the result of upheaval. Pirate attacks on the coastal town of Remedios exhausted the inhabitants until many fled to start a new life inland, close to the former Indian settlement of Cubanacán. Cubanacán is long gone, but the name still echoes as the place Christopher Columbus believed – in a remarkable illustration of wishful thinking – to be Cubana Khan, capital of the lords of Mongolia.

Land-bound and without the artifice of towns dedicated to tourism, Santa Clara reminds me of Camagüey, though it lacks that town's older colonial architecture and intimate streets. It also reminds me of provincial towns in Middle England – small towns minding their own business. Despite its Che Guevara connections, Santa Clara is mostly a place foreigners ignore or pass through on their way to somewhere else.

My ninth-floor hotel room gives a view of Parque Vidal; a clean, late colonial square with a circular heart of faded grass, palms, shrubs and a white bandstand. Schoolchildren run and roller-skate around the broad moon of pavement where, in colonial times, black and white strolled, separated by a fence. Elderly men chat on the many red benches around the park. Enrico Caruso's voice once echoed here when he sang at the nearby Teatro La Caridad. These days Santa Clara must be satisfied with its own municipal band; which a notice in the hotel lobby informs me is playing tonight in the bandstand.

It's dusk when I cross Parque Vidal to the sound of the theme from *Star Wars*. The band, which is exclusively wind instruments with a lot of Latin brass, has a wide repertoire of Hollywood film music. The musicians are old, young, black and white. There are even one or two women, including the lead flautist, a black woman with scarlet Afro hair. The square is full of people listening with interest and attention and there's something quite moving about the ingenuous playing of this pseudo-epic music: the sound of the enemy, of the 'beast across the water'. Black and white people listen side-by-side, boys and girls hold hands and sometimes kiss. An old mulatto man with flapping shoes listens and applauds with care and discrimination to something he clearly feels a part of. No-one rejects him or turns away from the overwhelming stench of dirt and urine. Perhaps this is that Utopia of the poor, that ideal of Cuba so many Westerners carry in their hearts like a prayer. But the elderly man looks hungry – he's certainly unwashed and possibly homeless – and though no-one objects to him, no-one talks to him either. Watching the band, the audience and the applause, my awareness of bread-and-circuses wars with a very real sense of inclusivity.

Back in my room I turn on the television hoping for 'La Fuerza del Deseo' but find only a Colombian music channel. A brass blonde divette is thrusting her hips while smelling her exposed armpits in that peculiarly Latin movement perfected by Ricky Martin and members of the Iglesias family. This spectacle is interrupted by the funeral of Alberto Vasquez, one of the youths who died falling from a British Airways plane the previous month. A young woman is giving a hectoring speech to a large crowd about *el imperialismo yanqui* and the *farsa* of Vasquez' death because he wanted the *yanqui* way of life. A long catalogue of U.S. sins, some forty years old, follows. I time the list of blame, the *culpables,* that the speaker hurls into the grief-stricken air – seven minutes and thirty-five seconds. The speech winds up with a shouted inventory of Cuba's medical, humanitarian, anti-racist and women's rights work underway around the world despite *la guerra de imperialismo*. The Vasquez family look poor, defeated and like they don't give a shit about imperialism or any other 'ism'. They've lost their son, a promising young military cadet, one of the cream of Cuba's youth. But no-one mentions how easily seduced from career and duty the young man was and why that might have been. Alberto Vasquez was no-one until he fell to his death over west London and I stare, fascinated, as his cortege, complete with outriders, enters Colón cemetery, resting place of writers, artists and stellar revolutionaries. I'm beginning to see why Castro has lasted so long – I've never seen a defeat turned so skilfully to victory.

★

The homeopathic pharmacy has no homeopathic medicines and the pharmacist is out so I can't buy any standard cough medication either. Leaving the building I walk into a man carrying a long cardboard tube who attempts to draw me into conversation. Tired and worn down by relentless coughing my immediate reaction is to apologise and keep on walking, but something different about the man makes me pause and respond rather than ignore him. He walks beside me, talking incessantly and smiling anxiously.

'I'm an artist,' he says, waving the cardboard tube in the air. 'These are some of my paintings, I am trying to sell them.'

He's very thin and seems consumed with nervous energy, his eyes over-bright and much older than the rest of his face. He asks what I'm doing here in Santa Clara and when I say I'm a writer his whole manner changes, the smile leaves his face and he talks even faster, his English clear but febrile.

'I understand Cuba from the high to the low. Let me tell you about the things I know. One day,' he adds breathlessly, 'I would like to write about my own life here.'

We eat in a stand-up peso place. He says he's not hungry but his breath tells me that is untrue and I can't eat with a hungry man watching me. He swallows a few mouthfuls of yam and cabbage and then takes the meat, which I didn't order and didn't want, puts it into his own food carton and lays it at the bottom of his bag.

'For my girlfriend and my baby,' he says. 'They never have meat and babies need it to grow.'

His shoes are in tatters and he tells me that his white jeans and orange T-shirt are the only clothes he possesses. He repeats this at least four or five times in fifteen minutes until I begin to wonder whether he is suffering from much more than mere nervous anxiety and is maybe seriously ill or on drugs. When we sit on one of the red benches in Parque Vidal he relaxes a little and tells me he has a degree and postgraduate qualification in computing.

'The government wants me to work in some IT job for ten dollars a month and I refuse. Of course I refuse, I have no choice . . . I cannot feed my family with ten dollars a month and the authorities know that and humiliate me by expecting me to do what they know I cannot.' He pauses, rage flashing briefly across his face. 'I hate Cuba, I hate it because I feel I was born in the wrong place. I hate the weather, the people, I have no friends because friends cost money here. I can't afford to live with my girlfriend and my baby because I cannot support them. If I leave this country I will lose them, if I stay I will lose them because I cannot afford to keep them. I have told her to find another man who will look after her and my daughter. These are cruel choices, no?'

I nod uncertainly. 'So how do you keep yourself?'

He shrugs. 'For many years I lived by travelling from here to Varadero, selling things to tourists – paintings, cigars. It is illegal of course and the police have stopped me many times. They ordered me to leave Varadero and never come back. There are places Cubans are not allowed to go – we are not allowed to do business with you or even to walk in the street with you in Varadero. Here it is not a problem, but in a tourist place . . . we could not sit and talk together like this without the police appearing.'

'Why is that?'

'They don't want Cuban people to mix with foreigners, they don't want us to trouble you, or steal from you, or tell you the problems of our lives. My father was an architect, he designed one of the biggest hotels near Trinidad, but he is never allowed to go to this hotel as a guest because he is Cuban. He cannot go where he wants in his *own country* – places he created and built himself. We are all humiliated.'

Seeing the look of surprise on my face he says, 'I can tell that you have not visited these resorts.' He grins wolfishly. 'Now I believe that you are a writer.'

He carries pictures of his girlfriend and baby – a close-up of the baby's mouth pressed to a large, milky breast. His story seems a little too neat; everything except the agitation which is very real. Maybe it's just the way he tells it. He denies drugs and doesn't even finish the beer I buy him. I look at his arms for track marks, but there's nothing – only repetitive, self-obsessed ranting, and I feel a flash of discomfort assuming that political and social repression would be insufficient cause for his behaviour.

I'd planned to spend the afternoon visiting the monument to Che Guevara. Learning this, Erich offers to take me there, but the thought of his relentless complaining following me for the rest of the day is more than I can bear. 'Thank you,' I say, 'but this is something I want to do alone.' But I know, even as I say this, that our conversation is unfinished.

The Plaza de la Revolución is a rallying point lined with loudspeakers and big stadium lighting; there are few people here today and the space in front of the towering statue of Che is mostly empty. Music plays softly from the massive speakers followed by the eerie sound of Guevara's voice echoing through the air. I told Erich the truth when I said I wanted to come alone. There's an almost pilgrimage feel to the experience of being here, at *the* shrine of one of the twentieth century's most enduring icons.

Erected in 1987, the statue marks the twentieth anniversary of his death, showing Che in combat fatigues, weapon in hand. It's a fairly standard piece of communist imagery, but its scale against the backdrop of brilliant Cuban sky is affecting, as is the inscription of his last letter to Castro on a nearby slab, which concludes '*Hasta la victoria siempre*'. Ever onward to victory. It sounds trite now, but I try to hear the slogan as it would have been heard in the sixties, without the intervening years of cynicism and growing materialism to deafen me.

The statue stands on high ground dominating everything; it is a symbol of revolution and idealism, of change bought with violence, of a life of action. Looking up at this icon of masculinity I remember a few throwaway Chatwin lines from *In Patagonia*. 'On my right was a lady novelist. . . Some years ago she knew Ernesto

Guevara, at that time an untidy young man pushing for a place in society. "He was very *macho*," she said, "like most Argentine boys, but I never thought it would come to *that*.'" Underground beneath the statue is the result of '*that*' – the physical remains of Ernesto 'Che' Guevara and sixteen of the thirty-eight revolutionaries who died with him in Bolivia in 1967.

Cubans, Bolivians and Peruvians are buried together in the simple underground chamber. It's quiet and peaceful, a place of wood and pale, honey-coloured stone. The bones of the dead lie in individual niches each sealed with a name and a carved portrait of the dead person. Every image has something individual about it, as if the stonecutter truly wanted the dead to be remembered as people, not just revolutionaries. There's one woman here – Tania, Tamara Bunke – a thirty-year-old German Argentine killed, along with other guerrillas who lie here beside her, in a Bolivian ambush on 31 August 1967, a week before Che's capture. With so many friends and comrades lost, Che, the consummate commander, must have known then that it was hopeless, that it would be sui-cide in the tradition of Martí. His niche in this tomb is distin-guished from the others only by being slightly raised from the wall and having a softly focused white star shining on its stone.

Tourists arrive by the coach load in Santa Clara only to disap-pear again after an hour with Che. There are quite a few foreigners in the Museo Memorial and together we stand in silence and watch the man himself on a grainy black-and-white film that plays on a loop in the museum's entrance. I realise I have never seen him move, never seen that face and heard the voice together until this moment. Like most people outside Cuba, my vision of Che is of the iconic Korda photograph taken at a funeral rally in March 1960: there's a slight frown as his eyes fix on some invisible horizon above the heads of the mourners. It's strange, almost sacrilegious, to see that image brought to life. I don't think I ever imagined Ernesto Guevara as a real person, and though this black-and-white film is far from 'real', it's the nearest I'll ever get.

Like many icons, Guevara seems uncomfortable in the public eye, moving stiffly across the screen, a cigar too often between his lips for a chronic asthmatic. His voice is slightly grating, perhaps it's his Argentine accent, and there's little of the ease and confidence that Castro exudes in front of the camera. Che speaks carefully, as if he has difficulty adequately expressing all that he wishes to say. In this too he is unlike the young Castro who seems quite unable to rein in his flow of self- expression. There are school certificates, notes in childish writing signed 'Ernestito' and pictures of him as a rugby fanatic. The images trace his life from cosseted, middle-class youth to medical student and motorbike traveller. There are the photos he took on the two long bike journeys through Latin America that marked the start of a much longer adventure on the road of revolutionary idealism. There are photos of Che on horseback, in a GI helmet, beside Camilo Cienfuegos with whom, the accompanying text declares, he had a very special understanding, a very special *amistaḍ.*

Despite seeing his dental equipment in a glass case I find it hard to imagine this man as a doctor. More bizarrely, I find it hard to imagine him as a man of action in spite of the many images to the contrary. For me there is an ambiguity about him, an almost Hamlet-like quality that seems to stretch him between thought and motion. What comes across most strongly is a life of the intellect, of ideas translated with great difficulty into action – this was literally true, as photographs of him recovering from asthma during the Sierra Maestra campaign illustrate. There is of course a copy of 'that' picture and beside it a glass case containing 'that' jacket. The jacket, a kind of green imitation leather with black stretch fabric at the neck and cuffs, looks surprisingly modern and smaller than I imagined. The label says 'Havana' and looking at it I think how difficult it would be to find such a fashionable, well-made garment anywhere in Cuba today.

After the Triumph of the Revolution Guevara gets plump fast, despite the well-recorded physical work and 'shared struggle' ethos, another point of departure from the comfort-loving Castro. In the last photograph taken of him in Cuba, Che is unrecognisable, having disguised himself for his journey to Bolivia by shaving his beard and most of his head. He wears thick glasses, a Mafia-style

LOS CANTOS DE LOS HOMBRES

suit and trilby. He looks utterly, unimaginably different and rather repellent. The beautiful man of Korda's image has disappeared and been replaced by a pasty, bug-eyed creature. I look for the intent, charismatic face and cannot find it.

On the wall of my study in London hangs a photograph of Che taken a few hours after his murder on the orders of the Bolivian government with the connivance of the CIA. The British photographer, Brian Moser, who photographed the body at Vallegrande on 9 October 1967 shortly after it arrived from La Higuera lashed to the skids of helicopter, described the scene:

> These pictures, taken as his corpse was laid out on the concrete washbasin of the hospital, show him before he was cleaned up ready for presentation to the world's press the following day. His body was covered in blood and all the bullet wounds in his legs, stomach, chest and neck were clearly visible. He had been wounded in the legs on October 8th, then summarily executed just after 1pm on the 9th. Two Bolivian doctors, accompanied by a CIA agent, inserted a plastic tube into his neck to conduct the formalin into his body to preserve it prior to secret burial at the side of Vallegrande airstrip.

When I look up from my desk I see the man of Korda's photograph again. The weight is gone, the beard and long, curling hair are back. He looks young again in death, only blood and gloved fingers grasping an artery in a neck wound with forceps, indicate that he is not sleeping.

Erich is waiting for me on a red bench. He seems, if anything, even more agitated than at our earlier meeting. I wonder if it's cocaine, but he says he hasn't slept well for years because of anxiety. He asks me again if I would like to buy his paintings for five dollars as he needs money to get a German visa and if he doesn't get one soon his ticket will expire. He has a passport and a ticket to Düsseldorf which he shows me, seeming very anxious that I believe him. He says he is desperate to escape from Cuba any way he can. The ticket was given to him by two German friends, gay men living in Düsseldorf – men from the former East Germany who understand his situation and his desire to escape and who have helped him for that reason. Knowing he's a *jinetero,* or at least a con artist of some kind, I neither believe nor disbelieve his story. I doubt if the paintings he offers me are even his own, he seems to think so poorly of them. I don't entirely like him, but he's unique in my experience of Cuba and I stay and listen mostly from fascination: if he's a con man, he's the very best I've ever met – anywhere. I try to catch him out, ask questions in different ways and from different angles but his answers are always the same. He seems more desperate to be believed than to be helped and says repeatedly that he never takes anything without giving something in return, even if its only information or advice.

'I have never been to Varadero,' I say. 'Tell me about it.'

'I spent years on the streets of Varadero, many of them sick, cold and hungry. I told you that I was often stopped by the police – the last time they took my paintings and my money. I have a caution against my name now. One more caution and I get four years in prison. I hate Varadero and I hate the tourists who go there.' He pauses, lips pressed hard together, then whispers, 'I lost everything there, my dignity, my pride and I have much pride . . .' he looks away from me as he says this, his eyes unnaturally bright.

I consider all the things he might have done: lying, stealing, cheating, screwing elderly foreigners for pitiful sums of money, and for his sake I say, 'Don't tell me . . .' though I'm eager to know.

But he wants to tell me and instead of words he shows me his arm and the pale white line running between his wrist and his elbow. 'I cut myself,' he says slowly.

This is not the answer I was expecting and I must look confused.

'I cut myself,' he repeats, 'for five dollars.'

When I say nothing he continues, 'They were drinking and I said I would do anything and so they asked what would I do, and I said anything, really, anything. And then one German man laughed and asked would I bleed, would I show them my blood. So I did. I took the money and cut myself from there to there . . .' he draws his forefinger along the outline of the scar. 'Not too deep of course, just enough to make a lot of blood.'

I stare, open-mouthed, until he blushes and looks down.

'I know. I am ashamed. I have no pride.'

I realise I'm still staring and it dawns on me that I'm not horrified by what he did, but by someone wanting him to do it. I believe him, for the first time I really believe him. It's surely too bizarre to be invented. Too vile.

His eyes film with water but he blinks and continues, 'I hate telling you my problems and always, always it's about money. I am sorry, but it is my life, what else *can* I tell you.'

'But what about all the things we hear of Cuba, the good things – education, health care – there must be something here you think is good.'

He laughs nastily and opens his mouth to show me the stumps of three teeth. 'There's no free painkilling medication and there is a limit to what I can endure. If I had money these would have been removed without pain.' He closes his mouth and is silent momentarily. 'You ask about education. Education is more than just something you learn from a book. *I* am educated but not in the way that you are, we are not taught to think for ourselves and that is what *real* education is. I try to think for myself and look where I am. I'm a fighter and a hard worker but none of those things matter here, in fact they make problems for me. I just want to use my brain and get paid for what I do – is that wrong?'

I wonder if it's possible to blush on demand, whether tears can be called up as required. Erich is a clever man but whether it's intelligence or low cunning I still can't decide. It's all too much, yet it fits with what others have said, others whose honesty I never questioned. He offers me the pictures again – two large canvases with bright slashes of thick colour depicting a cockerel and something surreal I don't recognise – and says he wants five dollars for both. Five dollars towards his visa to Germany? Or five dollars for cocaine, or to repay some crushing debt?

Somehow it doesn't matter. I offer him twenty-five dollars, the amount he says he needs for his visa. His shock is unfakeable.

'No,' he says. 'They aren't worth even five and I can tell you don't like them.'

'I think they're worth twenty-five.' I'm getting good value regardless of who painted them. In London the materials alone would cost twice that and I really like the cockerel picture; it has genuine energy and inventiveness.

'Tourists usually want both for one dollar.' He starts to smile as if suddenly remembering what I've just offered him and then he beams. I wonder if he's happy because he has what he needs for a new life. I pause before handing him the money, but the truth is I don't really care what he wants it for – even if everything he has told me is a pack of lies. I'm being offered the chance to feel that for a very small sum of money I've contributed to a very big change in a man's circumstances, and there's something strangely irresistible about that.

He hands over the pictures, takes the money and jumps up. 'I'm going to call my mother and my girlfriend now but I will see you later, here on this bench.'

I watch him walk away to the public telephones on the other side of the square and wonder if he's calling his dealer. Are there such things as dealers in Cuba? Perhaps Pebbles was right and I am cynical.

Parting he'd said, 'Africans are poorer than Cubans, much poorer in every way, but they can leave, go to another country. But this is an island and we are prisoners, prisoners of the system, of the ocean. I am thirty-one, but in ten years time my life will be over. I want to live now.'

Watching him speak into the phone I wonder if he has any real idea of what African poverty is like, whether he knows what Europe is like – the stress and endless effort. But what do I know of his stress, his effort?

He did not make our meeting that evening. I was not surprised.

★

I've got used to sitting on toilets without seats, light switches in the shower cubicle and electrocuting showerheads fixed directly above projecting taps that don't work. I haven't got used to the absence of real food and realise that maybe I never could. With luck I'll probably never have to. Looking at the puffy, faded faces in the pizza place that calls itself an Italian restaurant, I wonder how many of these customers are old enough to remember real food and how it tastes. It's cold outside, and raining again, but the restaurant's air conditioning is turned right up, making the full-length net curtains flutter. A keyboard player starts playing 'New York, New York' accompanied by a drummer using a brush like an egg whisk. I'm alone at one end of a rectangular table until a waiter shows a youngish man to the other end. We sit in silence like a Victorian couple, both coughing and sneezing. He consumes soup, then spaghetti and orders two pizzas. When my small, solitary pizza arrives I poke it, looking for the ham, then realise it's not mine but his. Like Victorians, we needed an excuse to speak and the pizza does well enough.

We discover that we are both writers and of a similar age. We even look somewhat alike, fleshy and with dark, curly hair. He tells me his name is Aristides, that he writes poetry, that his first novel is about to be published in Costa Rica.

'Why in Costa Rica?' I ask.

'Because you can't publish novels here, not anti-authority ones anyway.' He asks if I've met any other Cuban writers and I mention Enrique Cirules in Havana. He snorts dismissively.

'Cirules is like this . . .' he crosses his first and second fingers, 'with the army and the government. It *is* possible to be a writer here and to be honest,' he says, shaking his head, 'but it's hard to live. Most of the money for my novel will go to the Cuban government for permission to publish abroad. Only a very little comes to me.'

He looks tired, his face is unshaven, hair unkempt, teeth caried, but he has real charm as he speaks and I guess that his softness of body is counterbalanced by a sharp directness of mind. He asks if I know any communists. The question feels strange, particularly here in Cuba, but I say I'm not sure; one or two expats in Havana, maybe one person in London. I realise as I speak that I'm not even certain what the word means any more; it ceased to have real meaning ten years ago when the Soviet Union imploded, but the political, though not the economic, implications of that seem to have passed Cuba by.

He pays for my pizzas. I consider refusing to accept this but then say nothing. He pays for coffee in a bar despite me claiming my turn. Passing a bookshop, he darts in and buys me a copy of his poems.

'Do you have plans for today?' he asks as we shelter in a doorway from the rain, his book inside my jacket.

'To see the armoured train, that's all. Is it far?'

He shakes his head. 'I will show you if you would like me to.'

We walk together under my small umbrella to the site where an armoured troop-carrying train was derailed and captured by Che's men during the Battle for Santa Clara in December 1958. Batista had sent more than 10,000 troops to Santa Clara to block the westward advance of the rebels using armoured trains for transportation. In a brief hour-and-a-half skirmish, fewer than twenty rebels overcame more than 350 heavily armed but disheartened government troops and seized the town. In a prophetic expression of conflicts yet to come, Batista used American and British bombers to attack those parts of Santa Clara where the rebel forces were located, but succeeded in killing only civilians.

'They say it was a great victory,' Aristides says, 'and maybe it was, politically. But my father was there. He watched it and says it was all much quieter than they make out now.'

The site is surprisingly small, a few carriages painted red-brown set among trees and paving stones beside a work of modern sculpture that could be anything The tractor used to tear up the rails is mounted on a podium and in one of the carriages, now a museum, is the wrench used to upend the track. I have a vision of the Wild West, of Butch Cassidy and Billy the Kid. Perhaps that's who Guevara was after all, a brilliant outlaw. Standing in front of a photograph of Che I ask Aristides what he thinks of him.

'He was a man,' he says, 'an interesting human being, an ideologue, an adventurer. But he couldn't last, not here, and I think nothing has turned out as he hoped. That's the trouble with adventures.' He points surreptitiously to the uniformed guard standing under a bush on open-air museum duty and presses a finger to his lips.

'Cuba has changed a great deal, even since five years ago,' he says as we walk through streets of terrace houses back to the town centre. 'My daughter had no toys until I went to Argentina and Costa Rica for a few months with my work. She was eight then, and when I gave them to her she was so very, very happy.' He ducks suddenly and makes a grab at my bag. Seeing my surprise he looks serious. 'That's what it was like then, you could not walk in the street and be safe. Foreigners were the particular target of thieves. People robbed just to be able to live. I had no food, no clothes, no soap. It was wash or eat, walk or dress.'

'Why do you think that happened?' I ask, thinking he will blame the collapse of the Eastern bloc. Instead he shrugs and says, 'Ask Castro, or, better still, ask your foreign communist friends in Havana.'

'I will,' I say and laugh.

He looks at me for a moment then smiles broadly. 'You're the first British person I've met – I always thought the British were very serious, but you're not at all like I expected.'

'Oh I'm very serious,' I say, 'serious and funny, sometimes at the same time.'

'Me too. I think we have much in common – our jobs, Greek names, bronchitis.'

It's still raining when we reach Parque Vidal so I buy beer in a tiled bar that sells chicken, chocolate and fries and smells strongly of stale fat. I ask what kind of chocolate he likes but he shrugs noncommittally and I buy the dark, bitter kind. We sit in a littered courtyard at plastic tables and talk about his eleven-year-old daughter Salma, about his Lebanese grandfather, and his parents with whom he lives less than 100 metres from my hotel. We drink the beer and I open the chocolate, take a square and push the rest towards him. He's very quiet and glancing up I notice a small muscle twitching in his cheek.

'Can I make a confession? Is that the same as in English, *confesión*?'

I nod, wondering, after my experience with Erich, what I'm about to hear.

To my surprise his eyes fill but he smiles, and says, 'I have never eaten real chocolate before.' A tear runs down his face before he can brush it away.

I don't know what to say and just press one of his hands, unsure whether he is happy to have real, by which I understand 'foreign', chocolate at last, sad because he has never had it before, or both. Why has he never had this chocolate before? Then I remember what he told me about choices – wash or eat, walk or dress.

'You have many poor in England I think. Have your poor tasted chocolate?'

The question stuns me momentarily as an abyss of priorities yawns before me. 'Yes,' I say eventually. 'Our poor have chocolate . . . it's different in England, there the poor have no homes or maybe no beds. It's just a difference of scale. I don't think the English poor are any happier than the Cuban poor, probably the opposite – in England everyone knows what they don't have, but at least everyone has chocolate.'

That evening I visit Aristides' home and meet his parents and his daughter. His father is still handsome with vivid leaf green eyes, his mother looks frail but wears pink lipstick and a brooch at the neck of her long housecoat. I feel an effort has been made because I'm a visitor, and there's something touching about that. The house is filled with paintings and works of art and craft – the house of educated, middle-class people. The small room Aristides shares with his daughter is lined with books, many of them religious. When his wife, a clinical psychologist in a remote rural hospital, is able to come home all three sleep here.

I talk with his parents and Aristides disappears and returns holding a large envelope in one hand. He spreads half a dozen small ink sketches in front of me and offers me a choice. I choose a bespectacled man sitting at the table, a glass of rum in one hand. The sketch is in blue ink over the wrapping of an old cigarillo packet – *Popular*, the label states boldly, *superfinos negros*.

'Thank you,' I say, 'I will treasure it. You know, this is my only Cuban gift.'

He smiles lopsidedly. 'I am fortunate in having something to give you.'

In three hours' time I will be leaving on the *madrugada* bus for Havana and the west of Cuba. I spend this time walking and talking in the wet, black and silver streets of Santa Clara with a man whose soft, relaxing voice drains away a little of the tiredness that's setting in.

'*Mira*, Soay,' he says and I barely recognise my name. 'See, this square is full of people looking as if something important is about to happen, but all they do is stand and of course, nothing happens. Nothing could.'

Young people kiss and are openly sexual, undeterred by rain and company. Remembering Cecilia Vaux' words I ask about this.

'Mostly people want physical relationships, they meet and make love in the streets and then they part. Cubans are afraid of relationships, afraid of love . . . it is too complicated to make a relationship. It's easier to say "I am me over here with my problems and my life, and you are you over there with yours." Many people live together only for sex. They do not share other parts of their lives, that would be too risky.'

We part outside my hotel and he tells me how much meeting me has meant for him, and not only because of the chocolate. When we hug goodbye I know that he is one of the few people I have met here with whom I will keep in touch, and who – one day, when everything is different – I would like to meet again. My only regret is that my Spanish wasn't good enough to understand all he needed to say. Despite his patience, I sensed his sad frustration at having a foreign writer to communicate with and knowing the communication could be only partial.

When my bag is packed, I look for the last time over the rain-drenched heart of Santa Clara. One hand holds a book of poetry entitled *El riesgo de la sabiduría – The Danger of Knowledge –* the other a dictionary. Moving from one to the other I can hear the poet's voice reading to me above the sound of salsa music, among chicken bones and empty beer cans in a café with white plastic tables:

> No me entusiasma el juego
> porque mi ojo es de cristal
> y un país es todo cuanto refleja.

> I have no enthusiasm for the game
> because my eyes are crystal
> and a country is all they can reflect.

WEST

★

Viñales

The one time I get to travel on public transport in daylight there's a distraction. The video playing on the bus is a kind of hallucinatory soap opera about the lives of several *habaneros* on the Feast of Changó/Saint Barbara, a fateful day. There's a middle-aged woman who gave up her child twenty years earlier and is now in psychotherapy because she faints every time she hears the word 'sex'; a psychologist who loses his job helping the same woman; a ballerina who has to choose between dance, love and God; a musician whose long-absent mother is called Cuba and who wanted him to be the perfect New Man. Torn between watching the artifice of these characters' lives and traumas on the small television hanging above the bus driver's head, or looking at the very real countryside passing me by, I shift restlessly in my comfortable seat.

The film director has used Havana cityscapes to dazzling, if unrealistic effect. This is not the Havana I've just left for the second time, but a glamorous, sharp-edged place where grown men spend whole days watching snails crawl on the sea wall of the Malecón and beautiful dancers prefer God and chastity to sex with godlike young men. The bus speeds south and west while the muscular, mustachioed musician rails at the Santería statue of his mother, Cuba, and a white-haired, real-life man cuts the grass at the roadside with a pair of brass-handled machetes. The old man bends from the waist, flicking his wrists so rapidly that the only thing clearly visible is the grass flying up from between the slicing blades.

It's 200 kilometres from Havana to the small town of Viñales in Pinar del Río province. Between the capital and the provincial border the land is a flattish region of yellowing grass and cows.

Low, scrubby bushes shiver beside small pools that feed into glassy, rectangular ponds that might contain anything from breeding fish to rice shoots or a submersible weapon. A small river runs alongside the road, shallow and stony in this landscape of dust and water. After half an hour the beginnings of tobacco appear, emerald and vivid beside the red tractor ploughing through red earth, furrows broken by straggling lines of white tick-birds. Desiccating leaves, in too many shades of brown to count, hang like animal skins or parchment on low racks at the edge of tobacco fields, and the high, pointed roofs of the drying sheds give space and air to the precious crop.

We enter Pinar del Río province near San Cristóbal, but I barely notice because the macho musician has got a *gringa* girl-friend and they are making out in front of the Santería shrine in his lush, plant-filled garden. As the film unfolds on the small, distant screen I realise, surprised, that 'Life is to Whistle' is a comment on the state of the nation wrapped in a form of magical realism. But the text is unambiguous. The musician was rejected by his mother, Cuba, when she realised he would not be her idea of a New (Che-like) Man; the ballerina has made vows that bring success but leave her without human love. The middle-aged woman cannot forgive herself for surrendering her child to the State; her psychologist attempts to cure her by running into the street shouting words like 'falsehood' and 'hypocrisy' until there's no-one left standing – all faint when confronted with words they don't want to hear. The psychologist undertakes this cure, knowing it will cost him his career. The metaphor is plain enough. Much later I learn that the director has been having a few difficulties with *his* career and hasn't been seen outside of Cuba recently. Perhaps the metaphor was too plain.

Pinar del Río is a small, pleasant city – hardly even a city – whose main streets give tantalising glimpses of exotic buildings set among the usual pastel-painted houses. Under long pillared porticoes, the enterprising sell pizzas and *bocadillos* from glass cabinets, beside cobblers seated in a sea of shoes. It looks like every other Cuban town, yet there is that small something that begs you to notice it, wants your rapidly passing eye to see its uniqueness. Children stare up at the luxurious bus with its television, curtains and on-board toilet. Some wave, the rest just stare as if looking at a meteorite passing overhead.

After Pinar del Río the land changes yet again, becoming suddenly more productive, more cultivated, as if belonging to different people. Vegetables appear as if by magic and the viridian of tobacco is everywhere, its soft, rabbit-eared leaves maturing in the sun. Then we are rising up and up into the mountains on steeply twisting roads through forests of mixed palm and pine until we can look down before and behind into tobacco-filled valleys that sweep, green on red, from hillside to horizon. In a roadside garden, a seated woman plays with her baby in the sun, rocking the child over her knees and laughing as its head hangs backwards almost to her ankles. We pass a row of pretty thatched houses painted in blue, pink and pale yellow, and through an open door I see a wooden bed with a distinctive blue-and-white cover, a glimpse of a spotless, spartan home among a garden of roses.

Higher still, the palms give way to the dark of pines and the grey-green of aerial plants that cling to every telephone wire and hanging vine like living ash. On a flat stone set in the pink earth of the road-side bank someone has carved the words, *Dios te ama*, and I think of Juan and the two leaves handed to me like a benison at his door in Santiago. That seems a long time ago and very far away from here as I look back to Pinar del Río across a floodplain that glints like polished steel under the midday sun. Ahead the mysterious *mogotes* of Viñales are already visible – domes of limestone, swaddled in creeping vegetation, that rise sheer from the valley floor much like the limestone crags of Vietnam's Halong Bay and the Guilin region of China. These pincushion mountains are filled with caves and beneath them seasonal rivers hide in the blackness of karstic caverns waiting for the rains to rise again like liquid souls. But as we start to descend there is nothing of darkness about the land before me. My impression is only of colour: green hills against the bright blue of a cloudless sky and green crops against vivid ochre earth.

★

Viñales is a two-oxen town of around 4000 people; though leisurely it's bustling enough today in the sunshine. A first glance shows a strangely un-Cuban place reminiscent of Raj hill stations. There are well-kept benches along the neatly swept, conifer-lined streets. Brilliant orange creepers hang from railings, telephone wires and houses and white trumpet flowers droop in profusion above neatly manicured grass. There's an air of prosperity though it would be hard to say why. It might simply be that, at only 125 years of age, Viñales is the newest place I've been in Cuba, and something of that almost-modernity hangs in the air.

The handful of foreigners who arrived with me on the bus disappear without trace, as if absorbed. The town of Viñales, hardly more than a village, rapidly resolves itself into a few parallel lines cut by squares: main roads, a central square with church, an art gallery displaying local work, a gallery for foreigners which sells high-quality art, and a few small gift shops selling T-shirts adorned with Che Guevara's face. In the large, empty dining area of a *paladar* that's neither closed nor open because it was too popular, is an elderly piano covered in fake paper money. One bill has a naked Monica Lewinsky pressed against a smiling President Clinton in the place where Washington would normally be.

My *casa particular* has a garden with avocado and mango trees and a gigantic black boar that snuffles happily in its large wooden home beside a muddy wallow. There are mosquitoes even in daylight, but they're slow and heavy and killing them is easy. I sit in the sun as vast, painted butterflies flutter around the hibiscus bushes and gold brown lizards warm themselves on the garden wall. Cary, the owner of the *casa*, places a plate of fresh mango and a glass of home-made lemonade on the table beside me and I watch, soporific, as she pours boiled water into a natural stone basin. The water drips quickly through the stone, catching the light as it falls into the jug beneath. Only in Pinar del Río province, Cary tells me, can such purifying stones be found, where water has worn away the landscape since the Cretaceous era, 100 million years ago.

In the late afternoon I stroll across the road through strutting cockerels to look at the Jardín Botánico de Caridad and its house. The gateway is hung with slices of drying citrus fruits and the decapitated heads of dolls, and through the open front door I glimpse three elderly black women dressed in black woollens staring fixedly at the television, as if possessed. The garden's tall trees are heavy with starfruit, tamarinds, avocadoes and white orchids, and the scent of cinnamon and citrus drifts through the bushes and into the road. Deeper among the trees, more heads and body parts are stuck on spikes and dangle from nooses. It looks like an ancient German oak grove where shamans hung the remains of enemies. Perhaps these are bloodless offerings to the spirit of the place in that same tradition. When I ask, no-one has an answer.

The following day I wander through the small square beside the church. In the gallery of local artwork is a painting that stands out from the other amateur efforts – a surreal image in vivid oranges and greens, a painting of this region focused on a man pinning green clouds across the sky from a ladder supported only by air. The gallery attendant notices me looking at the picture and asks if I would like to meet the artist. Before I can answer she disappears through arched double doors and into the colonial courtyard beyond, returning quickly with a handsome, youngish man in a dusty jacket with frayed cuffs who shakes my hand and seems pleased by my interest in his work.

'My name is Ismael Sidonia and this gallery is meant to stimulate people to make art,' he says. 'Nothing here is for sale, it is only for looking at. But if you would like to see more of my work . . .' he gestures towards the courtyard. 'I am teaching now and I must go back . . . come, I will show you.'

I follow into a dark classroom where sloping desks face each other in a line down the middle of the room. A sketch of José Martí's face is pinned to the blackboard and a group of young boys is learning to draw the proportions of the human face from its five sections. Another man with the same narrow, olive face and black hair as Ismael Sidonia appears from behind a screen.

'This is my brother.' The faces are very alike, though Ismael's hair gleams in long coils around his neck and his brother's is brushed straight and quaffed in a 1950s rockabilly style. These men look Syrian or Lebanese, and I scan their features for resemblances to Aristides. When I ask if they are of Middle Eastern descent they deny it. 'We are from Oriente,' the brother says in strangely clipped English. 'Our family are from Contramaestre. Look . . .' he points to where his brother's paintings lie in a scattered heap. He pulls one out and lays it on the desk before me. With a sense of *déjà vu*, I see again the landscape I drove through with Pieter, the mule train crossing the river far below the bridge on which we travelled, the *vaqueros* in their straw *sombreros*.

'Come,' Ismael says and draws me into the small space behind the blackboard. There's a bunk bed and scattered belongings. The top bunk is covered in paper, sketches and folders. The lower is scattered with personal items including a guitar. Now I understand Ismael's crumpled, dusty appearance, the marks of chalk on his jacket, threads hanging from his shirt. Close up, neither man looks well fed.

'The painting of Viñales in the gallery, is it for sale?' I ask.

The artist shakes his head as the brother says 'maybe'. A long rapid discussion follows and eventually I'm told that if I return that night, when they've had time to remove the painting from the gallery and replace it with another, it will be mine. I feel guilty, as if I've asked to buy a national treasure, and wish I hadn't spoken. The artist looked crestfallen. He doesn't want to sell it, perhaps is anxious at tampering with the gallery's display, but I sense that he loves it and doesn't want to part with it. The brother, who neither paints nor has money, manages us both.

That evening after an excellent dinner of chicken and potato stew, I make my way back through the dark potholed streets, past the bank and the Masonic lodge, past the church where Mass is just ending, and around to the back of the gallery. A door opens and I'm slipped quickly into the classroom once more. The painting looks naked without its frame – cheap acrylic paint on what looks like photographic paper. It's beautiful. I love the humour and the hope of the *campesino* hanging emerald clouds on the vine that crosses the picture from one copper-coloured *mogote* to another. As Ismael Sidonia rolls the painting carefully between an x-ray of his father's lung cancer and a piece of card with the words *Policía, Pinar del Río* on it, I wonder if I am that decadent Westerner Castro warns his people about.

Pepito drives a 1956 Chevrolet with original leather upholstery and a black and chrome body as smooth and shiny as the film stars he watches every Saturday in the local cinema. He's probably a relative of Cary's, my landlady seems to know or be related to everyone who passes her door. I can't imagine such lack of privacy, as no doubt she couldn't imagine my London existence.

Pepito's eyes and hair, which are almost the same colour as his car, gleam in the rear-view mirror as he tells me proudly that he is Viñales' sole projectionist and cinema manager.

'I love films. I love all films, but my favourite are action films – Steven Segal, Claudio Van Damme. These are the films most Cuban people like. But I also enjoy dramas – *Pretty Woman* is the best because Julio Robertas and Richard Gayé are so good.'

'And what about women?' I ask. 'What kind of films do they prefer?'

'The same as me – action, drama. This is the Cuban taste.'

'And what about Cuban films – do you like them?'

'Sure, they're okay, but most people like Hollywood films best. Action, big scenes – that's the great thing about film. I love it. Really, I love it.'

We drive at about forty kilometres per hour through the Valle de Viñales winding around the base of Las Dos Hermanos – The Two Sisters – *mogotes* whose limestone peaks are shrouded in vines and ferns. We turn off the main road and drive even more slowly along a rutted dirt track. Clearly visible among the hills ahead are a group of houses belonging to Los Aquaticos, a community founded in 1943 by Antoñica Izquierdo, a mystic who believed in the healing power of water at a time when locals had little access to conventional medicine. Izquierdo and her followers settled the hillside and, despite her death in a Havana mental institution only a few years after the community was born, at least a dozen families still live there today.

'Many people die up there from lack of medical treatment,' Cary had said to me. 'Children and women giving birth often die because they believe only in water. I think sometimes they die because of the water – my neighbour told me they bathe three times every day and then let the wind dry them . . . even the old people and little babies!' She had sounded almost indignant. 'That can't be right.'

'It's an interesting place, Los Aquaticos,' Pepito says. 'They never come down into the valley, except sometimes maybe for salt or things they cannot grow. But they are clever too,' he grins. 'They must be the only people in all Cuba who live as they want without any government control – no-one looking to see what they do. Okay, some of them die without medicine, but the ones that survive live to be very old. Feliz Rodriguez, the head of the community, is ninety-three years old. I don't think we will live so long despite our doctors.' He slows. 'You want to go there? You will have to walk or take a horse, no cars can get up there.'

Without thinking I shake my head. It occurs to me then that I am tired of histories. I want to see the valley and its colours, touch the tobacco leaves and crumble the earth between my fingers. Los Aquaticos and I can do without each other.

Pepito is worried about his beloved.

'This road is no good for my car,' he says anxiously. 'The suspension is a big problem for old cars on bad roads.'

We stop between a field of *malanga* and a stand of banana plants, many bowed under the weight of unripe fruit or a cochineal red flower shaped like a human heart. Green and red: Viñales is a place of contrasts, from violent cadmium orange to darkest crimson, and the dusty green of epiphytes to the clear emerald of young tobacco. Pepito gets out and, for the fourth time in an hour, lifts the hood of the car and peers into its arcane interior. He doesn't actually do anything, just stares anxiously at what's left of American engineering almost half a century old and shakes his head. In the wide-open spaces between *mogotes,* men are ploughing with oxen harnessed to ancient ploughs. Since fuel rationing, pragmatic Cuba has returned to animal power, to domestic carts and racing traps.

Deciding the car needs a rest, we stop beside a small tobacco sorting plant where Pepito knows the manager, a pleasant young woman in jeans who offers to show me around the place.

After the brilliant colours of the outside world, the high-roofed, echoing building is very brown: the long piles of fermenting tobacco plants, the workers, the packing crates, the chairs and desks, the floor, the walls. Even the sunlight shafting through cracks in the roof and walls is a dusty, glowing sepia.

'This is where we grade and sort the leaves,' the manager says, showing me between desks where twenty or thirty women are tying leaves into bundles. 'We call these "chickens",' she says, handing me a bunch, 'because they look like tail feathers.'

I lift the bundle of tough, papery leaves to my nose and inhale. Nothing at all like the rich scent of cigars or even the acrid perfume of cigarettes. Just an organic plant odour.

'Then we lay all the "chickens" like so.' We move towards a perfect rectangle of tobacco leaves about hip height and five metres long. 'This is sprayed with water very frequently to stop it drying out and to encourage the fermentation of the leaves.' (I never knew that tobacco was fermented.) 'Look,' she lifts up several bundles and thrusts her hand deep into the warm, ammonia-scented interior of the rectangle, encouraging me to do the same. My hand emerges smelling of urine and I wonder if water is all that's sprayed on these leaves. 'We check the temperature at the centre of the pile very frequently,' she says as she waves a vast, threatening thermometer between us like a baton. 'There is an optimum temperature that we must always look for, particularly with these mixed "chickens".' She picks up a bundle again and holds it out to me. 'These, with leaves of different colours, we use to make mild, high-quality cigars like Romeo y Julieta or

Montecristo for export.' In the semidarkness she touches and names each leaf: red, grey red, brown red, brown, grey – where she sees a world of change I see only the slightest variation.

At the far end of the plant, slender black men are standing in large crates lined with dried palm leaves and jumping up and down on the fermented bundles, stamping them down into the crates which are then sealed with more palm and tied with string. Each crate bears the stamp of weight, quality and destination. I see the words *France*, *Holland*, *Italy* marked in English.

'What stays here in Cuba?' I ask.

'Two types,' the manager says, 'one type for local cigarettes, the other for *puros,* the cigars Cubans smoke. Do you smoke? '

I shake my head. She smiles. 'Nor me. It's very bad for the health, no?'

Beside the factory an almost empty general store sells rubber shoes, rope and canvas cloth. It's like the Company Store, except it has too few goods to buy anyone's soul. Three elderly, weather-beaten *vaqueros* are drinking *ron cana* and coffee, their straw hats tipped back on their heads, machetes swinging from their belts. Pepito orders coffee, which comes in green plastic egg cups and smells like ear wax. When I ask one of the men if I can take his photograph he seems delighted to have been singled out, happy to pose outside where the bright sun illuminates the deep, ochre creases of his face and neck. There's a small place below the open collar of his checked shirt where dark, sunburnt skin meets smooth white flesh, a glimpse, of something hidden and delicate.

Returning to Viñales town we pass a school decorated with revolutionary pictures and a gleaming white bust of José Martí, the Cuban flag drooping above him in the cool, windless air. Seen in this idyllic landscape the Revolution, communism, seem realities to be admired, though life is surely no easier or pleasanter here than anywhere else in Cuba, just more picturesque.

'Tell me what these songs mean,' Pepito says, as he presses a tape into a car stereo that certainly wasn't in the '59 Chevy.

The Beatles' 'Yesterday' is relatively easy to translate. Simon and Garfunkel's 'The Sound of Silence' is a different matter

we agree to differ – which is what Europeans are supposed to do. The Belgians seem to accept some of my points on Cuba and I appear to agree with some of their thoughts on the West. We shake hands when it's time for me to head to the bus: large, firm handshakes. Walking fast up Viñales' main street towards the little knot of foreigners waiting to board the bus, I'm aware of feeling quite invigorated. I had no idea that day in late January 2001 how the artist's words would echo less than eight months later. I had thought him a bigot, masquerading as something else.

★

Our Man in Havana

> Passing the Cathedral he gave his usual coin to the blind beggar who sat on the steps outside. Beatrice said, 'It seems almost worth while being blind in this sun.' The creative instinct stirred in Wormold. He said, 'You know, he's not really blind. He sees everything that goes on.'
>
> Graham Greene, *Our Man In Havana*

From the balcony of Simon Wollers' thirteenth-floor apartment I watch the brightly painted Olds and Chevys drift along Linea full of fare-paying passengers heading towards downtown. I'm here because Simon is kind and because I arrived in Havana from Viñales to find my hotel reservation had been cancelled, my magic letter of introduction refused. Remonstrating with hotel staff I was told the head of the company had rescinded it personally and without explanation. Now I'm glad – it's better up here where I can look towards the Hotel Nacional, airline and tourist offices, banks and dollar shops, the Malecón and the sea. There are no curtains on the louvred windows of my bedroom and at night I can stand on the bed and look out at the lights of Havana and the darkness that is the Caribbean. I am poised between worlds: the vivid, unsubtle world of Cuba, and the calm, English world contained within these walls. This is the perfect place to be at the end of my journey. Speaking English with Simon I feel myself already slipping away from here towards home.

Giolvis and I shop for money, breakfast and dinner. Attempting to confirm my homeward flight in the airline offices, we find a whole section of roof collapsed and twenty-seven people waiting in the queue for information. Back at the apartment Giolvis sorts every-thing out by phone in only an hour and a half, then tries to teach me salsa. I can't keep up with him of course, so he dances alone to the thumping strains of 'Yo Soy Malo', shoulders swaying and hips writhing. Deciding that dancing alone is no fun, he flops down, puts on the headphones and picks up Malraux' 'La Condition Humaine', which makes him giggle until Coralia, the cleaner, arrives.

'She is completely deaf,' Giolvis says. 'Sometimes we play tricks on her for fun. The best one is when Simon stands behind her and asks if she would like chocolate – when she doesn't reply we say "If you don't want any we'll eat it all."' He grins.

'That's horrible!'

'It's a joke. She plays much worse tricks on us and, of course, she always gets the chocolate!'

It's impossible to know how old Coralia is. She has no teeth, which makes her seem elderly, but her face is oddly youthful and was probably pretty once. Her nose is broken and she speaks in a nasal whine that's hard to understand, though her lip-reading is very sharp. My Spanish is adequate now, but it's still strange to have someone watching my mouth as I speak their language and actually understand me.

'Her husband battered her,' Giolvis says, 'more than twenty years ago. She lost her sense of smell and hearing. She's a very good woman and we help where we can. She says we are like her sons.'

As she cleans, she seems to make almost as much mess as she clears up, pottering slowly and idly from room to room, then suddenly rushing at the dirt as if to take it by surprise.

In the afternoon she asks Giolvis to help her make a phone call and for the next twenty minutes I'm mesmerised as the young black man and fifty-something white woman sit opposite each other and stare intently into each other's faces. Coralia holds the handset upside down like a microphone and shouts at some official on the other end of the line. Giolvis listens and repeats the responses, con-scientiously, patiently. I remember Simon telling me when we first met that Giolvis and people like him are the true heroes of the

Revolution. Then I wondered what that meant. Now I wonder if the compassion I'm seeing has much to do with politics.

Several months later I received an email from Simon. The message said that Coralia was dead. Not long after I left Havana she'd been diagnosed with cancer and died within weeks. When I thought of the life of brutality and hardship she'd endured I felt tremendous sadness for this woman I'd known so briefly. Then I remembered her laughing and giggling as she hung out men's underwear to dry on Simon's balcony.

'We cleared her things after she died,' Simon told me when we spoke in England later in the year. 'She had nothing, just a few rags of clothes and some plants that she could never get to flower. We kept one of the plants and it flowered after her funeral. It's not stopped flowering since.'

The day after my return to Havana I finally meet a woman I've been trying to contact since arriving in Cuba: Estela Bravo, documentary film-maker and winner of awards from Rio de Janeiro to Moscow and Bilbao. A Brooklyn-born American, Estela Bravo moved to Cuba in the early 1960s with her Argentine husband, now a professor of bioethics at Havana University. They met at a student congress in Poland in 1953. Estela, raised by union activists in immigrant New York in the 1930s, was there as Brooklyn College's leader of Students for a Peaceful World. Ernesto Bravo was receiving medical treatment following his torture by the Peronist authorities in Argentina for organising student protest. These are people who have fought all their lives for what they believed and standing outside their door in a pleasant area of Vedado I find myself wishing I'd met Ms Bravo before I experienced Cuba.

A petite, brown-haired woman, Estela Bravo is almost seventy but looks younger.

'Please, come in,' she says and we shake hands as her husband appears and offers to make tea. She asks me to remind her who I work for and what I'm writing, then starts to talk about her life.

'We came to Cuba in 1963; Ernesto was invited to teach at the medical school and then we just stayed. I knew a lot of musicians at the time, people like Pete Seeger, so I worked in radio and music at first. Later I worked with Ewan McColl and Peggy Seeger on the first music protest in the States in 1967.' She shakes her head. 'It's a terrible thing about Kirstie isn't it?'

'I'm sorry?'

'Kirstie McColl . . . her being killed like that.'

I realise just how out of touch I've been. 'She's dead? When?'

'Quite recently – a boat accident in Mexico. It's really a loss,' she says, before pressing on. 'We worked in the *encuentro* movement with Cuban musicians like Pablo Milanese and then in children's television. I made my first documentary, "Those Who Left", in 1979. It was about Cubans who left during the Revolution and went to the States. It took a while to get on television but it was the start; after that point I became well known and began to work increasingly on films about Latin America and peoples' lives. Now I've made twenty films, mostly about the social struggles in Peru, Argentina, Chile. One of my next projects is about the "found children of Argentina" – children "lost" during the dictatorship and now returned to their families.'

Thinking of Pieter and his problems with the authorities I ask, 'How do Cuban film-makers feel about your work?'

'Oh there's been jealousy of course, but that would be the case anywhere I'm sure.'

'You made a film recently about Castro I think.'

'Yes, for British television. I enjoyed that because Channel 4 wanted a fair, balanced view.' She smiles and offers me the peach tea and small biscuits that Ernesto has laid on the coffee table.

'What did Castro think of it?'

'When I approached him first he said I should wait until he was dead to make such a film, but it wasn't about him as a political leader, it was about Fidel the man. Of course, some people abroad said it couldn't possibly be objective, but that kind of talk really makes me angry. Fidel didn't even see it until it had been out for some time.'

here long enough to make judgements, you can't see everything that happens.'

'I agree,' I say. 'But I listen and try to make space for others to speak. That seems only fair.'

She peers at me suspiciously. 'Who did you say you write for?'

The door opens and a Swedish journalist and his New York wife arrive. Saved by the doorbell. 'Thank you so much for your time,' I say as I take my leave. 'It's very much appreciated.'

At the door Ernesto, the doctor, comments with concern on my cough.

'I call it Cuban Lung,' I say, and smile. 'I've had it some time but it's almost gone now.'

He returns the smile. 'I believe most of the infections we get here every winter are brought by foreigners escaping the cold in their own countries.'

I wonder if he's joking but it's impossible to know.

The cold rain of December has given way to vivid azure skies and bright, sun-filled days. Habana Vieja is alive with tourists on day trips from the beaches of Varadero and Playas del Este. Light filters through the stained glass of newly restored mansions, casting red and green across the tiled floors of palmy courtyards. Walking towards Maria's home through the mix of old and new-old architecture, the shiny and the decaying, I'm aware that my feelings on many things are significantly different to when I last saw her. I think too how very different my experience of Cuba would have been without her teaching.

When Maria opens the half-door to her home and sees me standing there, she seizes me and holds her daughter Ana's arm up next to mine.

'Look at the colour! You are like a mulatto now!' she says laughing. 'Tell me everything – what you saw, where you went.'

At a knock on the half-door she jumps up, calling to her mother, 'Mama it's Juana.' Then, 'This is my sister,' she says

turning to me and introducing a slender, grey-haired woman
wearing a wool checked skirt and tailored leather jacket.

When the question of where I went and what I saw is repeated
there are three generations of *habaneras* listening to my story. I
tell them about Santiago – the people I met, the Santería ceremony
at Elena's house. Maria cringes and tuts at the tale of blood and
death, though whether from embarrassment at the 'primitive' practices of her compatriots, or something more general, I can't tell.
Her mother nods as though she has seen and heard it all before,
Ana looks mildly interested, Juana starts rocking and giggling on
her stool when I mention the word *cojones*.

'This is not a word respectable people use in Cuba,' Maria says
in her best pedagogic tone.

Juana shrieks with laughter. 'Except when we talk about
Castro's *cojones!*'

Maria gasps and shakes her sister's knee, muttering in a low
voice, 'She's a writer, don't forget she's a writer.'

I'm unsurprised by these words, aware that through all the
many hours we spent together she was holding back, a model of
communist propriety: polite, thoughtful, wall-like. I realise now
that I never had any idea of what she must have been thinking,
worrying about, and the level of trust she placed in me to take me
into her home knowing what damage I could do if I chose. Would
she have done it if she didn't need the money? Probably not. But
there's still that slight twinge, that disappointment at not being
entirely trusted, though I understand the reasons very well.

Juana doesn't look remotely sorry for having spoken. 'But it's
true . . . we do talk about Castro's balls. Why not say it out loud?'

Ana is giggling now too and even Antonia has a slight smile
curling her lip. Looking at Maria's face I see decades of anxiety and
silence. I know that she and her husband believe in the Revolution,
are trusted members of the party, but her home is still falling down
around her ears, her mother is a virtual servant, her brilliant husband earning fifteen dollars a month as a senior engineer.

'I would never repeat anything you say to me – that anyone
would say to me and use their real names or even location. I've

written about countries like Vietnam, Croatia and Burma, so I do know that it's not always possible to say what you would like and feel safe.' I mention my meeting with Estela Bravo and her anxiety about what I might write.

She nods and seems to relax.

'You met Estela Bravo?' Juana asks. 'What is she like?'

'Kind and polite,' I say. 'Very official.'

Juana laughs and pats her sister's shoulder. 'You see,' she says, 'everyone worries, not only you! Laugh! What else is there to do?

'My husband was a high-ranking officer in the navy,' she says turning to me. 'He loves the Revolution, he loves Castro. Men are so stupid and it is always us women who are left to deal with the problems and difficulties they make. What do they know about things we endure – like menstruation and how it is every month making rags to stuff in your underwear because you have no money for anything better.'

Ana says, 'My mad aunt is right! It really is terrible. Every month we get ten lumpy sanitary towels on our ration card. I think they're made from cardboard and bits of wood chips, but they're okay I suppose, if you don't bleed that much. But if you do . . .' she lifts her shoulders and grins as her aunt mimes tearing cloth to rags and shoving them under her skirt. Maria laughs with embarrassment and to help her I say that my mother told me everyone did this during the war.

'Exactly! Exactly – during the war! But we are not at war, there's a blockade, yes – an embargo – but that's an excuse for everything!' Maria speaks as if the gates have opened. 'We've been made to feel that we are at war for forty years and we are tired. What kind of war continues for forty years?'

'What kind of house does Estela Bravo have?' Juana asks. 'Better than this, no? And I am sure she has never used her clothes for rags.'

Maria tuts and shakes her head at her sister and says 'Foreigners come here, they mean well, work hard, maybe they live here for many years, but it does not make them Cuban, it does not mean they ever really share our troubles because, in the end, they are always free to leave, to return to their own country. We have no other country, no passport to anywhere else, this is home.'

There is no bitterness in her voice as she says this; it seems merely a recognition of limitation for all concerned.

I ask Antonia about life in Cuba before the Revolution. She's a quiet woman in company but I sense a massive and powerful presence affecting Maria and probably the whole household, despite her role of semi-servant which, it seems, the elderly in this society must take on if they are to justify the food they put in their mouths.

'It was very different then, very different,' she says. 'We had little money but there was always plenty of food and food was cheap. Socially it was a terrible disaster: chaos, Mafia everywhere and corruption. There was no honesty in the government or in the country, no law. If you did something wrong and you were rich, you bought yourself out of the problem, even if it was murder. Now it is much better in that respect, but not in any other.'

'But what do you say,' I ask of all of them, 'to people who say you are very fortunate in comparison with most Latin American countries. That you complain about not being given enough, that you at least have a ration card?'

'But we don't want to be given anything!' Juana blurts as Ana and her mother mutter in agreement. 'We want only to be able to get what we need for ourselves, to be independent . . . and that we have always been denied, as you would deny children because they don't know what's best for themselves.'

'We are all intelligent, educated women here,' Maria says, 'but you see where and how we exist. If we lived in Latin America we would have very different opportunities, some might be harder, more difficult, more painful, but at least there would be opportunities, to move, to study, to exchange ideas freely, even maybe to make money and be comfortable. The people of Latin America have suffered very much over the years and in this we are more fortunate than them – but now, today? No, I don't think we are more fortunate. The cost of what we have has been too high.'

As I prepare to leave, Maria looks sad, knowing this may be the last time we ever meet.

'I hope I'll be in France in the summer for a language course,' she says, as if trying to distance the realisation that I am leaving and she cannot. I can't imagine how that must feel.

'What are you doing tomorrow?' she asks as I kiss Ana and Antonia goodbye.

'I have a meeting with a journalist, Martin di Giovanni,' I say, assuming she won't have heard of him.

She looks taken aback, then quickly smiles. 'Be very careful,' she says as we hug outside her door, 'and remember – we are good people, please don't write anything bad about Cuba.'

I'm surprised by her words and the tears filling her eyes, uncertain if the emotion is at parting from me, or an expression of her feeling for Cuba.

'That's what Estela said to me,' I say.

'Of course,' she replies. 'But this is my country.'

I walk through the picturesque squares of Habana Vieja towards the church and former monastery of San Francisco de Asís thinking about what I just heard. I feel privileged to have been allowed a real glimpse into Maria's life beyond the polite surface we scratched all those weeks ago as I laboured over verbs and tenses. I think of Estela Bravo's comments on lies and Simon telling me that Cubans are 'spoilt'. These squares and streets are being gradually and beautifully restored to their former colonial glory, but the talk all around me is of food and dollars, and I wonder how much room this constant anxiety about the basics of life leaves for the 'higher things' that Estela Bravo talked about so passionately; whether it doesn't force a kind of triviality on life. I think of the people I've spoken to over the months who have referred to humiliation – their own and other people's. Erich cutting himself in Varadero; Simon Wollers who believes the United States is trying to humiliate Cuba through the pointless embargo; Martin di Giovanni who says Castro humiliates his own people through lack of information and press freedom. The one thing almost everyone agrees on is that Cuba is proud of its independence, proud to have avoided becoming a satellite of the United States in the face of years of political and economic antagonism. No-one has ever told me they would prefer to be 'American' and there's plainly a residual affection for the 'bearded tyrant', much like an only child might feel for its stick-wielding single parent. Despite the complaints, the frustration, the desperation, I have what I doubted having when I arrived here – a very clear picture of the head-high stance of Cuba's people. And that, there's no doubt, is the result of revolution. Not just the last one of course, but a century and a half of it.

The blonde woman's high, pure voice fills the church. Like the other singers and musicians she's wearing costume from the time of Columbus. I recognise 'Rodrigo Martinez', a lively, fast-paced piece whose remarkable musical verve echoes Spain's driving imperialism at the end of the fifteenth century. What follows is equally rich with Sephardic, Middle Eastern and Maghrebi sound; a vibrant amalgam which even the composers of the up-and-coming Tudor dynasty could not match for energy and variety.

Looking around at the audience for this concert of early Spanish music, I cannot see one black person: this must be what the white middle classes of Havana do in their spare time. After less than fifteen minutes the concert ends – *Cartelera*, a free magazine aimed at tourists, has got the time wrong.

Feeling cheated I inveigle my way backstage into the monastery's beautiful cloistered courtyard where I'm welcomed as a foreigner, a writer, but mostly as an *aficionado* of early Renaissance Spanish music. The young singers change out of their costumes into respectable, sober street clothing – no glittering Lycra here – as we chat about music. A short, broad man appears and introduces himself in a cockney accent.

'I'm Genesio mate, Italian. Lived here twenty-three years. Do you like the cockney or would you prefer Mayfair, or maybe Welsh?'

'What's he supposed to have done?'

'Worked for the U.S. – been too closely identified with American interests.'

'And what do you think is going on?'

He shakes his head. 'Who knows? I've wondered if there is any truth in the allegations, but logically it would be foolish for any government to use someone as obvious and exposed as Martin simply to gain information. He has too much to lose and he's been here too long to be useful to anyone covertly.'

I stare, shocked that Simon has given the accusation a moment's credence. It had never even occurred to me there might be any truth in it, and every reason to think that what Martin had been fearing and almost expecting had actually happened. But what do I know of intrigue or how it manifests in a place like this? How paranoid is it possible to become if you live here long enough?

Cecilia is upset and the atmosphere between her and Simon is somewhat tense as they stand side-by-side in the kitchen chopping vegetables with large blades in their hands.

'It's terrible what's happening to him, ridiculous and terrible!' Her voice echoes through the high-ceilinged rooms. 'And of course it just makes you feel so vulnerable, reminds you how it's possible to go along on the surface, forgetting what's underneath it all – that when it really comes down to it you have no control at all over your life here.'

Simon, trapped by his various allegiances, tries to soothe her and the situation. I escape into the sitting-room and the calm that is Giolvis.

'Look,' Simon says as we all sit, subdued, around the dining table. 'I feel very sorry for Martin and for what has happened, truly I do. But there are rules here and we either follow them or we don't, and there are many things to take into consideration.'

Cecilia shakes her head, her eyes fixed on her dinner. I want to ask Simon the same question I asked Martin: 'Why do you stay here?' But I'm tired and my mouth is full of scraped-together pasta and I look at Giolvis and know part of the answer anyway.

'So, you either accept that and take what is good and honest about this place,' Simon continues, 'which to my mind is the greater part of life here, or you don't.'

I wait for Martin in front of the cathedral, wondering if I'll recognise him among such a crowd of foreigners. There's a troupe of mummers performing for the tourists, who stand around in shorts, waving cameras and laughing. I recognise Joel up on his stilts in full make-up. Seeing me he lurches forward waving his hands camply and demanding money with humorous menace. Apart from Joel, the Plaza de la Catedral is almost unrecognisable as the place where I spent Christmas Eve. Despite the crowd I feel conspicuous, even anxious about the Graham Greene-ish nature of my situation. All my tapes and notes, two months' work, are sitting in the home of someone who recently told me he and his apartment are regularly observed, and now I'm waiting for Cuba's Most Unwanted Man.

When Martin arrives I do not mistake him; his fair, floppy hair and wired manner are quite distinct. We shake hands and he seems more relaxed than I expected, more relaxed than at our first meeting – perhaps because the worst has happened. We sit and drink coffee in the expensive and conspicuous café bar beside the cathedral and Martin tells me a complex story involving Spanish diplomats, Czech former diplomats and two boys who fell to earth.

'So many things have happened this month,' he says after our coffee arrives. 'It began a week after New Year with the Epiphany parade organised by the Spanish embassy. Some Spanish diplomats and businessmen dressed up as the Magi and threw sweets to kids in the crowd. There was an almighty row about it, the papers talked about Cuban children being humiliated by foreigners and called the diplomats "clowns", "scarecrows", that kind of thing.' He sighs. 'Five days later two Czechs were arrested for organising meetings with dissidents.'

'I heard there are no dissidents here.'

He snorts. 'So, these Czechs are accused of being agents of U.S. interests, of working with anti-Castro elements in America.

They should have known better really: one guy was a former finance minister, the other an ex-student leader. The same day, the identities of the two boys who fell from the British Airways flight were confirmed. All these things happening in such a short time started a kind of xenophobic backlash, which in turn is playing into government plans to backtrack on a lot of the social changes there have been over the past few years.'

As he speaks, the tense atmosphere that I'd been aware of since mid-January begins to make sense: the immigration officer in Trinidad, the problems in the hotel there, trouble with the hotel right here in Havana. It feels now as if I've been on the furthest edge of a shock wave, unaware of the epicentre's existence.

'But what are they saying *you've* done?'

'I told you when we first met that this was on the cards, but it was like some part of me never thought it would really happen.' He twists his cup with his fingers. 'There were two things really that finally turned the screw – my commentary on the Epiphany celebrations and my commentary on Castro's New Year speech.'

'What did you say?' I ask.

'Nothing much different to usual – the main issue was that I said he'd spoken with typical "bravado" – which translates into Spanish as "boastful". The translator offered me the opportunity to change the word. I thought about it and refused.' A flash of what might or might not be regret crosses his face. 'There are so many things counting against me, like my insistence on his age – which I've been told Castro himself finds offensive – so it's become almost personal.' He lifts his hand for another coffee. 'You'd be surprised at how very mild the foreign press here is, how much it toes the line.'

All around us the throng of tourists in bright clothes continues amid the toings and froings of *habaneros*. Joel is drawing a big crowd and money is pouring into the hat held out by his fellow entertainers.

'So why stay? If it's so hard to do the job, so pressured and stressful, why would any journalist stay? It's not even as if there are exciting stories to be had.'

He smiles, leaning back in his seat. 'I disagree, it's a very interesting place. There are so few tyrants left in the world, so few non-Third World countries where lack of democracy is tolerated. And there's a grandiosity about the regime which stems from Castro's more than forty years in power. For example, when the Pope visited Cuba two years ago the headlines said things like "clash of the titans".'

'Have you heard directly from the authorities?'

He shakes his head. 'That isn't how they work; nothing is ever direct here. I watched that "Martin di Giovanni Round-table Debate", just as I was supposed to, and heard what they said about me, about my buying information on the sugar industry.' For a moment he looks almost angry, the surface ruffled. 'Everyone here buys information, that's no secret. There's no other way to get it, and in that instance I was approached, not the other way round.' He looks at me. 'I should tell you that when we met in my office we were probably overheard.'

'What do you mean "overheard"? Overheard by your colleagues?'

'No, I mean bugged. And now I'm being watched of course.' I must look shocked or at least surprised because he grins before turning serious again. 'Perhaps I've been naïve. Those people on television had lists of my contacts and meetings going back over ten years – lists of every meeting I've ever had with American companies, American interests. Of course, they didn't mention any of the other meetings, the other, far more frequent, meetings with everybody else. Black or white, there can be no middle ground; if you aren't for this government you're against it – simple as that. Now they're using my legitimate professional meetings to claim I work for the U.S. government and so justify their actions.'

'I'm really very sorry,' I say, knowing that anything else would be quite useless. I ask about his family and how they are coping. He tells me that his son who used to work in computing has now been moved to menial duties.

'His boss called him in and asked two questions: do you read your father's articles and do you have access to his files?' He

criollo / a / s – Creoles, Cuban-born Cubans
cucaracha – cockroach

encuentro – encounter
estancia / s – farm
extranjero / a / s – foreigner

gallo – cock, rooster

habanero / a / s – a person from Havana
hombres – men

jabón – soap
jején – midge
jinetero / a / s – a place where cockfights are held

loco – crazy

madrina – godmother
madrugada – the time between midnight and six in the morning
malanga – a root vegetable
maricón – gay man, a "queen"
mira – expression of impatience
mirador – a viewing point
mogote – a limestone hillock
muerte – death

nada – nothing
negro – black

orisha / s – gods and goddesses of Santería religion

padres de familias – heads of the households, family men
padrino – godfather
paladar / s – privately-owned restaurant

pabellón – housing
patria – country, homeland
peninsulares – Spanish-born Cubans (colonial period)
ron caña – cane rum
rumba – a form of Cuban music

santero / a / s – a Santería priest
son – an early form of salsa music
suerte – luck

tinajón – large earthenware water jar
todos – all

valla de gallos – a place where cockfights are held
vaquero – cowboy

yanqui – Yankee, American

THE LONELY PLANET STORY

Where it all began...

A beat-up old car, a few dollars in the pocket, and a sense of adventure. That's all Tony and Maureen Wheeler needed for the trip of a lifetime. They met on a park bench in Regent's Park and married a year later. For their honeymoon, they decided to attempt what few people thought possible – crossing Europe and Asia overland, all the way to Australia. It took them several months and all the money they could earn, beg or borrow, but they made it. And at the end of it all, they were flat broke... and couldn't have been happier.

It was too amazing an experience to keep to themselves. Urged on by their friends, they stayed up nights at their kitchen table writing, typing and stapling together their very first travel guide, *Across Asia on the Cheap*.

Within a week they'd sold 1500 copies and Lonely Planet was born. Two years later, their second journey led to *South-East Asia on a shoe-string*, which led to books on Nepal, Australia, Africa, and India, which led to... you get the picture.

Fast-forward over 30 years.

As Lonely Planet became a globally loved brand, Tony and Maureen received several offers for the company. But it wasn't until 2007 that they found a partner whom they trusted to remain true to Lonely Planet's principles. In October of that year, BBC Worldwide acquired a 75% share in Lonely Planet, pledging to uphold Lonely Planet's commitment to independent travel, trustworthy advice and editorial independence. BBC Worldwide is the main commercial arm, and a wholly owned subsidiary of, the British Broadcasting Corporation (BBC).

Today, Lonely Planet has offices in Melbourne, London and Oakland, with over 500 staff members and 300 authors. Tony and Maureen are still actively involved with Lonely Planet. They're travelling more often than ever, and they're devoting their spare time to charitable projects. And the company is still driven by the philosophy in *Across Asia on the Cheap*: 'All you've got to do is decide to go and the hardest part is over. So go!'